ST THOMAS CANTILUPE
BISHOP OF HEREFORD

ESSAYS IN HIS HONOUR

Seal of Saint Thomas Cantilupe, Bishop of Hereford.

ST THOMAS CANTILUPE BISHOP OF HEREFORD

ESSAYS IN HIS HONOUR

Edited by

MERYL JANCEY

Published by
The Friends of Hereford Cathedral
Publications Committee for the
Dean and Chapter
1982

ISBN 0 904642 04 6.
Printed by Orphans Press Ltd., Hereford Rd., Leominster.

FOREWORD

In the year in which the 700th anniversary of the death of St Thomas Cantilupe, Hereford's saintly bishop is especially remembered in this diocese, I am glad that the Friends of Hereford cathedral have sponsored the publication of this book. It is not easy to find information about Cantilupe's remarkable career or to understand the reputation he enjoyed in medieval times. The contributors of these essays have set him in the context of the thirteenth century, and in doing so, have shown in what ways he still stands as a figure of relevance for the twentieth. I commend this book to you all in the knowledge that in reading it you will be keeping company with a great saint of the church.

+ John Hereford.

The Bishop's House,
The Palace,
HEREFORD.

30th March, 1982

PREFACE

As the date of the 700th anniversary of the death of St Thomas Cantilupe drew near, it became evident that there was very little material available to give us an understanding of the significance of his life and sanctity. The Publications Committee of the Friends of Hereford cathedral, with some courage, decided to fill this gap by sponsoring a book of collected essays in honour of the saint. With the encouragement of the Council of the Friends, the committee, under the chairmanship of Major-General A. H. Dowson, made funds available and sought advice in getting the book together. Council would like to thank here all those who helped us at this stage—Professor Christopher Brooke, Miss K. Major, Miss B. Smalley, Mrs. Elizabeth Hallam Smith, and Professor E. L. G. Stones. The book came into being as scholars and churchmen generously gave their time and learning to write for us. Their essays have brought forward new material relating to Cantilupe, corrected old errors and set him before us in a new and clearer light.

Miss Meryl Jancey, by her skilful and patient editing of the book, has earned our most sincere gratitude.

Although the Publications Committee have been responsible for the issuing of small booklets about Hereford cathedral, this is the first time it has published a full-scale work of scholarship. May it not be the last!

Roger Mynors,
Chairman of Council

CONTENTS

ILLUSTRATIONS

INTRODUCTION

by Meryl Jancey

Dom. David Knowles has said that the thirteenth century is a period that keeps its own silence, an age in which we are given fewer insights than in some others for the inner lives of outstanding personalities. This is certainly true of St Thomas Cantilupe. He wrote nothing that has survived to us, and the evidence for his life and work given by witnesses at the inquiry for canonization in 1307 has been often misunderstood and even misinterpreted in succeeding times. A reputation for courage in litigation, for careful virginity, for austere practices in the wearing of hair shirts with their accompanying plenitude of lice, taken together with extravagant stories of miraculous healings at his tomb, does not bring us very far in understanding the man, though it does show us something of what his own age looked for in one that it needed as a saint. In his own life-time he was reverenced. The interesting point in the story that little birds flew to the window when he was singing at the celebration of Mass at Wallingford is not whether this was, or was not, a miraculous obeisance of creatures to a saint, but that observers thought that it was.

In this, the seven hundredth year after his death, it seemed right to do honour to this saint of Hereford and to try to discover the qualities for which his own age revered him. Contributors to this book have taken topics covering phases of Cantilupe's life or aspects of his character and examined the significance and effectiveness of his career. They have provided an account of one who emerges as totally consistent. Judgment, discernment, brilliant administrative powers were in him the fruits of the unremitting self-discipline of a brave and lonely man, whose inner sanctity was guarded by a deep reserve.

As administrator, councillor of state, bishop, and specialist in canon law, he is no inconsiderable figure in the history of the thirteenth century, but it is because he achieved sanctity and canonization that he is especially remembered to-day. Shorter contributions in this book are concerned with some of the effects of that sanctity in years long after his death.

As sponsors of this book, the Publications Committee of the Council of the Friends of Hereford Cathedral owe a great debt of thanks to the contributors who have so generously given of their time and learning. Many people have helped in preparing the book. Miss K. Warry and Mrs. Carol Morgan have typed for us, Miss Nona Martin and Dr. Margaret Roberts have checked references. Some financial help has been given by the Institute for Advanced Musical Studies towards the publication of the article by Professor Trowell and Mr. Wathey.

The book stands as a miscellany of essays written in honour of St Thomas of Hereford. There has been no attempt to strain after too much uniformity and so break down its character as an anthology, though a few general practices have been adopted, notably the dropping of the 'de' element in the Cantilupe family name for Thomas Cantilupe himself. The printers of the Orphans Press have saved an inexperienced editor from an even greater number of ineptitudes than those that may still be detected. Miss Joan Bookham, Secretary of the Council of the Friends of Hereford Cathedral has been an unfailing source of encouragement and support.

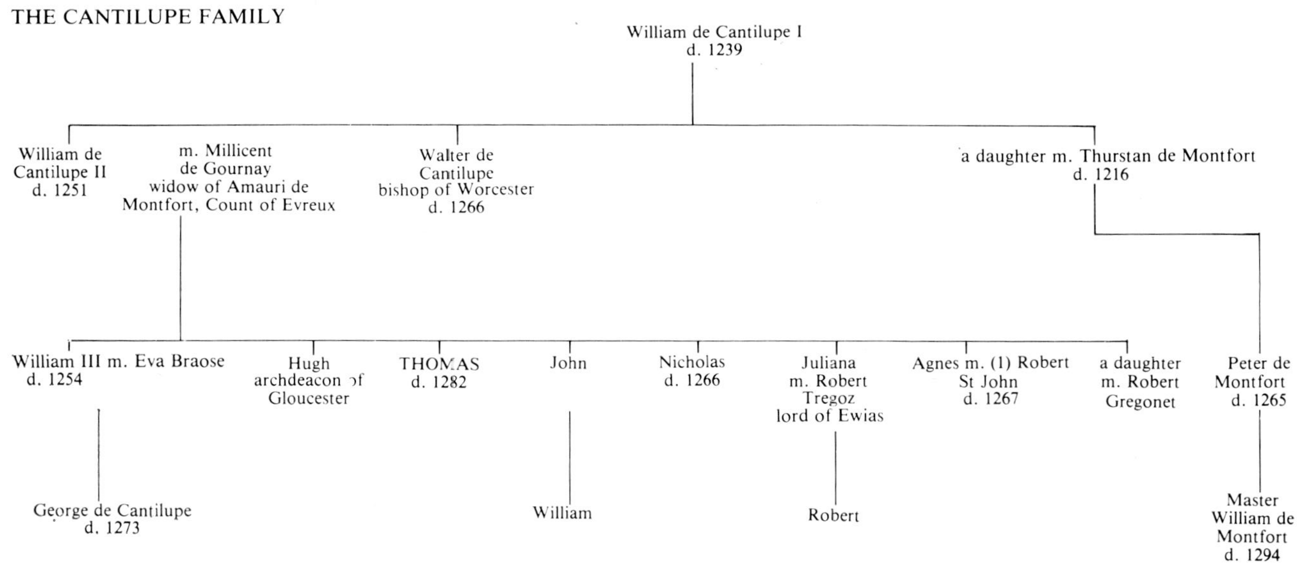

I. A FAMILY TREE SHEWING THOMAS CANTILUPE'S NEAR RELATIONS

THE LIFE OF SAINT THOMAS OF HEREFORD

by Nona D. S. Martin

Thomas Cantilupe was born about 1218[1] at his father's manor of Hambleden, near Great Marlow in Buckinghamshire, and was probably baptized in the village church there. He was descended on both sides from Norman barons. His father, William, second baron Cantilupe, held, like his father before him, the office of seneschal of the royal household. His mother, Millicent, was the daughter of a Norman lord, Hugh de Gournay, and had been first married to Amauri de Montfort, count of Evreux. His uncle, Walter de Cantilupe, who became bishop of Worcester in 1236, was one of the most distinguished men of his time, the close friend of Simon de Montfort and his staunch supporter throughout the Barons' Wars.

Thomas was one of five brothers, the eldest of whom, William, third baron Cantilupe, acquired by marriage with an heiress of the great Braose family the lordship of Brecon. Another brother, Hugh, who is known to have been older than Thomas, became archdeacon of Gloucester and the two others, John and Nicholas, became knights. His three sisters all married into noble families, and Juliana, the one with whom he seems to have had the closest ties, was the wife of the Marcher lord, Robert Tregoz of Ewias.

Although as a child Thomas once expressed an ambition to be a soldier, he was destined, like his brother Hugh, for the church and received his early education under the guidance of his uncle, Walter. In 1237, according to Anthony Wood, he went 'to be initiated in Academical learning'[2] at Oxford, where his chief tutor was the Dominican, Robert Kilwardby, afterwards archbishop of Canterbury. A few years later, about 1242, he was sent to read Arts at Paris, joining his brother, Hugh, who was already a student there. A large household was maintained for them, in which they lived in almost princely style, with their own chaplain and tutor, and were honoured by a visit from St Louis, the King of France. In 1245 Thomas, accompanied by Hugh, attended the first Council of Lyons, where he was appointed a papal chaplain by Innocent IV and also received a dispensation allowing him to hold benefices in plurality, of which he was to make full but scrupulous use.

1 The generally accepted date of c. 1218 for St Thomas' birth is based on Richard Swinfield's statement at the canonization process that Thomas was aged 63 'or a little more' when he died in August 1282, but other witnesses differed from him on this point and recent research suggests that a slightly later dating for the birth, c. 1222, is more likely to be correct.

2 Anthony Wood, *The History and antiquities of the university of Oxford,* [ed. J. Gutch], (Oxford, 1792-6), I, 221.

By this time Thomas had taken his Master's degree in Arts and he next embarked on a long course of legal studies, going first to Orleans, where he studied civil law under Master Guido, and then back to Paris to study canon law. About 1255 he moved to Oxford to teach canon law and, having incepted as doctor in that faculty, he was elected in 1261 as chancellor of the university, an office then normally held for two years. During his tenure Thomas won respect by the strictness and impartiality with which he maintained discipline among the large and unruly body of students.

It was probably about 1263, when the dispute between Henry III and his barons was drawing towards its crisis, that Thomas began to take part in political affairs. His sympathies, as might be expected, lay with the de Montfort cause with which his uncle, Walter de Cantilupe, was so closely involved. In December 1263, having vacated the chancellorship of the university, he went to Amiens as one of the representatives of the barons at the arbitration which St Louis had undertaken to make between them and King Henry. The issue largely turned on the barons' claim to a share in the choice of the King's counsellors and Thomas was well qualified by his legal training to act as chief baronial proctor and to draft the three documents in which their case was presented.[3] There was little hope, however, that it would prevail and St Louis' verdict, given on 23 January, 1264, supporting King Henry, led immediately to civil war. After Simon de Montfort's victory at the battle of Lewes in May, a council of magnates was set up which ruled in the King's name. In February 1265 the council nominated Thomas, who was as acceptable to the King as anyone of his party could be, as chancellor of England. He held the great seal for only a very short time,[4] but he retained the office of chancellor and exercised some of its functions until the defeat and death of de Montfort at the battle of Evesham on 4 August brought the baronial government to an end.

After this brief experience of political life, Thomas retired to Paris and, though he was formally restored to the King's favour in February 1266,[5] and apparently never deprived of the archdeaconry of Stafford, the highest ecclesiastical preferment he had so far obtained, he remained abroad for several years. In Paris he devoted himself to the study of theology under, among other masters, the Franciscan, John Pecham, who was later to become archbishop of Canterbury. He gave lectures in the university on the Epistles and the Apocalypse, and about 1272 he returned to Oxford, where in June of the following year he became doctor of theology. His inception in the church of the Dominicans was presided over by

3 P. Walne, 'The Barons' argument at Amiens, January, 1264', *English Historical Review*, LXIX, (1954), 418-25.

4 F. M. Powicke, *King Henry III and the Lord Edward*, (Oxford, 1947), II, 492.

5 PRO, *Calendar of Patent Rolls, 1258-66*, 549.

his old teacher and confessor, Robert Kilwardby, archbishop-elect of Canterbury, who spoke in high praise of him, declaring 'that he never perceived him guilty of any mortal sin'.[6] Soon after this Thomas was again appointed chancellor of the university and it was during his second chancellorship that a serious riot between the opposing factions of the northern and southern scholars broke out in January, 1274. Thomas himself intervened in an attempt to make peace and the front of his cloak was slashed by a northerner.[7] It seems that his term of office as chancellor was cut short when he went to attend the second Council of Lyons, convened by Pope Gregory X to end the schism between the Eastern and Western churches, which met on 7 May, 1274. On this occasion he was accompanied by his nephew, William Cantilupe, and he was again made a papal chaplain.

During the years between the first and second Councils of Lyons, which Thomas had spent mostly in academic life, he had received many ecclesiastical preferments which brought him great wealth. In addition to being archdeacon of Stafford, precentor and canon of York, and canon of London, he held many widely-scattered parochial livings, largely acquired through family influence. Among them were Deighton in Yorkshire, Coleby[8] in Lincolnshire, Aston-Cantlow in Warwickshire, Bulwick in Northamptonshire, Dodderhill in Worcestershire, Bradwell in Essex, and Sherborne St John in Hampshire. But Thomas was the most conscientious of pluralists. Not only did he take care to provide good and competent vicars, he also made frequent visits to his parishes, celebrating mass, preaching, and hearing confessions, and gave generous alms to the poor and sick. He used his wealth to repair or rebuild dilapidated church properties and exercised his influence to protect the rights of his benefices. At Dodderhill, for example, he had barns and other buildings repaired and recovered for the rectory tithes of salt owing to it.[9]

In his middle age Thomas lived frequently in London, where he entertained lavishly, though himself extremely abstemious, and was known as a cultivated and sociable man, as Brother Robert of St Martin, the sacristan of St Bartholomew's, affirmed in his testimony at the canonization process in 1307. It is to the same witness that we owe the only detailed description

6 Wood, *op. cit.*, I, 65.

7 A. B. Emden, *A Biographical register of the university of Oxford to A.D. 1500*, (Oxford, 1957-9), I, 348; *Acta Sanctorum*, New ed., (Paris, 1863-75), Octobris, I, 546.

8 Thomas was rector of Coleby from 1265 to 1275 and it is possible that he had property in Lincoln as the land of a Master Thomas de Cantilupe is mentioned in a grant of c. 1273 in the cartulary of the Vicars Choral of Lincoln, (Lincs. Archives Office, V.C./2/1, no. 180). I am indebted to Miss K. Major for this reference.

9 Vat. Cod. Lat. 4015, fo. 19r.

which exists of Thomas' personal appearance. Brother Robert had known Thomas for four years while he was canon of St Paul's and, remembering him as he had often seen him officiating there, said that he had an angelic countenance (*quasi vultum angelicum*), a fresh complexion, a good beard, and a long nose; and that the hair of both his beard and head was of a reddish colour streaked with white.[10]

About 1274 Thomas, whose family had interests in Herefordshire, was appointed by John le Breton, bishop of Hereford, himself a distinguished lawyer, to the prebend of Preston in Hereford cathedral. In May, 1275 le Breton died and Thomas, whom he had intended to be his successor, was elected as bishop by the canons on 15 June. The royal assent was signified a few days later and Thomas was consecrated on 8 September at Canterbury by Archbishop Kilwardby.

Thomas now became a favoured adviser of Edward I and regularly attended his councils, but he was chiefly occupied in the administration of his large and disordered diocese. As well as fulfilling his pastoral responsibilities with the utmost zeal and firmness he gave careful attention to the management of the episcopal estates. He also devoted much of his energies to the strenuous defence of the rights and properties of his see against the encroachments of the neighbouring lords, spiritual and temporal. In a litigious age this involved him in many long disputes in which he engaged with all the skill acquired in his legal training and the martial spirit of the class from which he came. One of his fiercest conflicts was with Gilbert de Clare, the mighty earl of Gloucester, whom he forced to surrender his claim to the right of hunting in the episcopal chase on the western side of the Malvern hills.

In 1279 Kilwardby was succeeded as archbishop of Canterbury by John Pecham who, like his predecessor, had once been Thomas' teacher. But he and Thomas were opposed by temperament and training, and a bitter quarrel soon arose between them about an appeal in a matrimonial suit made direct to the court of Canterbury without the cognizance of the bishop's court. In order to avoid an interdict Thomas withdrew to Normandy, where he stayed from the late summer of 1280 till the autumn of the following year, spending some of that time at the Benedictine abbey of Lyre, in Evreux, which had close links with Herefordshire. Early in 1282, soon after his return to England, he was again in dispute with Pecham over a testamentary jurisdiction claimed by the court of Canterbury. His stubborn support of the court of Hereford in resisting what he felt to be an infringement of its rights finally brought excommunication upon him.

10 *ibid.*, fo. 49v.

Thomas immediately appealed to the pope and, though in failing health, he soon came to the decision to lay his case against Pecham, and two others which he had long been prosecuting through proctors, in person before the papal court. In the early spring of 1282 he set out for Italy, where he arrived safely and was kindly received by Martin IV at his court at Orvieto. He then retired to 'Castrum Florentini' (Ferento), near Montefiascone. Here he caught a fever to which, worn out by age, overwork, and his ascetic way of life, he succumbed within a few days. Having received the last sacraments from Nicholas, his chaplain, he died at dusk on 25 August, held in the arms of his faithful servant, Robert Deynte.

In accordance with medieval practice, Thomas' body was boiled to separate the flesh from the bones. The flesh was buried in the church of the monastery of San Severo, near Orvieto, and a funeral sermon was preached by the cardinal of Praeneste, afterwards Pope Nicholas IV. The heart and bones were brought back to England by Thomas' steward, John de Clare,[11] one of the small band of officials and servants who had accompanied him to Italy. The heart was deposited by Edmund, earl of Cornwall, who had known and venerated Thomas, at a small college of canons under his protection at Ashridge in Buckinghamshire. The bones were laid to rest in the cathedral at Hereford, where their miraculous powers soon manifested themselves and inspired a pilgrim cult. After many appeals to the pope by Richard Swinfield, Thomas' successor as bishop of Hereford, and others, a careful inquiry was made into the life of Thomas and the miracles, which eventually resulted in his canonization as a saint of the Western church in 1320.

11 *ibid.*, fo. 47r.

THE CULT OF ST THOMAS BECKET IN THE THIRTEENTH CENTURY

by Anne Duggan

At first sight there seems to be little to link St Thomas of Canterbury with St Thomas of Hereford, save for the superficial similarities of name, occupation of the office of chancellor, episcopal rank, and exile. Becket was a parvenu, Cantilupe a member of an established administrative family, whose path was smoothed by the patronage of his influential uncle, Bishop Walter of Worcester, the life-long supporter of Simon de Montfort. Becket, though educated sufficiently well to be clerk to archbishop Theobald and chancellor to Henry II, was neither a scholar nor of scholarly disposition; Cantilupe spent the greater part of his adult life learning and teaching in Oxford and Paris, proceeding through the faculties of Arts, Canon Law, Civil Law, and Theology. Becket was murdered in his own cathedral by four knights of the king's immediate entourage, in the course of a major dispute about the respective rights of church and state; Cantilupe died near Montefiascone while pursuing a technical legal dispute with Becket's successor, John Pecham. Becket's claim to sanctity rested on his martyrdom and the cause for which he died, Cantilupe's on his life and character. Each immediately became the centre of a cult, but Becket's was on a European scale, whereas Cantilupe's rested largely on his local reputation in Hereford and the assiduous devotion of Richard Swinfield, his successor in the see; and, while the Canterbury saint retained a powerful grasp on the popular imagination for the rest of the middle ages, Hereford's saint slowly declined in popularity from the time of his canonization in 1320. The second Thomas did not inherit the mantle of the first—nor did he seek to assume it—but neither he nor any other conscientious English bishop could escape the influence of the long shadow cast by the heroic martyr; and his admirers made what they could of the coincidences between his life and Becket's to find in St Thomas of Hereford some echoes at least of St Thomas of Canterbury. This desire resulted from more than the natural inclination to link and compare two saints who bore the same name; it reflected the pre-eminence still enjoyed by the cult of Becket more than a century after his death, and the survival of a particular pattern of sanctity which his life, and especially the manner of his death, was thought to exemplify.

In order to understand the influences which moulded Thomas Cantilupe in his formative years as a student in the schools, it is necessary to examine the extent of Becket's cult and the nature of its appeal to kings, scholars, and churchmen, as well as to the thousands of ordinary men and women who flocked to his shrine in Canterbury cathedral. For the image of the martyr exercised a pervasive influence on the mentality of the thirteenth-century church. Becket became a figure of epic quality, the hero of reformers, and one of England's patron saints. It is also necessary, however, to look at the broader currents of spirituality which produced both Becket and Cantilupe, and which explain the persistence of the Becket image of heroic virtue. For both were men of their times, canonized by popular acclaim as well as by official process, because their contemporaries recognized in them special qualities of moral and spiritual grandeur which set them apart from the rest of their world, and made them worthy of veneration.

The murder of Thomas Becket in 1170 caused an immediate reaction throughout Europe; his assassination, like that of President Kennedy in recent times, shocked contemporaries as did no other piece of violence. Within three years he was canonized by Alexander III, one of the swiftest canonizations in the history of the medieval church;[1] within ten years, his cult had penetrated to the boundaries of Latin Christendom, and beyond;[2] and his tomb in the crypt at Canterbury had become the goal of pilgrims from the whole of Europe;[3] after fifty years, the translation of his remains to a magnificent new chapel, dominating the east end of Canterbury cathedral, was one of the grandest state occasions of the century,[4] and inaugurated the Jubilee of St Thomas, which was celebrated every fifty

1 Thomas was canonized on 21st February, 1173, at Segni, less than 26 months after his murder. The five equally rapid canonizations are those of St Hugh of Grenoble, d. 1132, can. 1134; St Francis of Assisi, d. 1226, can. 1228; St Anthony of Padua, d. 1231, can. 1232; St Peter Martyr, d. 1252, can. 1253; and St Clare of Assisi, d. 1253, can. 1255.

2 M. Barth, 'Zum Kult des heiligen Thomas Becket im deutschen Sprachgebiet, in Skandinavien und Italien', *Freiburger Diözesan-Archiv* 80 (1960), 97-166; J. Becquet, 'Les sanctuaires dédiés à St Thomas de Cantorbéry en Limousin' in R. Foreville, ed., *Thomas Becket: Actes du colloque internationale de Sédières, 19-24 Août 1973,* Paris (1975), 159-62; R. Foreville, 'Le culte de St Thomas Becket en Normandie', *ibid.*, 135-52; eadem, 'Le culte de St Thomas Becket en France. Bilan de recherches', *ibid.*, 163-88; H. Martin, 'Le culte de Saint Thomas Becket dans les diocèses de la province de Tours', *ibid.*, 153-58. For a general view of the artistic results of the cult, see T. Borenius, *St Thomas Becket in Art,* London (1932). The wide dissemination of Limoges caskets made in the period *c.* 1195-1215/20, to enshrine relics of the new saint, is a good index of the spread of his cult throughout Europe at the end of the twelfth century. M.-M. Gauthier lists the present location of 45 Becket châsses: 7 in Germany, 2 in Austria, 1 in Spain, 11 in France, 11 in Great Britain, 3 in Italy, 1 in each of the Low Countries, Poland and Sweden, 3 in Switzerland, and 4 originally from Europe, now in the United States. These are in addition to 23 further reliquary caskets whose precise identification is uncertain. More significantly, 12 caskets are in or very close to their original location: M.-M. Gauthier, 'Le meurtre dans la cathédrale, thème iconographique médiévale', in Foreville, *Thomas Becket,* 247 n. 3, and 248 n. 4. His feast is even found in calendars of the Armenian church in Cilicia: *AA.SS, Prop. Decembris,* 606 n. 2.

3 D. J. Hall, *English mediaeval pilgrimage,* London (1965), 148-65; H. Loxton, *Pilgrimage to Canterbury,* Vancouver (1978).

4 See below, n. 96.

years from 1220 to 1470, anticipating by eighty years the declaration of the Roman Jubilee by Boniface VIII in 1300;[5] and after more than two centuries, the 'oil of St Thomas' was used in the anointing of English kings.[6] In Canterbury itself, three feasts of St Thomas were celebrated each year,[7] and Tuesday was recognized as his special day.[8] No other English saint enjoyed such widespread veneration;[9] no other English shrine achieved so high a reputation. Part of the explanation for this extraordinary phenomenon lies in the nature of the cause in which Becket suffered, and part in the European context within which the controversy occurred. Thomas's six-year exile in France, protected by the pope, the king of France, and the archbishop of Sens, brought the English dispute into the forefront of European politics. The questions at issue, clerical immunity from lay jurisdiction, right of appeal to the pope, and the election of bishops, were matters of importance to every province in the Western church, and Becket's fate carried a significance that extended far beyond the confines of the English kingdom.[10] Had Henry II been able to carry

5 R. Foreville, *Le Jubilé de Saint Thomas Becket, du XIIIe au XVe siècle* (1220-1470), S.E.V.P.E.N. (1958); see below n. 97.

6 See below, n. 72.

7 The *Translatio,* 7th July, the *Regressio,* 2nd December, and the *Natalitio,* 29th December. For the feasts of the Translation and 'Birthday', see *Breviarium ad usum insignis ecclesiae Sarum,* edd. F. Proctor and C. Wordsworth, 3 vols, Cambridge (1879-86), III (1886), 445-51, and 1 (1882), ccxlvii-cclxi. Only fragments of the liturgy for the feast of the Return have survived in the 'burnt breviary' (Canterbury, Dean and Chapter Library Addit. MS 6), but there is evidence that this rare feast was celebrated in monastic houses which had specially close associations with St Thomas; see F. Wormald, *English Benedictine Kalendars after AD 1100,* I, Henry Bradshaw Society LXXVII (1939), 65 n. 2 (Arbroath), 79 (Christ Church, Canterbury).

8 Details of the Canterbury observance of St. Thomas's Tuesdays have recently been recovered through the fortunate acquisition by the British Library of Brit. Libr. Addit. MS 59616, formerly Phillipps MS 8113 (Heber Catalogue 322). The first section of the MS (fos. i^r-xiv^v) comprises the customary drawn up in 1428 by John Lyel and Edmund Kyngyston, keepers of the shrine. It details the daily ceremonies associated with the shrine, and provides (fo. iii^r-v) an account of Becket's Tuesdays, and the special observances attached to their celebration; see also n. 105, below.

9 Although both of Becket's parents had been born in Normandy (see below n. 40), he took his name 'Thomas Londoniensis' from the place of his birth and childhood, and contemporaries described him simply as *natione anglicus.*

10 For the most contentious clauses of the Constitutions of Clarendon, relating to these matters, see D. Knowles, *Thomas Becket,* Edinburgh (1970), 89-90; and for a general discussion of the significance of the Becket dispute, see C. Duggan, 'The significance of the Becket dispute in the history of the English Church', *Ampleforth Journal* LXXV (1970), 365-75, reprinted in idem, *Canon Law in medieval England: The Becket dispute and decretal collections,* Variorum (1982), no. I; see also, idem, *Thomas of London: An address in commemoration of St Thomas of Canterbury,* and 'From the Conquest to the death of John', in C. H. Lawrence, ed., *The English church and the papacy in the middle ages,* London (1965), 63-116, both reprinted in Variorum, *op.cit.,* nos. XVI and XV; see *ibid., passim.*

the day against the archbishop, then the secular powers would have achieved a signal victory over the church, whereas Becket's triumph by martyrdom was readily received as a divine judgment in favour of Alexander III and the church,[11] and against Henry II and other likeminded monarchs. It vindicated resistance to political authority and demonstrated that the inexorable advance of royal power could be contained.

Becket's life and death thus became an inspiration to the leaders of churches struggling in similar circumstances to free themselves from secular restraint, and the propagation of his cult became a symbol of ecclesiastical resistance. In Norway, where Eystein of Trondheim (Nidaros) brought to his office all the idealism and reforming zeal of the Victorines, the struggle with King Sverre (1177-1202) was so severe that Eystein was compelled to spend three years in exile in England (1180-83), and his successor Eirik together with all his Norwegian suffragans remained outside the kingdom for twelve years, from 1190 to the death of the king in 1202.[12] Not surprisingly, the feast of the English martyr was immediately received into the new liturgy which Eystein constructed for Trondheim through the 1170s,[13] and the Translation offices were duly added to the office books in 1221.[14] Thomas the martyr was second only to St Olaf in veneration by the Norwegian church down to the end of the middle ages, though the surviving evidences are now few. Among the small number of artifacts described by Borenius are an interesting altar-piece, now in the Bergen museum, from the church of Luro, which shows St Thomas in the company of St Olaf, St Edmund of East Anglia, and St Magnus Dux,[15] and an extremely fine châsse in the church of Heidal in Valdres, made by a Norwegian craftsman in the mid-thirteenth century, and bearing a remarkably accurate depiction of the murder.[16] From Norway's neighbour, Sweden, Borenius cites only two examples, but both are important works of art. An enamelled châssc, manufactured in

11 Benedict of Peterborough, *Miracula Sancti Thomae* in *Materials for the history of Thomas Becket, Archbishop of Canterbury,* edd. J. C. Robertson and J. B. Sheppard, Rolls Series 67, 7 vols, London (1875-85), II (1876), 24-5.

12 Lilii Gjerløw, *Ordo Nidrosiensis ecclesiae, Libri liturgici provinciae Nidrosiensis medii aevi* II, Oslo (1968), 29-30, 109. The province of Nidaros, organised by Nicholas Brakespear 1152/3-1157, included the dioceses of Bergen, Stavangar, and Hamar in Norway, Skálholt and Hólar in Iceland, and Sodor, comprising Greenland, the Faeroe Islands, the Orkneys, and the Western Isles of Scotland. Earlier (1103-1152/53) Norway had been part of the province of Lund (Sweden, but then in the kingdom of Denmark), and earlier still (*c.* 1043-1103) it had been included in the province of Bremen-Hamburg.

13 *ibid.,* 30, 162-63, 166 n. c, 168, 169 n.f, 170, 171. With the exception of some small borrowings from other sources (*ibid.,* 440-41), the basic liturgy for St Thomas's day corresponds with the Sarum use, and was therefore probably derived directly from Canterbury in the 1170s or 1180s.

14 *ibid.,* 76 and 364.

15 Borenius, 20 and plate VI, fig. 3.

16 *ibid.,* 76 and plate XXIV, fig. 2.

Limoges before 1215, in the church of Trönö[17] and an extremely vigorous representation of four scenes from Becket's life on a font in the church of Lyngsjö in Southern Sweden, carved *c.* 1190-1200, attest the progress of the cult in that country.[18] In Iceland, only slightly later, Gundmund Arason, bishop of Hólar (1203-37) was regarded as a second St Thomas in his unsuccessful attempt to secure clerical immunity, and Becket became the object of a pervasive cult, again second only to that of St Olaf.[19] Magnússon listed 13 churches dedicated to him in medieval Iceland, and 17 effigies or paintings;[20] but even greater evidence of Becket's popularity is provided by the three Thomas Sagas composed in Old Icelandic in the thirteenth and early fourteenth centuries. Two now survive as mere fragments, but the *Thómas Saga Erkibyskups* is a unique and valuable source for the history of St Thomas, since it preserves extracts from a lost Latin life by Master Robert of Cricklade, prior of the Augustinian house of St Frideswide in Oxford.[21] In Poland, a similar movement for ecclesiastical emancipation provoked similar devotion to the new martyr. The foundation of the collegiate church of St Thomas at Racibórz marked the reconciliation between Thomas II (1270-92), bishop of Wroclaw, and prince Henry IV, after a long struggle over ecclesiastical rights,[22] but the martyr's office had been included in breviaries and his feast featured in calendars from the end of the twelfth century.[23] So influential was the witness of St Thomas considered to be that Polish historians have argued that the movement in the 1250s for the canonization of St Stanislas, bishop of Cracow and patron of the Polish nation, was directly inspired by the precedent of Becket, and some have gone so far as to suggest that the *Vita* of St Stanislas, prepared to support his cause, was modelled on John of Salisbury's Life of Becket.[24]

Elsewhere in Europe, various networks of influence, friendship, and diplomatic connections played decisive parts in the early stages of dissemination of Becket's cult. The Cistercian and Augustinian Orders were foremost in encouraging devotion to him; friends and admirers in high places almost vied with one another in honouring their dead colleague; and, paradoxically perhaps, the marriage alliances of Henry II's three

17 *ibid.*, 90 and plate XXXV, fig. 2.
18 *ibid.*, 80 and plate XXX, fig. 2: now in the museum of Lund university.
19 *Thómas Saga Erkibyskups,* ed. E. Magnússon, 2 vols, Rolls Series 65, London (1875-84), II xxiv-xxvi.
20 *ibid.*, xxix-xxxii.
21 For a discussion of the Saga's use of Robert of Cricklade's Life of Becket, see *ibid.*, lv-lvi and lxxiv-lxxv, and M. Orme, 'A Reconstruction of Robert of Cricklade's Vita et Miracula S. Thomae Cantuariensis', *Analecta Bollandiana* 84 (1966), 379-98.
22 W. Uruszczak, 'Les répercussions de la mort de Thomas Becket en Pologne (XIIe-XIIIe siècles)', in Foreville, *Thomas Becket,* 117.
23 *ibid.*, 116.
24 *ibid.*, 119-24. Stanislas, bishop of Cracow, had been murdered by King Boleslas in 1079; he was canonized by Pope Innocent IV on 17th December, 1253.

daughters (and one daughter-in-law) played some part in spreading devotion to their father's chief ecclesiastical adversary. The duchy of Saxony, for example, to which princess Matilda was sent as bride to Duke Henry the Lion in 1168, became an important centre of Becket's cult in northern Germany, because of a combination of dynastic, political, and economic links with England. Matilda's son, Henry of Brunswick, conceived a very strong devotion to the saint and declared him patron of the duchy, and the new cathedral in the city of Brunswick, dedicated in 1226 to St John the Baptist, St Blaise, and St Thomas, housed a substantial frieze depicting the martyr's life and death.[25] In the north, in lands dominated by the Hansa, four cities had magnificent altar-pieces which included scenes from his life, sometimes in significant conjunction with other saints. The retable in St Jürgen in Wismar linked three Thomases, the Apostle, Aquinas, and Becket,[26] and that in Tettens in Oldenburg paralleled his life with that of St Martin of Tours.[27] A further retable, which formerly belonged to the church of St Nicholas in Stralsund, shows four scenes from his life;[28] and two scenes from a four-panelled altar piece survive from the cathedral in Hamburg.[29] But the earliest dedications to St Thomas in German lands owe their existence to other influences. The foundation, by 1179 at the latest, of the Cistercian nunnery of St Thomas an der Kyll, near Trier, reflects the interest of the Cistercians;[30] and the dedication on 17th March, 1178, of a chapel in Salzburg in Austria, to Saints Thomas, Patrick, and Gertrude, reflects the devotion of archbishop Konrad.[31] The cult of St Thomas penetrated widely and deeply through German-speaking lands.

In Castile, when Henry's daughter Eleanor married Alfonso III, Bishop Jocelin of Salisbury, who had accompanied the princess to her new realm, dedicated a chapel to St Thomas the Martyr in Sigüenza, and the queen later endowed a chapel in his honour in Toledo cathedral. The beautiful church of San Tomás Cantuariense in Salamanca dates from the

25 Borenius, 52-4 and plate XVII, fig. 2. A silver reliquary bearing an image of St John the Baptist, flanked by SS Thomas and Blaise (the three patrons of Brunswick cathedral), attributed to local workmanship, is now in the Cleveland Museum of Art, Ohio, U.S.A.: R. Foreville, *Le jubilé,* plate 12.

26 Borenius, 62 and plates XXI-XXII.

27 *ibid.,* 68 and plate XXVI, fig. 1.

28 *ibid.,* 68 and plate XXVI, fig. 2.

29 *ibid.,* 58-9 and plate XIX.

30 E. Müller, 'Die Geschichte des Konvents der Zisterzienserinnen von St Thomas an der Kyll bis 1802' in *St Thomas an der Kyll,* ed. Priesterhaus St Thomas, Trier (1980), 28. The cathedral of Trier formerly contained a substantial frieze depicting the life of Becket in the Nicholas Choir: Borenius, 54.

31 B. Fischer,'Der heilige Erzbischof Thomas Becket (1118-70) und die Anfänge seiner Verehung in St Thomas an der Kyll' in *St Thomas an der Kyll,* 17 n. 17. For a full discussion of the cult of St Thomas in German-speaking lands (and also in Scandinavia and Italy), see M. Barth, *art.cit.* in n. 2, above.

1180s, but the details of its foundation are unrecorded.[32] The church of Sta Maria in Tarrasa, north of Barcelona, contains an extremely interesting series of wall-paintings from the late twelfth century, which, if the identification of subject is correct, indicate the early entry of Thomas's cult to the neighbouring kingdom of Aragon.[33] Princess Joan's entry into the Norman kingdom of Sicily, to marry King William II in 1177, merely reinforced the strong ties between England and Sicily and the close personal links between the higher clergy of the two countries. William's new cathedral at Monreale, completed in the period 1174-88/99, contains a magnificent mosaic of the new saint,[34] and a very fine reliquary pendant in gold was commissioned by Reginald FitzJocelin, bishop of Bath and Wells (1174-79) and a former member of Becket's household, for presentation to Joan's mother-in-law, the Queen Dowager Margaret, who died in 1183.[35] This magnificent piece is now in the Metropolitan Museum of Art in New York. It may well have been a recognition of the patronage which the queen, then regent for her son, bestowed on Becket's relatives during his exile.[36] In Hungary, Lukácz of Esztergom was recognised as another Becket in his defence of ecclesiastical rights in that country.[37] To his foundation is ascribed the collegiate church of St Thomas in Pest (Budapest), dated *c.* 1175-80, and the introduction of St Thomas's feast in the Hungarian liturgies,[38] and possibly also the recognition of Becket as copatron of the kingdom, with SS Stephen, Adalbert, Emmeram, and others. The marriage of Margaret, daughter of Becket's protector, Louis VII of

32 Borenius, 48.

33 *ibid.,* 49-50 and plates XV and XVI. The alternative identification of St Narcissus of Gerona has been suggested, but that has not been established: see M.-M. Gauthier, 'Le meurtre', 252 n. 24. The iconographical theme of 'murder in the cathedral' presents serious problems of identification, since many saints, apart from Becket, were killed by sword or axe in similar circumstances. Nevertheless, Mme Gauthier argues for a presumption in favour of a Becket identification, unless there is good evidence to show the renewal of another cult in the area in question at the turn of the twelfth century: *ibid.*, 249-52, and n. 15.

34 Borenius, 13-14 and plate II, fig. 1. For the date, see E. Jamison, 'Alliance of England and Sicily in the second half of the twelfth century' in *England and the Mediterranean tradition: studies in art, history, and literature,* Oxford (1945), 25.

35 P. A. Newton, 'Some new material for the study of the iconography of St Thomas Becket' in Foreville, *Thomas Becket,* 260-62.

36 Becket's letter *Licet faciem vestram* thanks Queen Margaret for her kindness to 'coexsules nostros, proscriptos Christi et consanguineos nostros', *Materials* VII, 142.

37 Z. J. Kosztolnyik, 'The Church and Béla III of Hungary (1172-96): the role of Archbishop Lukács of Esztergom', *Church History* 49 (1980), 375-86.

38 P. Radó, *Libri liturgici manuscripti bibliothecarum Hungariae et Limitropharum regionum,* revised L. Mesey, Budapest (1973), 15, 17, *et passim.* Evidence of the early entry of St Thomas's cult is seen in Bibl. Nat. Hung. Nyelvemlékek 1 (Radó, no. 2), which was completed in 1192-95. The MS belonged to the monastery of Somogyvár in the period 1203-16, *ibid.,* 40-76, esp. 51.

France, former daughter-in-law of Henry II and widow of the Young King Henry, to Béla III in 1183, may well have advanced the cause of Canterbury's saint. The lady certainly had no love for her former father-in-law.

While Henry II's female relations helped to extend the cult to the corners of Europe, his own penitential foundations set an example in his own lands, which others could follow. His rebuilding of the church of the priory of St-Jacques-du-Mont-aux-Malades in Rouen in 1174, which was rededicated to St Thomas, has claims to be the earliest centre of cult in Normandy, though it is closely challenged for that honour by Reginald FitzJocelin's consecration of a chapel of St-Thomas in St-Lö on 28th July, 1174.[39] But other influences played their part in establishing the popularity of St Thomas in Normandy. Although he was known as the English St Thomas, *natione Anglicus,* his parents were born in the duchy, and he was Norman by race and language, and Normandy had equal claims on his patronage. These close Norman associations probably explain the popularity of his cult there, and its special concentration in the area from which his family derived, in the flood-plain of the river Seine.[40] No other area in Henry II's continental dominions revealed the same degree of devotion, although none was wholly without instances of his cult.[41]

Capetian France had been the land of Becket's refuge, its king, Louis VII, his patron, its monasteries at Pontigny and Sens, his places of retreat, and its most influential bishop, William *aux Blanchesmains*, bishop-elect of Chartres (1165-76), archbishop of Sens (1168-76), and finally archbishop of Reims (1176-1202), his constant support through the difficult years of the exile. It is not surprising to find widespread indications of Becket's cult throughout the provinces of the French church.[42] A very early example was the rededication of the Victorine chapel of St-Laurent, in which Thomas had preached just before he returned to England to die in 1170.[43] Louis VII's brother, Robert de Dreux, founded the royal collegiate church of St-Thomas-du-Louvre in 1180,[44] and John of Salisbury's most

39 Foreville, 'Le culte . . . Normandie', 137, 145, 150. The prior of Mont-St-Jacques, Master Nicholas, was a firm supporter of Becket throughout the dispute with Henry II, see A. Duggan, *Thomas Becket: a textual history of his letters,* Oxford (1980), 27 n. 9.

40 Foreville, 'Le culte . . . Normandie', 139-41. Professor Foreville identifies two locations with the name le Becquet, near Elbeuf and the monastery of Notre-Dame-du-Valasse respectively, from which the Becket family could have sprung: *ibid.,* 141 n. 8.

41 Professor Foreville lists 59 centres of cult in the former province of Rouen: *ibid.,* 139, 144-52; 15 in the province of Bourges: 'Le culte . . . France', 183-85; and 4 in the province of Bordeaux: *ibid.,* 186.

42 Professor Foreville lists 5 places of cult in the province of Lyon: *ibid.,* 174-75; 15 for the province of Sens: *ibid.,* 176-78; and 23 for the province of Reims: *ibid.,* 179-82.

43 *ibid.,* 177.

44 *ibid.*

precious gift to his cathedral church at Chartres in 1180 was the magnificent reliquary, now in New York, designed to hold two phials of the martyr's blood. This ranks with the FitzJocelin pendant as one of the earliest and most valuable survivals of the cult of the martyr.[45] As the great gothic cathedrals of northern France soared heavenwards in the thirteenth century, St Thomas was commemorated in the stained glass windows of Sens,[46] Chartres,[47] Angers,[48] and Coutances.[49]

In Italy, papal patronage ensured wide dissemination of devotion to St Thomas. The celebration of his feast was established in the papal curia,[50] his relics were enshrined in St John Lateran and Anagni,[51] and Cardinal Uguccione commissioned a frieze commemorating St Agnes, St Eusebius of Vercelli, St Thomas, and St Cecilia, in the early thirteenth century,[52] for the church of San Martino ai Monte in Rome. In the Sacro Speco, Subiaco, Thomas occurs in a mid-thirteenth century wall-painting with Saints Stephen and Nicholas,[53] and Padua has a thirteenth-century church dedicated to San Tommaso Cantuariense.[54] In Italy, as elsewhere, the cult entered early and spread quickly.[55]

It is against this almost universal devotion to St Thomas that the English segment of the cult must be set. Here, numerous interests combined to enhance the honour of the new saint. His supporters preached

45 Borenius, 78-9 and plate XXIX, fig. 1 and 2; cf. n. 35 above.

46 C. Brisac, 'Thomas Becket dans le vitrail français au début du XIIIe siècle' in Foreville, *Thomas Becket,* 221-26 and plate II.

47 *ibid.,* 226-28 and plate III.

48 *ibid.,* 230-31 and plate IV, fig. 2.

49 *ibid.,* 229-30 and plate IV, fig. 1.

50 Among surviving copies of Alexander III's letters announcing Becket's canonization and ordering the solemn observance of the new feast is *Qui vice beati Petri,* addressed to Bishop Walter of Aversa, *Materials* VII, 549-50. The Canterbury/Sarum lections for Matins are found in two late twelfth/early thirteenth-century lectionaries from St Peter's, Rome (Bibl. Apostolica Vaticana, Archivium S Petri MSS A7, fo. 38^{ra-rb}; C 107, fos. 77va-79rb); Master Euvrardus of Clairvaux's *Passio* occurs in a third: *ibid.,* MS A 6, fos. 98vb-101vb; and the Canterbury//Sarum Mass, *Gaudeamus omnes,* in *ibid.,* MS B 64, fos. 39ra-40ra, a missal *tempore* Clement VI (1342-52). The medieval papal library was rich in Becket materials, see A. Duggan, *Thomas Becket,* 124-25.

51 Borenius, 90; cf. M.-M. Gauthier, 'Le meurtre', 248 n. 4.

52 Borenius, 14-15 and plate II, fig. 2.

53 *ibid.,* 15 and plate III, fig. 3.

54 *ibid.,* 64 and plate XXIII.

55 One of the earliest examples is probably the crypt frescoes in Anagni: see R. Foreville, 'Mort et survie de St Thomas Becket', *Cahiers de Civilisation Médiévale X^e-XIIe siècles* XIV (1971), 26; cf. R. Brentano, *Two Churches, England and Italy in the thirteenth century,* Princeton (1968), 58. St Thomas is to be found in the Fra Angelico altarpiece painted for San Domenico at Fiesole, 1420-25, now in the National Gallery, London.

the glory of their hero,[56] the monks of Christ Church recorded his miracles,[57] his former enemies founded churches and hospitals in his name,[58] the city of London invoked his patronage,[59] and his successors in the see of Canterbury set the image of his martyrdom on their personal seals as a constant reminder of their responsibility to his cause.[60] By the beginning of the thirteenth century, the reputation of Becket was so well established that it was only necessary for controversialists to refer to the cause for which St Thomas had died: his name encapsulated all the claims of the church to independence and freedom, and his dispute with Henry II became an inspiration to later primates in their disputes with their own kings, his name a catch-word in political debate. If *Magna Carta* came to represent the rights of the 'people', the *causa beati Thome* became the symbol of the rights of the church throughout the thirteenth century,

56 There are four major independent biographies: two written by men who had known him well (William FitzStephen and Herbert of Bosham); and two by men who joined him at Canterbury after his return in December 1170, and were eye-witnesses of the murder (Edward Grim and William of Canterbury): *Materials* III, 1-154 and 155-534, II, 353-450, I, 1-136. These can be supplemented by two derivative accounts, of early date but uncertain authorship ('Roger of Pontigny' and the Lambeth Anonymous), and the large compendium made by Elias of Evesham for Henry of Crowland in 1198-9, which weaves together extracts from Herbert, Edward Grim, William of Canterbury, John of Salisbury, and Benedict of Peterborough, and known as the *Quadrilogus (=Quadrilogus II): Materials* IV, 1-79, 80-144, and 269-430. The two most widely-circulated Lives, however, were the short Passions by John of Salisbury and Master Euvrardus of Clairvaux: *Materials* II, 301-22; J. A. Giles, *Vita Sancti Thomae Cantuariensis,* 2 vols, Patres Ecclesiae Anglicanae, Oxford 1845. II, 164-80.

57 Two books of miracles were made at Canterbury in the immediate aftermath of the murder: the first, and possibly the most well-known, was begun by Benedict, later abbot of Peterborough, in early 1171 (*Materials* I, 137-546), and the second, by William of Canterbury, was begun in mid-1172 (*Materials* II, 21-281); see A. Duggan, *Thomas Becket,* 192-4.

58 Henry II founded St Thomas's abbey in Dublin for Augustinian canons regular in 1177 (A. Gwynn and R. N. Hadcock, *Medieval religious houses: Ireland* London (1970), 172; cf. J. T. Gilbert, ed., *The Register of the abbey of St Thomas, Dublin,* Rolls Series 94, London (1889), xi and xvii. It became a Victorine house in 1192); Gilbert Foliot, bishop of London, issued indulgences to assist in the building of St Thomas's Hospital, Southwark, 1173-80, and the Justiciar, Richard de Lucy, founded the Augustinian abbey of Lesnes in Kent in honour of St Thomas the Martyr (M. D. Knowles and R. N. Hadcock, *Medieval religious houses in England and Wales,* 2nd edn, London (1971), 392 and 164; and Ranulf de Broc, who had entertained the murderers, founded the chapel of St-Thomas in the castle of Vernay *post* 1173 (Foreville, 'Le culte . . . France', 168, 186).

59 Borenius, 23-24; cf. Walter de Gray Birch, *Catalogue of seals in the department of MSS in the British Museum,* I (1887), no. 5068. The motto ran: ME QUE TE PEPERI NE CESSES THOMA TUERI.

60 Borenius, 74-5 and plate XXVII, for the counter-seals of Hubert Walter (1195-1205), Stephen Langton (1207-28), Richard Grant (1229-31), Edmund Rich (1233-40), and the seals of Thomas Arundel (1397-1419) and William Warham (1504-32); cf. *Catalogue of seals,* 159-68.

from the days of Stephen Langton[61] to those of Robert Winchelsey;[62] and Innocent III warned King John that it would be perilous for him to oppose God and the church in the cause for which St Thomas had recently shed his blood.[63] Simultaneously, the monarchy continued to cultivate the English martyr: Henry II (and possibly Richard I) was associated with the foundation of the military order of St Thomas of Acon;[64] John visited the shrine on at least three occasions;[65] and although Henry III was chiefly concerned to advance the cult of his royal hero, Edward the Confessor, in whose honour Westminster abbey was so splendidly reconstructed under royal patronage, he never abandoned the blessed martyr, whose translation had adorned the early years of his reign.[66] His own betrothal to Eleanor of Provence was celebrated in Canterbury in 1236,[67] and princess Eleanor of Castile was provided with lavish gifts to present before the shrine on her arrival in England in 1255, after her marriage the previous year to prince Edward, later Edward I;[68] taxes due from Christ Church were remitted to maintain four great candles permanently about the saint's shrine,[69] and 800 candles were ordered in 1240 to celebrate St Thomas's feast in Dublin.[70] Edward I maintained the same devotion, visiting the shrine six times between 1279 and 1305,[71] and Edward II sought papal

61 See below, nn. 91-94.

62 He accepted his election as archbishop in 1273 in the name of the Holy Trinity, the Blessed Virgin Mary, and St Thomas the Martyr, and invoked the merits of St Thomas in valedictions (Rose Graham, ed., *Registrum Roberti Winchelsey Cantuariensis archiepiscopi,* 2 vols, Canterbury and York Society, Oxford (1952-56), II, 1273, 1282, 1288; cf. *ibid.,* 581). His letter to Boniface VIII expressed the link between Becket and the rights of the church very clearly—'Item cum multa nimis gravia contra ecclesiasticas libertates hiis diebus in Anglia fuerint attemptata pro quibus Thomas gloriosus martir occubuit auferendis . . .' (C. Deedes, ed., *Registrum Johannis de Pontissara, episcopi Wintoniensis,* 2 vols, Canterbury and York Society, London (1915-24), I, 202).

63 '. . . non esset tibi tutum in hac causa deo et ecclesie repugnare pro qua beatus Thomas martyr et pontifex gloriosus sanguinem suum recenter effudit.' C. R. Cheney and W. H. Semple, edd., *Select letters of Innocent III concerning England* (1198-1216), Nelson Medieval Texts, London (1953), 89.

64 The founding of the Hospital of St Thomas of Acon on the site of Becket's birthplace was only achieved *pre* 1191, but it was regarded as part of Henry II's penance. It was subject to the Hospitallers; *Religious houses: England,* 372.

65 Matthew Paris, *Chronica Majora,* ed. H. R. Luard, 7 vols, Rolls Series 57, London (1872-83), II, 475, 480, 484. It is significant that he had himself re-crowned at Canterbury by Archbishop Hubert Walter in 1202, before embarking on his Norman campaigns (*ibid.,* 480).

66 See below, n. 96.

67 Matthew Paris, *Chronica Majora* III, 336: 'Desponsata fuit igitur regi H(enrico) III Cantuariae. Nuptiae vero celebratae, Londoniis apud Westmonasterium'.

68 Curia Regis Roll 39 Hen. III, 144.

69 *ibid.,* 24 Hen. III, 175, 181, 208, repeated 26 Hen III, 374-75.

70 *ibid.,* 24 Hen III, 227; cf. Gilbert, *Register . . . abbey of St Thomas,* xi, xvii. Henry III had hoped to rebuild St Thomas's, Dublin, on the scale of Westminster abbey.

71 Foreville, *Le jubilé,* 15 n. 4.

recognition from John XXII for the ampulla of miraculous oil said to have been given to St Thomas for the consecration of English kings. The elaboration of this myth was clearly intended to give the English monarchy a sacred character equal to that of their Capetian rivals. The French claimed that their coronation oil was the chrism, miraculously renewed, with which St Rémi had baptised Clovis, and so inaugurated the line of Catholic kings in France. Despite John XXII's refusal to give papal authority to the story, the myth was established. Significantly enough Henry IV seems to have been the first king to have been consecrated with it, and thenceforward the coronation oil of the English kings was known as the *oleum sancti Thome.*[72] Where the French kings were anointed with oil brought by angels to St Rémi, the English monarchs were anointed with oil given by the Virgin herself to Becket. Thus, England's Thomas became the equal of France's Rémi! Even more surprising, perhaps, was the association of his patronage with baronial conspiracies. A hymn has been discovered, which invoked his aid for the earl of Leicester and the Young King in the 1173-74 rebellion against Henry II,[73] and the chronicle of St Martin of Dover attributed Simon de Montfort's victory at Lewes in 1264 to his miraculous intervention.[74] In both sources, Becket has taken on the character of a national hero, protecting not only the church, but the whole English people.

The application to Becket of the title of martyr depended on an extension of the early Christian concept of death in defence of the faith. The primitive exemplars of supreme Christian virtue, like Polycarp of Smyrna in 155/65, were executed by the Roman state for refusing to compromise or abandon their Christianity. Martyrdom was held to be like baptism—indeed a second baptism, by blood—whereby the victim was immediately sanctified and admitted to the company of the blessed in heaven, the final act of fidelity to Christ erasing any short-comings there may have been in his previous life.[75] In the course of time, and with changing circumstances, the concept was enlarged to include missionaries

72 W. Ullmann, ed., *Liber Regie Capelle,* Henry Bradshaw Society XCII, Cambridge (1961), 35-39, and 91 n. 3. For John XXII's refusal to sanction Edward II's use of the oil, see Reg. Vat. 110, II, ep. 439, fo. 136ra-vb: *Venientes ad nos.* The story put to the Pope included Becket's prophecy that the fifth English king after Henry II (i.e. Edward II) would be a great king and would help to deliver the Holy Land! The form of the prophecy was altered to suit changing circumstances, and by the end of the 14th century, when it took final form (Giles, *Vita S Thomae,* II, 246-7), it promised greatness, victory against the pagans, and peaceful recuperation of lost territories!

73 D. Stevens, *Music in honour of St Thomas,* London (1973), 10-11. Recorded by the Accademia Monteverdiana for Nonesuch Records, 1974.

74 C. L. Kingsford, ed., *The Song of Lewes,* Oxford 1890, 85 n. 358: 'Hoc ascribunt beato Thomae martyri et beato Georgio'. In a vision, Thomas explained 'quievi in pace; sed jam necesse habeo surgere et pugnare pro patria mea Angliae'.

75 Tertullian, *de paenitentia* 13; Clement of Alexandria, *Stromateis,* 4.9.75.

like Boniface of Crediton, cut down while preaching, and individuals like Alphege of Canterbury and Edmund of East Anglia, killed by pagan invaders. St Augustine's statement that it was the cause and not the blow which made the martyr[76] concentrated attention on the motives of slayer and slain, and emphasised the element of witness that is intrinsic to martyrdom. It was in the light of these examples and this definition that Becket was judged. Long before the murder, members of Becket's household were convinced that he would be a martyr, if the worst happened,[77] even though it could not be said that he would suffer in defence of the Christian faith; and afterwards, John of Salisbury proclaimed the justice of his cause and the validity of his witness: Thomas had died *pro libertate ecclesie,* for the freedom of the church, and was thus a martyr to whom, not for whom, prayers were due. Moreover, every aspect of his passion and death emphasised his conformity with the perfect example of Christ himself.[78] Every major biographer made the same points, and some concluded that Becket's martyrdom was even more illustrious than those of the early church, because he died for others, whereas the original martyrs died to save their own souls.[79] These views were transmitted to a wide audience throughout Europe in the short Lives composed by John of Salisbury and Master Euvrardus of Clairvaux.[80]

But the most pervasive image of St Thomas was transmitted in the liturgical celebration of his feast, where the public reading of a specially composed Passion formed the central element in Matins, the solemn night office which began the celebration of his festival. The Canterbury office is no longer extant, but the lections in the Sarum Breviary probably represent the most ancient tradition emanating from Canterbury, traceable in its origin to the first celebration of Becket's feast day on 29th December, 1173, the third anniversary of the murder in the cathedral. The Sarum lections therefore constitute one of the earliest accounts of Becket's life, written at Canterbury in the first flush of exaltation after the canonization of the murdered archbishop. Re-read every year, just before dawn on the morning of the anniversary, they kept the original image of Canterbury's martyr vividly alive, and passed down to succeeding generations a powerful evocation of the saint and his cause. In about 1500 words, the lections

76 St Augustine of Hippo, Ep. 89: 'Martyrem non facit poena, sed causa'.

77 William FitzStephen, *Materials* III, 58: 'Si enim eum pro causa justitiae et libertatis ecclesiasticae pati contigerit, praestante Domino, anima ejus erit in requie, memoria in benedictione'.

78 *The Letters of John of Salisbury, II, The later letters (1163-80),* edd. W. J. Millor and C. N. L. Brooke, Oxford Medieval Texts, Oxford (1979), ep. 305, esp. 726-31.

79 Master Euvrardus of Clairvaux: Giles, *Vita S Thomae,* II, 177-78.

80 See above, n. 6. At least 17 copies of John of Salisbury's *Vita* have been found in MSS of continental provenance (A. Duggan, 'John of Salisbury and Thomas Becket' in *John of Salisbury and his world,* ed. D. Baker, *Studies in church history,* Subsidia 3, forthcoming, n. 4), and 20 copies of the Master Euvrardus Passion.

give a succinct narrative of the main events in Becket's life, followed by a dramatic peroration on the horror of the murder and the glory of the martyr.[81] Image is superimposed upon image, and the readings build up to a dramatic conclusion. Thomas is the shepherd, returning to protect Christ's sheep or lay down his life for their protection, the intrepid defender of ecclesiastical liberty, the man of God, the fearless confessor of Christ, imitating the Saviour in His passion and death: 'And truly was that holy man glorified, who fought for the church, died in the church, in a sacred place, in the period of the Lord's nativity . . . Let the virgin mother church rejoice at the victory of a new martyr; let her rejoice for her new Zachariah, sacrificed in the Temple; let her rejoice for the blood of a second Abel crying out to God on her behalf against the men of blood. The voice of that blood spilt, and the cry of those brains scattered by the bloody swords of the devil's satellites, filled heaven and earth with a great noise. The earth trembled and was shaken by the violence of the sound, and the powers of heaven were so disturbed that, as if in vengeance for the spilling of innocent blood, people rose up against people and kingdom against kingdom; even the realm was divided against itself, and great signs and wonders were seen in the heavens.'[82] This reference to tumult among nations was no mere rhetorical device, but a direct allusion to the immediate condition of King Henry II's domains. The first feast of St Thomas occurred about mid-way through the great rebellion of 1173-74, in which the kings of France and Scotland conspired with Henry's sons against their father. The fate of Henry II's monarchy still hung in the balance when those doom-laden words were written, and the disorder and chaos which appeared widely throughout Henry II's dominions could be interpreted as divine retribution for the murder of Becket. The king's expiation before the tomb was still six months distant. Echoes of these emotive images recur throughout the liturgy for St Thomas's day in antiphons, sequences and responses,[83] reinforced by the choice of the Good Shepherd parable for the Gospel reading, with Gregory's commentary on the parable of the talents.[84] What emerges is the potent symbol of a

81 *Breviarium . . . Sarum* I, ccxlviii-cclviii; cf. Giles, *Vita S Thomae* II, 146-52.

82 *ibid.*, lections VIII and IX: cf. Giles, *Vita S Thomae* II, 151-52: 'At vere sanctus ille glorificandus erat: pro ecclesia certans, in ecclesia passus est in loco sacro, Dominicae nativitatis tempore . . . Gaudeat igitur virgo mater ecclesia novum martyrem reportasse triumphum; gaudeat novum pro sua liberatione Zachariam immolatum in templo. Gaudeat novi Abel sanguinem pro se contra viros sanguinum clamare ad Dominum. Vox enim sanguinis effusi, vox cerebri funestorum satellitum gladiis dispersi et mundum similiter et caelum celebri clamore replevit. A clamore namque sanguinis hujus commota est et contremuit terra; sed et virtutes coelorum motae sunt adeo ut quasi in ultionem sanguinis innocentis surgeret gens contra gentem et regnum adversus regnum, immo ut regnum in se ipsum fieret divisum terroresque de caelo et signa magna fierent'.

83 See for example, *Jacet granum, Clangat pastor, Pastor caesus,* and *Granum cadit: Breviarium . . . Sarum* I, ccxlv-ccxlvi, and cclvii.

84 *ibid.*, cclvi; the Gospel reading is *Ego sum pastor bonus,* John x 11-16; and the homily is Gregory I, Homilia 14, *super Lucam* xix 12-28.

Christ-like pastor, chaste, generous, disdainful of the world, fearless defender of justice and the liberty of the church, cut down by the swords of the impious. Another Abel, another Zachariah, another Christ, offering himself for the good of the church and triumphing, like the early martyrs, in death.

Modern historians have been surprised by the evident delight taken by the contemporary biographers in the grandeur of his life as chancellor, and his enjoyment of the fruits of office. He engaged in campaigns on the king's behalf, leading the Canterbury knights in his own person in 1156, against Henry's younger brother Geoffrey, in 1157 against the Welsh, and in 1159 in the campaign against Toulouse. His court outdid that of his master, and the embassy that secured the marriage alliance between the kings of England and France in 1158 was magnificent. Contemporaries did not share the modern observers' discomfort. Far from minimising the worldly splendour of the chancellor, they revel in the public esteem of their hero. 'Above and beyond all others', wrote Herbert of Bosham, 'he seemed magnificent: great of heart, large in stature, splendid in his accoutrements. There was about him nothing that was not great, nothing that was not magnificent'.[85] His former power and glory, his enjoyment of the king's intimate friendship made his spiritual conversion all the more striking to contemporaries, and all the more puzzling to later commentators. In his day and in the aftermath of his death, however, it enhanced rather than reduced his heroic stature. In a period when political and ecclesiastical offices were regularly combined in one person, when treasurers, chancellors, and even justiciars were normally rewarded with bishoprics, Becket's resignation of the chancellorship after his elevation to Canterbury provided a model for the upright. Here could be seen an example of the classic Christian rejection of the world, the bishop's rejection of political power and advantage for the glory of God and the service of the church: a story of courage and heroic self-sacrifice. The splendour of Becket's life as chancellor and the extensive power that he wielded as the new king's right-hand-man increased rather than diminished the scale of his sacrifice. His voluntary resignation of political office was seen as a conscientious rejection of the temptations of the world. Here was a primate who put service of the church above service to the state, defence of ecclesiastical rights above private advantage, suffering sequestration, exile, and death in defence of principle.

85 *Materials* III, 176: 'super omnes et prae omnibus apparebat magnificus, sicut magnus in corde magnus et corpore, magnus et apparatu. Nihil circa eum nisi magnum, nihil nisi magnificentia'.

This image fitted in exactly with the prevailing trends in progressive ecclesiastical thought in the late twelfth and thirteenth centuries. Three major theological and spiritual movements met and mingled in the schools of Paris. The ascetic spirituality of Bernard of Clairvaux and the Cistercians and the mystical theology of Hugh of St-Victor and the Victorines combined with the penetrating analysis and allegorical exegesis of academic theologians from Robert Pullen onwards, to provide an extraordinary blend of profound spirituality and commitment to the restoration and reform of Christian society, which reflected the deepest stirrings of the contemporary church.[86] By the last quarter of the twelfth century, Peter the Chanter and his pupils championed the twin ideals of a liberated church and a pastoral episcopate freed from secular concerns. They urged the withdrawal of ecclesiastics from secular pursuits, the moral regeneration of the clergy, and the establishment of canonical norms of conduct. For them, a bishop was to be a *bonus pastor,* the spiritual shepherd of his flock, promoted for merit, who dedicates his life to the welfare of the church, protecting it from the greed and exploitation of secular powers. As portrayed by biographers and proclaimed in liturgical celebrations, St Thomas conformed in an eminent way to the demanding pattern being proposed for the episcopate. This explains the immediate espousal of his cause by the Chanter and his school.[87] Master Peter defended Becket's title to martyrdom in disputation with Master Roger Normannus, probably before 1173,[88] and proposed him as a model of courage and rectitude. Becket became the hero of the reformed and reforming church, his martyrdom vindicating the dignity and freedom for which it had striven since the days of Gregory VII. St Thomas made some very influential converts among the students of Peter the Chanter. The later Pope Innocent III, Lothario di Segni, interrupted his studies in Paris to visit the martyr's shrine in the 1180s,[89] and the two renowned

86 B. Smalley, *The Becket dispute and the schools,* Oxford (1973), 18-58; J. W. Baldwin, *Masters, princes and merchants: the social views of Peter the Chanter and his circle,* 2 vols, Princeton (1970), I, 32-46, 296-311, 312-43. That extremely influential 'school' included renowned reformers and preachers like Foulques de Neuilly (d. 1202) and Jacques de Vitry, bishop of Acre, cardinal bishop of Tusculum (d. 1240), *ibid.,* 36-38. (See also nn. 90 and 91, below.)

87 *ibid.,* 5, 145-47, 172, 180-84. Commenting on Hebrews II. 4, Peter wrote 'ad hoc etiam loquitur abel exemplo quia suo exemplo nos ammonet ut iusti simus. Interemit eum mors sed fama eius non est extincta. Similiter ad hoc loquitur nobis beatus cantuariensis Thomas exemplo suffragio et verbo quod reliquit': *ibid.,* II, 184 n. 37.

88 *ibid.,* I, 5, 146; cf. idem, 'A debate at Paris over Thomas Becket between Master Roger and Master Peter the Chanter', *Collectanea Stephan Kuttner* I, *Studia Gratiana* XI, Bologna (1967), 119-32.

89 Smalley, 139; Foreville, *Le jubilé,* 4.

II. Saint Thomas of Canterbury and Saint Thomas of Hereford.

English masters, Robert de Courçon[90] and Stephen Langton,[91] who were destined for outstanding academic and ecclesiastical careers, became firm advocates of his cause. It was principally through Robert and Stephen that the views of the Chanter were passed on to the younger generation of scholars at the end of the twelfth century, and remained part of the common heritage of the Oxford and Paris schools during the first two decades of the thirteenth. It was in this milieu that the English scholar-bishops—Edmund of Abingdon, Robert Grosseteste, Richard of Wyche, Oliver Sutton, Thomas Cantilupe—received their theological formation. It was an austere training-ground, and set a demanding standard of episcopal and clerical duty, for which the model was St Thomas of Canterbury.

Stephen Langton was one of the principal architects of the thirteenth-century cult, responsible for the translation and first jubilee in 1220, and for the propagation through liturgy and sermon of a particularly elevated image of the martyr. The circumstances of his appointment as archbishop of Canterbury, the long-drawn-out controversy with King John, and the six-year exile at Pontigny, all inclined Stephen to regard himself not only as the heir of Becket's see, but as the inheritor of his responsibility and his cause. Indeed, his own career seemed to be a re-enactment of Becket's, and the glorious martyr was persecuted anew in his person. His use of the phrase *salvo ordine nostro et ecclesie libertate* in 1210 was a deliberate and telling allusion to Becket's defence of his clerical order and the rights of the church,[92] and even the style *minister humilis*, which his chancery adopted from 1220, was derived from Becket's practice.[93] The coincidences between himself and Becket were useful propaganda ploys in his contest with the king, but his own personal regard for St Thomas rested on deeper foundations. Stephen was one of the most brilliant products of the school of Peter the Chanter in Paris, and it was there in the 1180s that he acquired not only his theology but his reverence for the recently martyred archbishop, whose canonization had vindicated the cause of the

90 Robert de Courçon (Curzon), canon of Noyon (1204), canon of Paris (1209), cardinal (1212), papal legate to France (1213-15), d. at Damietta 1219: Baldwin, *Masters, princes, and merchants*, 19-25.

91 Cardinal Priest (1206), archbishop of Canterbury (1207-28): *ibid.*, 25-31. He numbered among his students Master Thomas of Marlborough, abbot of Evesham (1229), and Master Richard Poore, successively bishop of Chichester (1215), Salisbury (1217), and Durham (1228).

92 *Acta Stephani Langton Cantuariensis Archiepiscopi, 1207-1228*, ed. K. Major, Canterbury and York Society 50 (1950), 3: 'non nos immo ipse in nobis potius infestatur'.

93 *ibid.*, 10-11 and xxi-xxiv. His counter seal bore a fine depiction of the martyrdom, with the device: MORS EXPRESSA FORIS SIT TIBI INTUS VITA AMORIS, see *Catalogue of Seals* I, 160.

reformers.[94] When, therefore, he had the opportunity to elevate the relics of St Thomas, he was honouring both his predecessor and the hero of his youth, and he was proclaiming to the world the continuing relevance of Becket's cause.

The unusually long delay of fifty years between the canonization and translation of St Thomas, which resulted from a series of misfortunes affecting Canterbury,[95] enabled Stephen to preside over the most splendid religious occasion in thirteenth-century England and to inaugurate a revival of devotion to Becket. For the archbishop, the translation marked the triumph of his ecclesiastical policy; for the monarchy, it marked the establishment of its authority under the protection of the papal legate; and for the generality of the people, it marked the restoration of peace and order, and the beginning of a more settled and prosperous period in national life. In the presence of the young king Henry III and his Justiciar, Hubert de Burgh, and a great company of magnates, the body of the martyr was conducted from the crypt to its new and magnificent resting-place in Holy Trinity Chapel by an imposing procession of ecclesiastics, headed by Pandulf, the papal legate, the archbishops of Canterbury and Reims, and an unnamed Hungarian archbishop. It was then placed in a golden casket, enriched with precious stones, and set upon a marble altar,[96] and a second feast of St Thomas was added to the English calendar, one which was destined to eclipse the original festival on 29th December. The date of the translation had not been a matter of chance. It had been

94 F. M. Powicke, *Stephen Langton,* Oxford (1928), esp. 23-48; A. d'Esneval, 'La survie de St Thomas Becket à travers son quatrième successeur, Étienne Langton' in *Thomas Becket,* 111-14; Henry, abbot of Crowland, paid tribute to Shephen's emulation of Becket, when he dedicated a new version of the *Quadrilogus* Life of Becket to him on the occasion of the Translation: 'Opera siquidem vestra, reverendissime pater, testimonium perhibent de vobis quod beatissimo martyri Thomae praedecessori vestro conformes fueritis et sitis, non solum per expressam morum similitudinem verum etiam per exilii caeterarumque molestiarum fortem et aequanimam perpessionem', Giles, *Vita S Thomae,* II, 40-41.

95 The solemn translation of a new saint's relics normally followed swiftly upon his canonization. In Becket's case, however, a series of misfortunes intervened: the delay in consecrating his successor, Richard of Dover, the great fire in Canterbury cathedral on 5th September, 1174, which necessitated the rebuilding of the choir and the chapel of the Holy Trinity, an enterprise which occupied 10 years until the death of archbishop Richard in 1184, the long dispute between archbishop Baldwin and the monks over his attempt to build a new collegiate church at Hackington, which occupied 15 years (until 1200), Richard I's crusade, and finally the difficulties of King John's reign, which resulted in the great interdict of 1209-13; see Foreville, *Le jubilé,* 5-7.

96 The best account is in Walter of Coventry, *Memoriale,* ed. W. Stubbs, 2 vols, Rolls Series 58, London (1872-73), II, 245-6; cf. Roger of Wendover, *Flores Historiarum,* ed. H. G. Hewlett, 3 vols, Rolls Series 84, London (1886-9), II, 254: 'nam dignissimum omnibus videbatur, ut sanctum martyrem Christi generaliter honorarent et colerent, qui pro universali ecclesia sanguinem suum fundere et ad finem usque non timuit fideliter decertare'; see also Matthew Paris, *Chronica Majora,* ed. H. R. Luard, 7 vols, Rolls Series 57, London (1872-83), III, 59-60; Foreville, *Le jubilé,* 8-11.

very carefully chosen in order to enhance the significance of the event. The day selected was not the ordinary fiftieth anniversary of the martyrdom, but the providential day of jubilee, calculated according to the details given in *Leviticus:* it took place on 7th July 1220, on the tenth day (by Langton's calculations) of the seventh month after seven-times-seven years from the event;[97] and for good measure, the day was Tuesday, corresponding with the special Tuesdays in Becket's life,[98] the date was the anniversary of Henry II's inhumation in 1189, and 1220 was a leap-year, a time of good fortune.[99] The pope, Honorius III, the papal legate, and the bishops who attended the ceremony, issued indulgences to a total of 540 days to all who should attend the solemnities at Canterbury, and the pope subsequently increased the amount and established the indulgence in perpetuity.[100]

There is no secure evidence concerning the authorship of the office for 29th December,[101] but a late Canterbury tradition attributes to Stephen Langton, or at least to a member of his entourage, the composition of the Translation liturgy.[102] If this assignment is accurate, and comparison of the lections and sequences with Langton's Translation sermon and the relevant papal bulls strongly supports that assumption,[103] then the liturgy affords an invaluable insight into Stephen's attitude to St Thomas. Four significant elements are found in the readings: the triumph of an Englishman,[104] the providential nature of the special Tuesdays in Becket's life,

97 *Leviticus* xxv 8-9: 'Numerabis quoque tibi septem hebdomadas annorum, id est, septies septem, quae simul faciunt annos quadraginta novem: Et clanges buccina mense septimo, decima die mensis, propitiationis tempore in universa terra vestra. Sanctificabisque annum quinquagesimum et vocabis remissionem cunctis habitatoribus terrae tuae: ipse est enim jubileus'. Stephen calculated his jubilee from 29th December, 1170, so that 7th July, 1220, was the *tenth* day in the seventh month, as the text required.

98 Stephen Langton, *Tractatus de Translatione Beati Thomae,* Pat. Lat. CXC, col. 421. (See also nn. 8 and 105).

99 *ibid.,* cols. 409 and 421-22: cf. *Breviarium . . . Sarum,* III, 446.

100 Walter of Coventry, II, 246: Foreville, *Le jubilé,* 165-66.

101 It is possible that the attribution of the lections to Master John of Salisbury (bishop of Chartres, 1176-80), made in the Sarum Breviary, is accurate: *Breviarium . . . Sarum,* I, 248, 'Passio sancti Thomae, edita a Johanne sanctae Recordationis, Carnotensi episcopo, prius cancellario Sarum ecclesiae'.

102 Instructions given to the Canterbury mission sent to Paul II in 1469 to seek papal approval for the 1470 jubilee claim Sephen's authorship (or at least that of a member of his entourage) for the Translation *lections:* Foreville, *Le jubilé,* 190, 'Que legenda creditur vel scripta a dicto domino Stephano cardinali vel *(ab alio ut)* in festo translationis legeretur ab eodem approbata'.

103 *ibid.,* 89-95.

104 *Breviarium . . . Sarum,* III, 448 and 451, 'unus ex anglicis inter angelos constitutus, qui intercessor sit pro salute populorum'. This echoes the language of the papal letter, *Rex celestis,* which authorised the Translation: Foreville, *Le jubilé,* 94.

revealing him as a man chosen by God,[105] the concept of martyrs as cornerstones in the edifice of the church, echoing Joshua's setting up of monuments to the twelve tribes of Israel,[106] and finally, the idea of jubilee, also derived from the Old Testament, as a period of repentance and remission of sins.[107] The elevation of Becket's relics was an occasion of jubilation, of grace, and divine mercy. In the course of a sermon, probably delivered in St John Lateran on 29th December 1220, Stephen applied to St Thomas the evocative quotation from *Ecclesiasticus* 50,1.8: *Ecce sacerdos magnus quasi flos rosarum in diebus vernis et quasi lilia in transitu aquarum,* interpreting the lily and the rose as symbols of martyrdom and setting Becket before his hearers as a model for their own day. 'Would that those who are set up as prelates had zeal for the souls of their subjects in the manner of St Thomas, who did not flinch from challenging the tyrant's anger and uncovering his head to the butchers' swords, in order to safeguard the church, to protect his people, and to

105 *Breviarium . . . Sarum,* III, 447. The belief that Tuesday (dies martis, feria tertia) was a providential day in Becket's life was established early, and almost certainly derives from oral tradition at Canterbury in the early 1170s. Its first occurrence is in the metrical *Vie de Saint Thomas* (ed. E. Walberg, Lund (1922), 198) composed by the French clerk, Guernes de Pont-Sainte-Maxence, who had come to Canterbury in 1172 to gather material for his epic. None of his known sources contains the item, and it may be presumed that he had it from Becket's immediate circle. From Guernes, it passed to Ralph de Diceto (*Ymagines Historiarum,* ed. W. Stubbs, 2 vols, Rolls Series, London (1876), I, 344), and from him to Roger of Wendover (*Flores Historiarum,* I, 85), and thence to Matthew Paris (*Chronica Majora,* II, 281); meanwhile it was adopted, in slightly changed form, by Herbert of Bosham *c.* 1186 (*Materials* III, 326). Guernes listed five Tuesdays: Becket's birthday, his flight from Northampton, his arrival in France, his return from exile, and his martyrdom. The addition of the translation and one other marvellous occurrence (the Pontigny vision in which Christ foretold the martyrdom) made up the sacred number of seven, thereby strengthening the prophetic implications of these coincidences. The keepers of the shrine (see n. 8) wrote that there were seven wonderful Tuesdays, but they listed only six, and Pope Pius II gave the full tale when he granted indulgences to visitors to the hospital of St Thomas of Acon in London in 1458 (Foreville, 'Tradition et conflit dans la chronologie de Thomas Becket', *Bulletin philosophique et historique (jusqu'à 1715) du Comité des travaux historiques et scientifiques, 1955 et 1956,* Paris (1957), 7-28; all seven are given poetic expression in the antiphon *Gaude lux Londoniarum,* found in fourteenth and fifteenth-century Books of Hours (e.g. Brit. Libr. MSS Arundel 341, fo. 16; Harleian 2846, fo. 34^{r}; 2900, fos. 56^{v}-58^{r}; 2982, fos. 13^{v}-14^{r}; 3000, fo. 31^{r-v}: these MSS were all executed in Flanders for English patrons. For the text, see J. A. Giles, *Anecdota Bedae, Lanfranci et Aliorum,* Caxton Society XII, London (1851), 202-3). This story of Becket's Tuesdays can be reconciled with the known historical circumstances, except for the Pontigny vision, to which no precise date can be assigned, and Becket's landing in France, for which biographers give the date of All Souls' Day, 2nd November, which in 1164 fell on a Monday. Professor Foreville reconciles the divergent evidence by suggesting that Thomas left England (i.e. boarded ship) late on All Souls' Day and landed in France before dawn on the morning of Tuesday, 3rd November 1164 (Foreville, 'Tradition et conflit', 19 n. 1).

106 *Breviarium . . . Sarum,* III, 448-49.

107 *ibid.,* 446; see also n. 97, above.

defend liberty.'[108] Two ideas are linked in this exposition: St Thomas as the good bishop, abandoning the delights of the world to devote himself to his spiritual responsibility, and St Thomas as the martyr for his time, laying down his life in the cause of ecclesiastical freedom. Even more splendid imagery was deployed six months later, when Stephen celebrated the first anniversary of the translation in a long commentary on the significance of Becket's elevation. St Thomas is a lantern, lit by God to enlighten the world, the elevation of his relics like the rising of the sun, his new tomb a signpost to mark the way of the just.[109] In a significant way, therefore, the liturgy of the Translation complements that of the original feast. The historical Becket, still discernible in the readings of the *natalitio,* has given way to the martyr and the saint, whose death was an affirmation of Christian verity, whose shrine is a symbol of grace, and whose continuing patronage is a source of divine favour.

St Thomas appealed to the thirteenth century on three levels. On the political plane, he was a symbol of the church's claim to independence from secular direction and control. The stark details of his martyrdom—an archbishop standing before an altar in a cathedral, cut down by four royal knights—created a potent image of the tension between sacred and secular, between church and state, and a statement of the ultimate triumph of the former over the latter. A king might murder the body, but the soul passed to eternal bliss, and God glorified His servant. In a society accustomed to paradox, symbolism, and allegory, the portrayal of Becket's martyrdom was a most effective piece of visual propaganda. It was because he represented the *libertas ecclesie,* the freedom of the English church as a part of the wider Latin Christendom under the papacy, that Henry VIII destroyed his shrine and ordered the deletion of his name from the service-books of the English church in 1538;[110] it was for the same reason that Thomas More,[111] three years earlier in 1535, had prayed that his execution might take place on the eve of St Thomas's Translation,

108 P. B. Roberts, 'Langton on Becket: a new look and a new text', *Mediaeval Studies* XXXV (1973), 44 and 47: 'Ut zelum animarum subditarum habeant qui in specula prelationis sunt eminenti, exemplo Beati Thome qui pro tuitione ecclesie, pro commisso grege, pro conservanda libertate non formidavit se furori tyrannico constanter obicere, et gladiis funestorum satellitum caput exponere'. The imagery of the lily and the rose had a distinguished ancestry in biblical exegesis and commentaries on martyrdom, reaching back to Cyprian, Jerome, and Gregory I: see J. O'Reilly, ' "Candidus et Rubicundus": an image of martyrdom in the "Lives" of Thomas Becket', *Analecta Bollandiana* 99 (1981), 303-14.

109 Pat. Lat. CXC, cols. 407-24, esp. cols. 422 and 424.

110 Borenius, 109-10.

111 'I should be sorry that it should be any longer than tomorrow for it is St Thomas Eve and the Octave of St Peter, and therefore tomorrow beg I to go to God. It were a meet day and very convenient for me': quoted in Foreville, 'Mort et survie', 32 n. 71.

which significantly coincided with the octave of St Peter (6th July). He was not disappointed. On the ecclesiastical plane, St Thomas was an example of supreme episcopal duty, the *bonus pastor* who laid down his life for his sheep. In this capacity he became an inspiration to generations of bishops and clergy who had to decide where their loyalties lay in the conflicting currents of political life. The prevailing climate of opinion demanded spiritual bishops, educated, contemplative, unencumbered by secular office. Thomas, who had resigned the chancellorship of England, who fed the poor at his table, who abandoned home and honour and comfort in fidelity to his office, became an ideal exemplar. So persistent was that image, that Thomas Brinton, the reforming bishop of Rochester in the reign of Richard II, used the theme of St Thomas as good bishop and model cleric to castigate the venality, self-seeking, and moral cowardice of the clergy of his day, putting Thomas forward as everything they were not.[112] It is evident that the power of the message had lost nothing in the preceding two hundred years, though it gained the added spice of a Saracen princess as mother to the saint.[113] And William Langland, in his turn, held him up as a reproach to worldly prelates.[114] On the spiritual plane, he was a saint whose life provided a pattern of virtue and whose continuing intercession could be invoked to heal the spiritual and physical ills of the world; his shrine was privileged with indulgences, and later archbishops relied on his merits in granting indulgences of their own.[115] It was the hope of grace, remission of penance, and healing that drew the thousands of ordinary pilgrims to Becket's tomb every year. To the church, Thomas was a symbol of triumph and future glory, to bishops and clergy, a model of that renunciation which they all expected to make sooner or later, to the laity, the pattern of a courageous and beneficent prelate, crowned with bliss when the king's men cut him down.

Only three thirteenth-centry Englishmen achieved canonization: Edmund of Abingdon in 1246, Richard of Chichester in 1262, and Thomas

112 Sr M. Aquinas Devlin, *The Sermons of Thomas Brinton (1373-1389)*, 2 vols, Camden Third Series LXXXV-LXXXVI, London (1954), sermons nos. 4, 10, 30, 91, and 92; see esp. no. 10, on the text *Bonus pastor animam suam dat pro ovibus suis*, and nos. 91 and 92, which depict Thomas as an exemplar of every episcopal and clerical virtue.

113 *ibid.*, II, 413. The 'Saracen Legend', which describes Becket's mother as a Saracen princess who had freed his father from moslem captivity and then followed him to England, where she converted to Christianity and married him, was concocted probably in the early thirteenth century, and secured a wide currency: A. Duggan, *Thomas Becket*, 178, n. 7; 193, n. 2.

114 W. W. Skeat, ed., *Langland's Vision of Piers the Ploughman*, Text C, Early English Text Society, London (1873), 324:

In sauacion of mannys saule seynt thomas of Caunterbury
Among vnkynde cristene in holychurche was sleye,
And alle holychurche honoured for that deyinge.
He is a forbusne to alle busshopes and a bryght myrour,
And souereyneliche to alle such that of surrye bere name.

115 *Registrum Winchelsey*, I, 27-8, 66; II, 796.

of Hereford, after some delay, in 1320;[116] and there is a remarkable general conformity between them. All three combine strict personal asceticism with academic learning and exemplary episcopal office; all three, therefore, conform, at least in essentials, to the contemporary ideal of the holy bishop so assiduously promoted by the Becket cult and by the reformist products of the schools of Oxford and Paris. So great was the influence of the image of St Thomas on prevailing attitudes that Eustace of Faversham modelled his Life of Edmund of Abingdon on John of Salisbury's Life of Becket,[117] and in so doing pressed Edmund into a mould that was not rightfully his. St Edmund was certainly a deeply spiritual and conscientious archbishop, who revered the memory of his legendary predecessor, but his struggle and death bore little resemblance to those of Becket. Nevertheless, the slight coincidences of his last days were exaggerated to provide a providential replication of Becket's exile at Pontigny,[118] a theme greatly amplified in the *Liber Sancti Edmundi,* and supported by an apocryphal prophecy in which St Thomas foretold that his saintly successor, exiled for the same cause as himself, would be entombed in Pontigny, as a recompense for the abbey's hospitality to himself.[119] Edmund's closest disciple and the companion of his last days, St Richard Wyche of Chichester, could not be quite assimilated to the same heroic pattern, though his election against the wishes of Henry III, his mortifications, and his fidelity to his episcopal office were counted as reflections of Becket. In the case of St Thomas of Hereford, a convenient prophecy ascribed to his uncle, Bishop Walter of Worcester, provided the necessary link. When asked what kind of life he would lead, when he grew up, the young Thomas declared that he wished to be a knight, to which his uncle replied prophetically that he would be a Knight of Christ,

116 There were three further canonizations of 'Englishmen' in the thirteenth century, but they had all lived in the twelfth: Gilbert of Sempringham (1202), Hugh of Avalon, bishop of Lincoln (1220), and William FitzHerbert, archbishop of York (1226).

117 C. H. Lawrence, *St Edmund of Abingdon: a study in hagiography and history,* Oxford (1960), 42, 43, and 203-21 *passim,* where Professor Lawrence has identified borrowings from John of Salisbury.

118 *ibid.,* 217.

119 E. Martène and U. Durand, *Thesaurus novus anecdotorum,* 5 vols, Paris (1717), III, cols. 1873-82, linking St Thomas, Stephen Langton, and 'non inferius successor beatus pater Edmundus . . . indutus lorica justitiae pro iustitia exsulans' (col. 1877); cf. Lawrence, *Edmund of Abingdon,* 8. The prophecy is found in a collection of materials relating to St Edmund, assembled at Pontigny soon after his death (Auxerre, Bibl. Municipale MS 125, formerly Pontigny MS 165). The *Vita,* with which it opens, attempts a very close assimilation of Edmund and Thomas. For the prophecy, see Giles, *Vita Sancti Thomae,* II, 297-311.

and fight for God and St Thomas of Canterbury.[120] No doubt contemporaries believed that the prophecy was fulfilled. The Hereford celebrations of his feasts echo in part the Becket liturgy. He is a good pastor, defender of the church's rights (in his case, Hereford's claims against the earl of Gloucester), ascetic and untouched by venality, and even a kind of martyr.[121] The second Thomas was seen to exemplify those virtues which the first had displayed.

120 *AA.SS,* October, I, col. 544D: 'responsum accepisset ab ipso Thoma, quod volebat esse miles, dixit idem episcopus, quod esset miles Christi, et pro Deo et S. Thoma martyri, Cantuariensi archiepiscopo, in clericali ordine militaret'. Richard Swinfield's letter to the pope requesting canonization of Thomas Cantilupe emphasised his defence of the rights of his church—'pro ecclesie sue juribus conservandis labores plurimos usque ad vite sue terminum cum omnia paciencia pertulisset': *Registrum Ricardi de Swinfeld, episcopi Herefordensis,* ed. W. W. Capes, Canterbury and York Society, London (1909), 234-35. And it is significant that Richard had a copy of Becket's condemnation of the Constitutions of Clarendon, together with the Constitutions themselves, copied into his register in 1285: *ibid.,* 108.

121 *The Hereford Breviary,* edd. W. H. Frere and L. E. Brown, Henry Bradshaw Society XXVI and XL, 2 vols, London (1904-1911), II, 310, 'in iuribus ecclesie defendendis'; 349 n. a, 'Carne licet non sensit gladium, corde tamen suplet martirium'; 354, 'manus penitus excutiens a munerum acceptione'.

THE ACADEMIC CAREER OF THOMAS CANTILUPE

by Jeremy Catto

Thomas Cantilupe's academic career spanned more than thirty years and encompassed six faculties in three universities. Unlike a multitude of contemporaries, however, whose books, lectures or lecture notes survive in some form, he left no record of his progress through the intellectual world of the thirteenth century, and his education must be reconstructed from the surviving evidence of the various milieu through which he passed. If this evidence, taken together, forms a coherent account of his passage through the schools and is reconcilable with what we know of his public career, it may be accepted as reasonable: without direct information about his studies, to go further would be impossible.

His education was certainly expensive, and almost, if not quite, all-embracing. As the grandson of William de Cantilupe, the steward of King John's household, he belonged to the office—holding and businesslike stratum of English society: the class of men in whose hands English royal administration had long been the most thorough in the European west. They were fully aware of the uses of education, and their appetite for knowledge of all kinds, plain or marvellous, was being met in the early thirteenth century by the production of encyclopaedias such as Alexander Nequam's *De natura rerum* or the *De proprietatibus rerum* of Bartholomaeus Anglicus. As the nephew of Master Walter de Cantilupe, a graduate, royal justice and finally bishop of Worcester, he was in touch with an active tradition of systematic learning: it is not clear whether Walter was an Oxford master, though it is possible, but whether he was trained in Oxford or Paris, his student days in the 1220's coincided with a formative period of the arts and theology syllabuses in both universities.[1] From about 1227 Walter was employed on Henry III's business at the Roman curia and in 1231 as a justice in eyre; in the latter capacity, he was a junior partner of the great clerical judges, Martin of Pattishall and William Raleigh, whose massive contribution to the making of English law was crystallising, during the 1230's, in the treatise *De legibus et consuetudinibus regni Angliae* which circulated under the name of Henry Bracton.[2] Unlike the common law judges of the end of the century, Walter's colleagues belonged to an intellectual world in which Roman notions of right, and even a philosophical conception of justice could influence the doctrine of the courts: the thorough knowledge of current Roman law in the circle

1 A. B. Emden, *Biographical Register of the University of Oxford to A.D. 1500*, (Oxford, 1957-9), (hereafter Emden), I, 349-50.

2 On its authorship see now S. E. Thorne's introduction to his translation of G. E. Woodbine, ed. *Henrici Bracton De legibus et consuetudinibus regni Angliae*, (Cambridge, Mass., 1968-77), III, i-lii.

of William Raleigh cannot have been unique. As a university master with judicial experience, Walter must have shared their skills and values and taken some part, albeit minor, in forming the still malleable common law of England in the light of larger principles; their endeavours must have influenced his plans for the education of his nephew. It was fortunate for Thomas that his inherited connection with the royal household should have been combined with so easy an access to the living intellectual traditions of his time, traditions which were at once speculative and practical.

Walter de Cantilupe, according to Thomas' companion and secretary Master Robert of Gloucester, 'sent his nephew to the schools and beneficed him', together with his other nephew Hugh, and some years before 1245 (perhaps about 1237) they set up their household in Paris where they studied the Arts course at the University.[3] According to the regulations of 1215, six years of study were necessary for the degree of Master of Arts, with a further two years of lecturing in the faculty, or 'necessary regency': we do not know, however, if these requirements were enforced by 1240.[4] But the main lines of the arts course can be reconstructed with some confidence. Its constituent elements—grammar, logic, rhetoric, arithmetic, geometry, astronomy and music—were derived from ancient schemes of knowledge; but in the twelfth century two subjects, logic and the natural sciences, had developed much more rapidly than the rest. The translation of the natural works of Aristotle and the systematic study of his logic had given these subjects coherent form: Aristotle's method of raising questions, to which only an outline solution was provided, was ideally suited to the disputative method of teaching which had developed at Paris. The 'new Aristotle' and his Arabic commentators Avicenna and Averroes, who were translated with the texts, had not been received into the intellectual world without much heart-searching and controversy. By 1231 his works on natural science had been condemned several times; but in the following decade this impossible ban was allowed to lapse, and Aristotle, usually seen through the eyes of his platonising commentator Avicenna, was universally read. Aristotle's teaching encouraged a methodical approach to the problems of nature and a healthy openness of mind; and these qualities were nurtured by the system of teaching. Though the texts were expounded in lectures, the questions arising from them were discussed in disputations, in which even undergraduates were required to take part: with 'opponents' and 'respondents' taking opposite sides, the questions were dissected and subjected to minute analysis, and were finally 'determined' by a master. The system involved the whole student popula-

3 *Acta Sanctorum*, (Antwerp-Brussels, 1643 sqq.), (hereafter AA.SS), Octobris, I, 544.

4 *Chartularium Universitatis Parisiensis,* ed. H. Denifle and E. Chatelain, (Paris, 1889-97), I, 78, no. 20.

tion in the active dissection of texts: assumptions were questioned and original perspectives encouraged; the emphasis was on a critical approach. Students were enrolled under their own masters, who presumably made them take part in less formal exercises: and like other rich undergraduates Thomas and Hugh Cantilupe brought their own master, Master Peter de Buttevilt, who was later Walter de Cantilupe's steward. Though he was probably a member of the bishop's household, nothing is known of Master Peter's academic career or of his place in the learning of his time.[5]

Little survives of the lectures and disputations of the Arts faculty in the years, perhaps 1237-45, when Cantilupe was studying in Paris. At this time the idea that universal knowledge could be attained by a single intellect had not quite faded: Robert Grosseteste, now bishop of Lincoln, was one of the last to aspire to complete mastery of all the branches of science. The age of philosophical or theological systems, each built upon a uniform coherent metaphysics, had not yet dawned, though the controversies they would engender raged about Cantilupe in his last Parisian period, around 1270. The second quarter of the thirteenth century was the age of the *Summa,* or complete exposition of a subject in a systematic form suitable for instruction. This was especially the case in the faculty of theology. The new gloss on the Bible by the Dominican scholar Hugh of St Cher was intended to summarise everything necessary for the understanding of the text, a massive task for a single scholar. Others produced the definitive work in cooperation, for instance the *Summa Alexandri,* the huge theological textbook ascribed to Alexander of Hales, but in fact compiled by some of his pupils and colleagues about 1245. By contrast, the textbooks of the arts faculty were more modest: the works of Aristotle provided brief but admirable introductions to most of the problems. Among the supplements which had been produced was the *Sphaera* of John of Sacrobosco, a brief exposition of astronomy. Sacrobosco may have taught in Paris, and his *Computus* was probably written in 1235. His *Sphaera* was certainly earlier, and it is not known whether he was still teaching in the schools in Cantilupe's day. But in any case it was one of the few authoritative works by a 'modern' which was universally read. It was provided with a commentary by the south Italian scholar Michael Scot, about 1233, a sure sign of its use in the schools. The *Sphaera* explained the nature of various 'spheres' surrounding the earth, in which the sun, moon and stars moved; the zodiacs or zones of the earth; the equator and the various earthly 'climes'; and eclipses. It was a plain answer to a very natural curiosity about the environment, in its widest sense. Like all such answers, it evoked many more questions than it solved, and Michael Scot's commentary, though probably not produced in

5 *AA.SS,* Octobris, I, 544. On the Paris arts faculty see Gordon Leff, *Paris and Oxford universities in the thirteenth and fourteenth centuries,* (London, 1968), 132-40.

the Paris schools, is doubtless typical, in the questions it raised, of discussion at Paris: is the world eternal? Is there one world or many? Are the skies moved by one 'motor'? Is the motion of the planets rational? Is the zodiac an oblique circle? Is the day as long in Capricorn as in Cancer? These are the questions which Thomas Cantilupe and his brother will have tried to reason out in the Paris schools about 1240.[6]

The brothers had led the aristocratic life of many rich scholars in Paris, with their own household and master. In 1245 they took their first public step and appeared at the first Council of Lyons, where Innocent IV rallied the international church to face the Emperor Frederick II. The rare occurrence of an oecumenical council presented unique opportunities of acquaintance and advancement, and Thomas took them, emerging with the title of papal chaplain and the valuable right to hold several benefices. Perhaps too his subsequent education was influenced by the example of the successful lawyer-pope: for the next eighteen years or so, he pursued a legal training, reading, disputing and eventually ruling in civil and canon law, first at Orleans, then at Paris and Oxford. The first step upon this slow if remunerative road was the school of Roman law at Orleans, where a powerful centre of legal learning was taking shape. In the twelfth century, Roman law had also flourished at Paris, and had received some encouragement from the French kings; but Philip Augustus came to suspect the Roman lawyers' exalted conception of the Emperor, and after the battle of Bouvines in 1214 he prohibited its study in his capital. Expelled from Paris, the masters eventually came to rest at Orleans, where the emerging university, dominated by its law faculties, received its first formal recognition in a papal bull of 1235. Here, according to Robert of Gloucester, Thomas studied under Master Guido.[7] On this occasion it is possible to identify his master: Guido de Guinis, a Bologna-trained lawyer and the first known doctor at the new French university. Guido had once studied under the two greatest exponents of Roman law, Azo, and Accursius: his surviving *Casus Institutionum* was compiled under the influence of Azo's doctrine, and he also made additions to the gloss of Accursius on the *Digestum Vetus.* Modern scholarship has made it possible to see the different emphases of the school of Orleans and its parent school at Bologna.[8] Whereas the Bolognese doctors were concerned to establish the underlying principles of Justinian's corpus, the Orleans school was more practical: it concentrated on matters of procedure, and on the question, which inevitably came up in various forms in the courts, of the validity of local customary law. In Italy the use of Roman law in the courts was already far advanced. In France, customary

6 L. Thorndike, *The Sphere of Sacrobosco,* (Chicago, 1949), translates both text and commentary.

7 *AA.SS,* Octobris, I, 545.

8 E. M. Meijers, *Etudes d'histoire du droit,* ed. R. Feenstra and H. F. W. D. Fischer, (Leiden, 1959), III, 27-35.

law still overwhelmingly prevailed. Guido was one of the first to confront the question how it should be reconciled with juridical principle; his consequent emphasis on procedure, which would characterise the law school of Orleans, was of the utmost relevance to English pupils like Cantilupe who were preparing for a public career in the church, with the variety of judicial and administrative duties it was likely to involve. But we know nothing of Cantilupe's activity at Orleans, beyond the dream of Archbishop Kilwardby's auditor of causes, that as a student at Orleans he had seen a vision of the mitred Thomas sitting in master Guido's chair.[9]

Perhaps about 1252, Cantilupe returned to Paris to complete his legal studies with a degree in canon law. The two legal systems, Roman and canon, were complementary: the law of the church was organised according to the same principles and was expounded in Bologna equally with the civil law, and indeed was hardly comprehensible without the preliminary study of the Code and Digest. To advance from one law faculty to the other was therefore normal, especially in France and England where there were almost no opportunities, at this date, for the practice of the Roman law independently. We can be sure, therefore, that at least from 1245 Cantilupe planned to graduate as a canonist. Of the nature of his studies, however, we know nothing: all that was remembered was that he and his brother Hugh, now studying theology, had separate households, and that he was generous to poor scholars.[10] Moreover, the teaching of the Paris canon law faculty itself is at this date obscure: a university document of 1248 lists as witnesses fourteen regent doctors or bachelors of canon law; several must subsequently have lectured to Cantilupe: but not one has left any literary remains or academic reputation.[11] Perhaps it is legitimate to look back a few years: it was barely a decade since the most famous canonist of the age, Henry of Susa (or Hostiensis as he came to be known) taught in the faculty. By 1252 his reputation was already considerable, and it is likely that his ideas and interests were also those of the other Paris masters. The quality of Hostiensis as a canonist lay in his breadth of vision. He sought to place the law of the Church on a firm basis of natural law and moral principle. Both Roman law and theology were pressed into service to clarify canonical concepts; he had studied Hugh of St Cher, and had learnt from the Paris theologians' debates on ethics.[12] It is tempting to regard his approach as characteristically Parisian, distinct from the Bolognese doctors' more strictly legalistic method. In the absence of known pupils the notion of a Parisian 'school' of canonical studies must be treated with caution, but

9 *AA.SS,* Octobris, I, 545.
10 *ibid.,* 545.
11 *Chartularium,* I, 209 11, no. 178. See for a few further details G. Peries, *La Faculté de droit de l'ancienne Université de Paris,* (Paris, 1890), 53-7.
12 C. Lefebvre in *Dictionnaire de droit canonique,* s.n. Hostiensis, V, 1211-27.

it is unlikely that the faculty could at any time escape being influenced by theologians who shared their concern with the same questions. In any case, the teaching of Hostiensis rendered the canon law an easier instrument for bishops, who had to take a broad view of issues, as distinct from practising canon lawyers; by bringing large moral concepts like sin, or good faith, or natural law into the interpretation of canonical decrees, he encouraged church authorities to apply them more intelligently and flexibly. If Cantilupe absorbed the tradition of Hostiensis his studies in both civil and canon law would fit him for the exercise of the complex *auctoritas* of an English bishop.

Cantilupe did not, according to Hugh le Barbur his servant, seek the doctorate in Paris, but returned at last to England to complete his studies at Oxford, having reached the degree in Paris of bachelor of canon law. He came to a university on the Paris model, devoted primarily to the teaching of arts and theology, but possessing also a tradition of legal education. By 1255, when Cantilupe is likely to have arrived, Oxford was already an established and recognised body: the privileges granted her by popes and kings since 1214 guaranteed her legal independence, and though her alumni had barely begun to be found on the episcopal bench and in the higher reaches of government, it was already fashionable for the kinsmen of bishops and civil servants to be educated there. Within a decade one of the greatest of the curial officers, Walter de Merton, would found the College which bears his name and in which he hoped future generations of his kinsmen would be educated. The nephews of ministers like John Mansel and Robert Burnell would be prominent figures in late thirteenth century Oxford. Indeed Walter de Cantilupe had been one of the first of these avuncular patrons, though on a more ambitious scale, and Thomas' decision to finish his education in Oxford marks the coming of age of the university as a centre of learning comparable to Paris. The teaching of the canon law faculty at Oxford is as obscure in the mid-century as that of the senior university: the names of very few of its alumni can be recovered. Its surviving statutes were compiled at an unknown date before 1313: if they represent the course as it was in 1255, three years would be enough for Cantilupe to proceed to the doctorate.[13] It is unlikely that those three years would have modified his training significantly. The only real distinction between legal study at Oxford and at Paris was the presence in the former of a civil law faculty, so that the two branches of the learned laws were more closely related. Indeed the role of civil law as a preparation for the career of the canonist was probably even more marked than in France; the old tradition of twelfth-century Oxford, of the study of both laws together, was still influential. As in

13 *Statuta Antiqua Universitatis Oxoniensis,* ed. S. Gibson, (Oxford, 1931), 45-8; L. E. Boyle, 'The curriculum of the faculty of canon law in the early fourteenth century', in *Oxford Studies presented to Daniel Callus,* Oxford Historical Society, (Oxford, 1964), 135-64.

Paris and Orleans, it is likely that procedure rather than juridical principle was the chief concern of the lectures: William of Drogheda, who had been the leading figure in the canon law faculty about 1240, had written a guide to procedure in church courts, his *Summa Aurea,* which is the only literary work to survive from the law schools of thirteenth century Oxford.[14] This accords with the future careers, so far as we know them, of the scholars educated in the faculty: like Cantilupe, they entered the world of high ecclesiastical government, as bishops' officials, archdeacons, or sometimes eventually bishops themselves.

In another way too, these years mark the culmination of Cantilupe's academic career, when he was beginning to enjoy the fruits of distinction and spread the political and administrative wings for which he had been nurtured. Several small marks of favour, like a series of royal gifts of oaks, indicate his friendship with Henry III, and his election to the chancellorship of the university in 1261 was probably a consequence of this. As chancellor, he secured the oath of the burgesses of Oxford to the university statutes; more generally, it must have been a substantial benefit to the university, during the ascendancy of Simon de Montfort, to be represented by a nephew of the Montfortian bishop Walter de Cantilupe, who had died in 1260.[15] The witnesses at his canonization process add only that as chancellor he made peace in the university; unless they are confusing his two chancellorships, this is one of the first references to those regional rivalries, soon to crystallise as the endemic conflict of northern and southern scholars, which would trouble the university throughout the fourteenth century. They were the consequence of the expansion of the university in the last generation, which had brought large numbers of strangers into Oxford, and Cantilupe's peace was only temporary. He would himself be compelled to repeat his mediation in 1274.

The doctorate of canon law, we may be sure, was intended from the beginning to be the crown of Cantilupe's academic career. His brother Hugh (of whom we hear no more) had followed a parallel path through the theological schools of Paris, and both careers were complete in themselves as varieties of professional training for the work of churchmen in the business of secular and ecclesiastical government. That Thomas Cantilupe subsequently returned to Paris to read theology can only be explained as the result of some interruption of a hitherto smooth career. This, presumably, was one of the side effects of his own prominence in the period of violent strife between political parties which ended at Evesham in 1265. Cantilupe, as the Montfortian nominee for the chancellorship of England, was naturally involved in the Earl's fall, though he

14 Emden, I, 594-5.

15 Emden, I, 347-9; *Mediaeval archives of the University of Oxford,* ed. H. E. Salter, Oxford Historical Society, (Oxford, 1917-19), I, 23-4.

suffered more lightly than other Montfort partisans; a period of residence abroad must have been deemed tactful. In any case, the Paris years, 1267-1273, were not a regular part of his academic career, and probably contributed little of direct value to his subsequent work. They were, however, years of particularly intense conflict in the Paris schools, and Cantilupe can hardly have avoided witnessing a cardinal episode in the intellectual history of Europe: the challenge of Thomas Aquinas to the traditional view of the human soul, during his second Parisian regency (1269-72).

Paris in 1267 had lost none of its leadership of the European intellectual world established in the twelfth century.[16] On the contrary, its theological schools had become the nursery of a mature professionalism: its theologians were systematically trained, and conducted their debates in the light of established principles. The Bible, their storehouse of wisdom, was now studied in a corrected text, divided for convenient reference into chapter and verse, and equipped with commentaries which explained its message in the light of historical scholarship and knowledge of nature. Speculative theological topics had been organised in the *Sentences* of Peter Lombard into four books, on God, creation, Christ and the works of Christ. Since the 1240's, every doctor of theology had lectured on the *Sentences.* As these topics raised philosophical questions, Aristotelian method, as interpreted by Avicenna and Averroes, was employed in analysing them; and as a result a precise philosophical vocabulary had been adopted, of substance and accident, matter and form, potentiality and act. Great theological *Summae* like that inspired by Alexander of Hales, or comprehensive commentaries on the *Sentences* like those of St Bonaventure, Robert Kilwardby or Thomas Aquinas, had interpreted theology according to metaphysical principles of growing consistency.

This process now of its own accord rent asunder the seamless robe of theological wisdom: the study of Aristotle had concentrated attention on the metaphysical assumptions which lay hidden in the premisses of theological discourse, and had finally brought into the open some fundamental divergences. By 1267 these centrifugal pressures were becoming institutionalised in the rival Franciscan and Dominican schools. Though united in condemnation of the unrestrained 'Averroism' of the Arts faculty, and in defence of their own mendicant status, on a deeper level these schools were mutally opposed. Albeit couched in abstract metaphysical language, the controversies of the schools derived their cutting edge from concern with the central problem of the human soul: was it a separate entity with its own form, distinct from the body, as theologians inspired by Augustine (and ultimately by Plato) had seen it since the

16 See in general F. Steenberghen, *La philosophie au treizieme siècle,* (Louvain, 1966), 413-74; J. A. Weisheipl, *Friar Thomas d'Aquino,* (New York, 1974), 272-92.

beginning, and as Bonaventure, the Franciscan minister-general, maintained? Or was the soul itself the form of man, integral to the complete human being, as Thomas Aquinas had come to hold? The new definition seemed to place in jeopardy not merely a theological doctrine but the whole tradition of christian spirituality with its theme of man as a pilgrim or stranger in the world, and its contraposition of ephemeral matter with a higher spiritual reality. By undermining the assumptions of the church's pastoral mission, it must, to say the least, have surprised the many theologians preparing, like Cantilupe, for a leading role in ecclesiastical affairs.

No evidence exists, however, of Cantilupe's response to the turbulent currents of opinion in his faculty, so different from the placid streams of unchallenged learning down which he had effortlessly floated in his previous experience of the schools. We know, on the evidence of his companion the Dominican Edmund de Aumari, that in the course of his baccalaureate he lectured *cursorie,* explaining the text without raising controversial questions, on the Epistles and Apocalypse; and he may well have followed the teaching of Aquinas on Romans, the book on which he was probably lecturing in 1270 and 1271. We know too that he once had to borrow money, and that another theologian called him a *rusticus,* a country bumpkin; these were common enough experiences of university life.[17] One famous incident however may have influenced the great controversy of his episcopate, though it can only be a speculation: the humiliation, at the hands of Thomas Aquinas, of a newly incepting young master whom the most recent students of the question have identified as John Pecham. William of Tocco, the biographer of Aquinas, recounting the incident of the inception ceremony at which the new master maintained a doctrine contrary to Aquinas' view on the eternity of the world; when he repeated it, the great Dominican master was provoked to defend his view so devastatingly that his opponent had to beg humbly to be enlightened. This incident seems to have happened in 1270, when Pecham became doctor of theology, and in the same year Aquinas published his *De Aeternitate Mundi* in which Pecham's (and indirectly Bonaventure's) ideas were refuted.[18] If Cantilupe witnessed this scene, as would be natural since Pecham and he were compatriots (indeed Pecham later called him his scholar), it may have diminished his respect for an impulsive colleague who was soon to be his metropolitan.[19]

In returning to Oxford in 1272-3 to incept as doctor of theology, Cantilupe followed the pattern of his canon law studies. The Oxford school, like that of Paris, was the furthest developed of the faculties, but

17 *AA.SS,* Octobris, I, 546, 552, 557.
18 Weisheipl, *op. cit.,* 287-8.
19 *Registrum epistolarum Fratris Johannis Peckham archiepiscopi Cantuariensis,* ed. J. T. Martin, Rolls Series, (London, 1882-5), I, 315.

its teaching followed closely that of the senior university, diverging only in treating lectures on scripture as a serious matter to be reserved for doctors. Many of its senior men, like Robert Kilwardby, the Dominican archbishop of Canterbury since 1261, had studied in Paris: all of them followed carefully the current debates of the Paris schools. Cantilupe was preceded to Oxford by John Pecham, who in 1271-5 was lector to the Oxford Franciscans; he is said to have introduced to Oxford the new Parisian practice of the *quodlibet,* a kind of theological press conference in which the questions to be discussed by a regent master were selected not by the master but by his audience, and were resolved by reference to consistent metaphysical principles.[20] Cantilupe is unlikely, therefore, to have learnt anything new in Oxford, and his return must be seen as a preliminary stage in the renewal of his public life. He must now have enjoyed Edward I's favour, or he would hardly have been elected to a second term as chancellor of the university in 1273: the chancellor's office, as principal defender of university privileges, demanded political and diplomatic ability. In the event, Cantilupe's aristocratic good manners and unflappability, attested by several anecdotes in his canonization process, was put to the test by a recrudescence of the feud of northern and southern scholars, in which he was set upon himself. His reconciliation of the parties was effected in January 1274.[21]

What are we to make of his almost unprecedented variety of academic experience? Although Cantilupe was three times a doctor, with the right to determine questions magisterially, no vestige of his teaching has been preserved, and it seems likely that his lectures never achieved the status of a copied and circulated text, or were modestly withheld from publication. There is no hint in the evidence of his canonization process that any notebooks or manuscripts were found in his possession at his death, though anything associated with him would have interested the church authorities at Hereford who promoted his cause. We must conclude that Cantilupe made no contribution to the original study of either law or theology, a surprising omission when active theologians like Kilwardby and Pecham were often advanced to episcopal office. It seems that his long years of study were devoted exclusively to preparation for public affairs; had it not been for the unfortunate association with Simon de Montfort, they would not have been so long. He was, therefore, strictly an amateur in the schools in an age of burgeoning professionalism; if it is not surprising that he had no ambition as a theologian, some employment of his legal training might have been expected. His friends remembered him not for learning but for his aristocratic virtues, his munificence, his self-control and impeccable manners. He could be riled, but *odium theologicum,* a common

20 *Chronicon de Lanercost,* ed. J. Stevenson, (Edinburgh, 1839), 100-1.
21 Emden, I, 348.

failing in his later years, was foreign to him. More in his style, perhaps, was the epic confrontation with the Earl of Gloucester in the woods they both claimed near Ledbury: when the Bishop, rapidly exchanging his crop for a crozier and donning cope and mitre over his riding breeches, solemnly excommunicated all who impeded him; and after they had slunk away, ostentatiously hunted the disputed country with all his hounds and huntsmen for three whole days.[22] Thirty years in the schools, it must be admitted, may only have furnished his native proud spirit with the dialectical weapons to defy with confidence earl and archbishop alike.

22 *AA.SS*, Octobris, I, 564.

ST THOMAS CANTILUPE: HIS POLITICAL CAREER

by David Carpenter

Thomas Cantilupe's tomb, erected not long after his death, survives in the north transept of Hereford cathedral. In niches around its sides are carved a series of weepers. Each represents a knight in full armour. A monument of this kind might seem more suitable for a baron than for a bishop who was to be made a saint. Yet it was perfectly appropriate. As Richard de Swinfield, Thomas' friend and successor, remarked during the canonization proceedings, it was 'well known throughout the kingdom' that Thomas came from 'the noble stock of the barons of England'.[1] The Cantilupes had risen through the service of kings. Thomas' grandfather, William de Cantilupe I (ob. 1239), a Norman by birth, was King John's steward of the household. William de Cantilupe II (ob. 1251), Thomas' father, held the same position under Henry III. Both Williams were richly rewarded for their royal service, and gained extensive lands in England.[2] Thomas was proud of his lineage. The fleur-de-lis of the Cantilupe arms were prominently displayed on both sides of his episcopal seal.[3] The weepers on the tomb would doubless appear as his kinsmen, had the blazons once painted on their shields survived. Family connections were of crucial importance in moulding Thomas Cantilupe's political career. That career was brief but significant. Apart from a sequel as a councillor of Edward I, it was confined to the years 1263-5 when Thomas emerged as a leading supporter of Henry III's great opponent, Simon de Montfort, earl of Leicester. For a few months in 1265, when Montfort was controlling the government of England, Thomas was chancellor of the realm. This chapter will consider the factors which led Thomas to embrace the cause of Simon de Montfort; it will examine his term as chancellor, which has not previously been studied; and it will look at the relationship between Thomas' Montfortian phase and his subsequent career as Edwardian councillor and bishop of Hereford.

To understand Thomas Cantilupe's role between 1263-5 it is necessary to glance briefly at the course of English politics in the preceding years.[4] 1258 in England was a year of revolution. Exasperated by many aspects of his government, the great magnates forced King Henry III to accept the Provisions of Oxford. These laid down that Henry must govern with the

1 *Acta Sanctorum* (Antwerp-Brussels, 1643 sqq.), Octobris, I, (hereafter AA.SS), 599.
2 For the Cantilupes, see Sir William Dugdale, *The Baronage of England* (London, 1675), I, 731; the *Dictionary of National Biography; Victoria County History of Warwickshire,* III, 36.
3 See frontispiece; *Rolls of Arms Henry III,* ed. T. D. Tremlett (Harleian Soc., CXIII-IV, 1961-2), 119-20.
4 For politics in this period see R. F. Treharne, *The Baronial Plan of Reform* (Manchester, 1932); F. M. Powicke, *Henry III and The Lord Edward* (Oxford, 1947); *The Thirteenth Century* (Oxford, 1953).

advice and consent of a council of fifteen. The great magnates were to have a major role in determining the personnel of the council and in controlling the king's choice of ministers. These restrictions lasted until Henry III's recovery of power in 1261. However, two years later a coalition, which included Gilbert de Clare, the young earl of Gloucester, revived the cause of the Provisions of Oxford, and summoned Simon de Montfort back to England to act as its leader. Montfort, an enthusiastic protagonist of the reforms of 1258, had retired to France in 1261, rather than accept their overthrow. In July 1263 he and his friends forced Henry to re-affirm the Provisions. The political situation was, however, very different from that in 1258. Many of those who had supported reform then, now stood aside, or were actively hostile to the earl of Leicester's party. When some of Montfort's allies deserted, Henry III was able to re-assert his independence. By December the country stood on the brink of civil war. All that could be agreed was to refer the dispute to the arbitration of Louis IX, the widely respected king of France. It is at this point that Thomas Cantilupe made his first appearance. In December 1263 Montfort sent him, with several colleagues, to plead the cause of the Provisions before Louis IX.[5] Their advocacy was to no avail. Louis' judgement, the mise of Amiens of January 1264, condemned the Provisions outright, and declared that the king could appoint and dismiss ministers 'at his own free will'. Since Montfort and his followers would not accept this verdict the result was civil war. This culminated in Simon's stupendous victory at Lewes in May 1264, which left both Henry III and his son, the Lord Edward, prisoners in his hands. Montfort had now to devise a constitution for the governance of England. The council of fifteen set up by the Provisions of Oxford had been broken up by death and defections. Instead, in the parliament of June 1264, three 'electors' were chosen (Simon himself; Gilbert de Clare, earl of Gloucester; and Stephen de Berksted, bishop of Chichester), who were to nominate a king's council of nine. On the advice of this council the king was to select his ministers and 'settle the affairs of the realm'. One of the councillors chosen by the 'electors' was Thomas Cantilupe.[6] The euphoria of Lewes soon evaporated. By early 1265 Simon's government was torn by dissension with Gilbert de Clare, earl of Gloucester; was defied by the lords of the Welsh March, who had been set free after Lewes; and was condemned by the papacy, which had ordered the excommunication of Simon and his supporters. It was at this point, on 25 February 1265, that Cantilupe was elected 'by the king and the magnates of the council' to the chancellor-

5 *Gervase of Canterbury,* ed. W. Stubbs (Rolls Series, 1879-80), II, 232; *The Chronicle of William Rishanger,* ed. J. O. Halliwell, (Camden Soc. 1840), 122.

6 *Documents of the Baronial Movement of Reform and Rebellion,* ed. R. F. Treharne, I. J. Sanders (Oxford, 1973), (hereafter *DBM*), 295-9. One of the council of three was always to be at court, and collectively they had power to dismiss the nine. In practice the government was run by Simon de Montfort and members of the nine.

ship.[7] His predecessor, John of Chishill, had been appointed by the king in December 1263, and was probably politically neutral.[8] In February 1265 a more convinced Montfortian was required.

Thomas Cantilupe, then, entered politics at a time of crisis, and as a partisan of Simon de Montfort. How can we explain Thomas' political allegiance? The most central and controversial feature of Montfort's programme was the demand that the great magnates, representing the community of the realm, should regulate the appointment of the king's councillors and ministers. The documents which Cantilupe and his colleagues took to Louis IX in December 1263 justified this claim on the simple grounds that the king had ruled badly before 1258 and must be controlled. Henry's heedless liberality, especially to his foreign relatives, had made him bankrupt; these relatives and other courtiers had placed themselves above the law, and 'justice was shut out from England'; the sheriffs had been corrupt; the church oppressed. In 1258 these indictments had secured wide support for the Provisions of Oxford. By 1263, and even more by 1265, great magnates had become increasingly aware of the difficulties and dangers of conciliar rule. Many were also antagonised by the personal ascendancy of Simon de Montfort. Yet, while others wavered, Thomas remained committed to the cause of reform and its controversial leader. In seeking to explain the strength of Thomas' attachment, the role of various influences may be considered: Thomas was a teacher at Oxford university; an ecclesiastic; and above all, a Cantilupe.[9]

Thomas Cantilupe's political convictions may have been reinforced by like-minded colleagues at Oxford. Cantilupe had been there since at least 1255, and in 1261-2 was chancellor.[10] An issue like conciliar control of the king, first demanded at a parliament in 1244, must have been eagerly discussed in university circles. Of course, Oxford is unlikely to have taken a uniform view of political matters.[11] Henry III had been a generous benefactor, and there is no evidence that the University was in disfavour after his recovery of power in 1265. Many of Henry's clerks were Oxford graduates. Cantilupe would not, however, have been alone in sympathising with Montfort and his cause. Two of the bishops closest to the earl of

7 *Calendar of Patent Rolls* (hereafter *CPR*) *1258-66,* 410.

8 T. F. Tout, *Chapters in the Administrative History of Mediaeval England* (Manchester, 1937), I, 297, 299, 307-9.

9 *DBM,* 257-67. (The documents of December 1263 are here dated—with equal validity—January 1264). In the absence of any writings it is impossible to know whether Cantilupe justified his politics in the light of some political theory.

10 *CPR 1247-58,* 412; A. B. Emden *A Biographical Register of the University of Oxford to 1500,* (Oxford, 1957), I, 347-8.

11 For Oxford in this period, see C. H. Lawrence, 'The University of Oxford and the Chronicle of the Barons' Wars', *English Historical Review* (XCV, 1980), 99-113.

Leicester in 1264-5 were Berksted of Chichester, one of the three 'electors', and Sandwich of London, who was with Thomas on the council of nine. Both, like Cantilupe, were fresh from the University where 'they had spent most of their adult lives . . . before they were mitred in 1262'. When the king besieged Northampton in 1264, at the start of the campaign which ended at Lewes, clerks of the University fought against the royal army under their own banner.[12]

Thomas Cantilupe's views, and those of masters and students at Oxford who thought like him politically, were probably coloured by the predicament of the church in England. Of all the groups in English society the church was the most solidly behind Simon de Montfort in the years 1263-5. Monastic chroniclers eulogised the great earl.[13] At the parliament of March 1265 nine bishops gave their support to his regime. Five of these bishops—Berksted of Chichester, Sandwich of London, Cantilupe of Worcester (Thomas' uncle), Gravesend of Lincoln and Gervais of Winchester—were later suspended from office by the papacy for being 'especial favourers' of the earl.[14] Only four bishops between 1263-5 were clearly on the king's side, and two of these were foreigners.[15] Ecclesiastical enthusiasm for Montfort derived from Henry III's subjection of the church before 1258—the manipulation of elections; the extortions during vacancies; the encroachments on jurisdiction; and the heavy taxation brought by Henry's misguided scheme to place his second son on the throne of Sicily.[16] Simon de Montfort's religiosity helped him benefit from these grievances. He cultivated the friendship of churchmen, and encouraged, to a degree unusual for a lay magnate, ecclesiastical reform. Robert Grosseteste, bishop of Lincoln, the greatest reforming bishop of the age (ob. 1253), had been 'a close personal friend of Simon's, perhaps in some sense his spiritual director'.[17] In 1264-5 Montfort did not disappoint the hopes of ecclesiastics. Several were given high office in his government, which showed itself continuously sympathetic to the claims and rights of the church.[18]

Thomas Cantilupe, then, may well have been drawn towards Simon de Montfort in much the same way as were other conscientious clerics. There was also, however, a more personal, and probably more potent

12 *ibid.*, 111, 100.
13 A. Gransden, *Historical Writing in England* (London, 1974), 415-35.
14 Powicke, *op. cit.* (1947), II, 490; Lawrence, *op. cit.*, 111; *Annales Monastici*, ed. H. R. Luard (Rolls Series, 1864-9), IV, 156; hereafter *Ann. Mon.*
15 The archbishop of Canterbury, and the bishops of Hereford, Rochester and Norwich; all were closely connected with the court; M. Gibbs, J. Lang, *Bishops and Reform 1215-72* (Oxford, 1934), 189-91.
16 *DBM*, 268-71, 278-9.
17 *Robert Grosseteste*, ed. D. A. Callus (Oxford, 1955), 205-6.
18 Powicke, *op. cit.* (1947), II, 484-5.

bond between the two men. Thomas' early career had developed under the wing of his uncle, Walter de Cantilupe, a son of William de Cantilupe I, and strong links remained between them. Walter, as the royalist chronicler Wykes put it, was a 'brave and intimate' adherent of the earl of Leicester.[19] Unlike the other bishops close to Montfort in 1263-5, Walter de Cantilupe was an old stager. He had been elected to the bishopric of Worcester in 1236, and was by far the most prominent ecclesiastical champion of the Provisions between 1258-61. His relationship with Simon de Montfort can be traced from at least 1248, when the Franciscan, Adam Marsh, remarked in a letter to the earl, 'the bishops of Lincoln [Grosseteste] and Worcester [Cantilupe] amongst all mortals are most favourably linked to you in special friendship'.[20]

The association between Walter and Simon de Montfort probably rested, in part, on similar views about the problems of church and state. Cantilupe was a committed churchman, and had quarrelled with Henry III on several occasions over ecclesiastical matters. In 1250 he defied the king's prohibition, and defended the jurisdictional rights of his see against the sheriff of Worcester by prosecuting a plea at the papal court. In 1255 he opposed the taxation of the church for the Sicilian venture.[21] These differences were the more likely to cement a political coalition with Simon de Montfort because Walter was not only a reforming bishop. He was also a councillor of the king. Both his family's connection with the court, and his own early career as a royal clerk pushed him in this direction. Dismissed from the king's council in 1255 for his opposition to Sicilian taxation, he was re-appointed two years later, and sent to negotiate peace with the king of France.[22] The experiences of Simon and Walter before 1258 were not dissimilar. Both were councillors of Henry III; both had felt the king's displeasure.

It has not, hitherto, been fully appreciated that this connection between the bishop and Simon de Montfort was part of a wider alliance which embraced Walter's nephew, Peter de Montfort, and perhaps another nephew, the son of William de Cantilupe II, William III. Peter de Montfort, who was no relation of Simon, had spent at least fifteen years as the ward of Walter's father (1216-31). In 1242 he journeyed to Gascony in the company of his cousin William de Cantilupe III. The tradition of

19 *Ann. Mon.*, IV, 180. There is a good account of Walter's career in the *Dictionary of National Biography.*

20 *Monumenta Franciscana,* ed. J. S. Brewer (Rolls Series, 1858), 270, 277-8; C. Bémont, *Simon de Montfort* (Paris, 1884), 19, n. 4.

21 *Close Rolls* (henceforth *CR*) *1247-51,* 525; *Ann. Mon.*, I, 143, 145; IV, 102, 440; *Chronica Majora Matthaei Parisiensis,* ed. H. R. Luard (Rolls Series, 1872-83), V, 525, 326; hereafter *Chron. Maj.*

22 Cantilupe was certainly on the council in 1255. His dismissal may be inferred from his re-appointment in 1257; *CR 1254-6,* 160; *Ann. Mon.*, I, 395; *CPR 1247-58,* 594.

the Cantilupe family was of loyal service to the crown, but when William III, by marriage a great Marcher lord, succeeded in 1251, his relationship with Henry III became strained. On his death in 1254 Peter de Montfort and Walter de Cantilupe judged money which was owed his executors. Simon de Montfort laid his body in the grave. Two years before, when Simon was on trial at Westminster for his conduct as seneschal of Gascony, only Peter de Montfort, Bishop Cantilupe and Peter of Savoy (the queen's uncle) stood by him. In 1258 Walter, Simon and Peter de Montfort were among the twelve representatives elected by the great magnates to assist in the drawing up of the programme of reform. In June all three became founder members of the council of fifteen. The following year Simon named Peter as one of his executors. In 1261 both Peter and Walter were his representatives in the process of arbitration which was to settle his differences with the king.[23] About this time Peter de Montfort told the king's clerk Walter of Merton, 'whatever you do to favour [our uncle Bishop Walter] we will count it wholly done for us.'[24] In 1264 the bishop absolved Simon's army before the battle of Lewes. After the battle Peter was elected to the council of nine. The next year Peter de Montfort died with the earl of Leicester at Evesham. The bishop of Worcester had said mass for the doomed army before the battle.[25]

The two Montforts and Walter de Cantilupe saw each other at court. They must also have met in the country. The chief seat of the Cantilupes was at Aston Cantlow in Warwickshire; that of Peter's family was at Beaudesert. The two places are but four miles apart. Simon de Montfort's great base in England was at Kenilworth; twelve miles from Aston Cantlow and nine from Beaudesert.[26]

Walter de Cantilupe, then, enjoyed a longstanding personal and political friendship with Simon de Montfort. The friendship also encompassed Thomas Cantilupe's cousin, Peter de Montfort, and perhaps his brother, William de Cantilupe III. There seems little doubt that Thomas was drawn by his uncle Walter into the same circle. Thus, as bishop of Hereford, one of Thomas' most trusted clerks was his 'kinsman', master William de Montfort, a son of Peter de Montfort of Beaudesert.[27] From the first, Walter de Cantilupe exercised a decisive influence on Thomas' career. The

23 *Complete Peerage,* IX, 123; Dugdale, *op. cit.,* I, 404, *Pipe Roll 26 Henry III,* 341; *Chron. Maj.,* V, 224-5; *CPR 1247-58,* 348; *Ann. Mon.,* III, 192; *Monumenta Franciscana,* 123; Bémont, *op. cit.,* 328, 196 n. 1. See Powicke, *op. cit.* (1947), 229, n. 2.

24 Public Record Office (hereafter PRO) SC/1/7/20.

25 *Ann. Mon.,* IV, 168, 174; *DBM,* 295.

26 *Victoria County History Warwickshire,* III, 32, 36, 45-6. Beaudesert was situated in a hundred held by the bishop of Worcester.

27 *AA.SS,* 555; *Reg. Cantilupe,* 111, 221, xix; *Reg. Swinfield,* 71, 101; *Roll of the Household Expenses of Richard de Swinfield,* ed. J. Webb (Camden Soc., 1855), cxxx; *Complete Peerage,* IX, 128 n.a. One of Thomas' benefices was at Aston Cantlow.

story that he prophesied that the infant Thomas would become an ecclesiastic may be apocryphal, but there seems no reason to doubt the evidence of Richard de Kimberle, who had spent ten years in Thomas' household and whose father had served Bishop Walter. 'He had heard it said that his uncle Walter brought Thomas up, kept him in the schools and beneficed him'. One of those in Thomas' *familia* in Paris was master Thomas de Buttevilt, who was later steward of Walter de Cantilupe. Thomas held several livings in the Worcester diocese which were of the bishop's gift. In 1255 he was pardoned a small offence connected with the royal forest on his uncle's 'prayers'. When Walter died in February 1266, Thomas was his executor, and was left that most personal of possessions, his hair shirt. Thomas' servants probably reflected the view of their master when they described Walter as a man of learning and of saintly and austere life, for whom, after his death, God worked many miracles.[28]

Thomas Cantilupe's politics, therefore, probably owed a great deal to his uncle Walter and to the company in which Walter moved. The same connections doubtless facilitated his elevation both to the council of nine and to the chancellorship. Thomas, however, was well known in his own right by 1263. On one occasion, while in Oxford, he had invited the Lord Edward and many earls, barons and justices of the king to a feast in London. His prestige and training as a scholar, and his familiarity with Louis IX, whom he had met whilst studying in Paris, made him an ideal choice to promote the cause of the Provisions at Amiens. In the period 1258-65 outsiders were quite frequently given charge of the chancery and treasury, but they had usually proved their administrative ability in other fields. Here Thomas' term as chancellor of Oxford may have been important. That he exercised a firm rule over the turbulent masters and students is suggested by his conduct during his second term of office in the 1270s, and by his complaint that another chancellor of Oxford was insufficiently 'stern and attentive in the administration of justice'. It was necessary, in Thomas' own words, to be a 'terror to fools'.[29]

Thomas Cantilupe kept the king's seal from 25 February to 7 May, 1265.[30] The chancellor was responsible for the writing and sealing of all royal letters and thus held a pivotal position in the government of England. Apart from a couple of stories told during the canonization proceedings, the sources for Thomas' term in office are the rolls of the chancery itself. The chancery recorded the royal letters which it issued, according to their

28 *AA.SS*, 544, 555; *Reg. Cantilupe*, xix, 134; *CR 1254-6*, 197; *CPR 1258-66*, 596.

29 *AA.SS*, 558; *Cal. Ancient Correspondence concerning Wales*, ed. J. G. Edwards (Cardiff, 1935), 38. For the firm discipline during Thomas's second term as chancellor, see *AA.SS*, 545.

30 *CPR 1258-66*, 410; *CR 1264-8*, 54.

type, on the close, patent, liberate and fine rolls. Charters were entered on the charter roll. All five rolls survive for the period of Cantilupe's keepership.[31] Although this comprised less than three months Thomas clearly took vigorous hold of his office. He rejected gifts and accepted a rise in the chancellor's salary. He refused to consent to at least one royal letter, and took more responsibility than his predecessors in the 'giving' of royal charters. He probably instituted the large increase in the number of notes on the chancery rolls indicating on whose authority royal letters were issued. It is difficult to be certain whether a common theme runs through all this activity. The interpretation of chancery practice has many pitfalls for the historian.[32] Nonetheless, a good case can be made for saying that Cantilupe was influenced by criticisms made of chancellors in office before 1258; criticisms like those found in the documents of December 1263. He wished to avoid the failures of these officials, and run the chancery in the spirit of the Provisions of Oxford and reform. Cantilupe's predecessor, John of Chishill, appointed by the king before Lewes, probably felt no such commitment.

Under the Provisions of Oxford, the council's control of the king rested upon the stipulation that the chancellor should seal no writs, other than those which were routine, without its orders. That stipulation was not repeated in the constitution of June 1264, but the king was to dispose of the affairs of the kingdom on the advice of the council of nine. The implication was that the chancellor should take instructions from king and council, and refuse to seal anything important on the sole authority of the king.[33] There are signs that Cantilupe did not think the king should be reduced to a mere cipher. He was clearly concerned to record that Henry had admitted him to office 'willingly'—*gratanter.*[34] Nonetheless, a story told by Cantilupe's nephew and former clerk, William de Cantilupe appears to show Thomas refusing to seal a letter on the king's orders: 'He

31 Each chancery roll ran for a regnal year. Thus Cantilupe's term was included in the rolls for 28 October, 1264-27 October, 1265, Henry III's 49th year. The close roll for 49 Henry III is printed in full in *Close Rolls 1264-8* (H.M.S.O., 1937). The patent, liberate, and charter rolls are calendared in *Cal. Patent Rolls 1258-66; Cal. Liberate Rolls 1260-7; Cal. Charter Rolls 1257-1300* (H.M.S.O., 1910, 1961, 1906). Excerpts from the fine roll are in *Excerpta e Rotulis Finium,* II, ed. C. Roberts (Record Commission, 1836).

32 For the chancery, see P. Chaplais, *English Royal Documents* (Oxford, 1971); H. C. Maxwell-Lyte, *The Great Seal* (London, 1926).

33 *DBM,* 102-3, 106-7, 296-7. In practice it is clear from the authorisations of royal letters that the chancellor received orders from the council of nine, or members of it, and from Simon de Montfort. The king later complained that Simon used the seal 'at his will'; *CPR 1258-66,* 436.

34 PRO C/ 66/ 83, m.18. This is said in the writ dealing with Thomas' salary; *CPR 1258-66,* 416; the statement (for which see below) that the king folded this writ with his own hands is another example of Thomas' concern for the position of the king. It is not impossible that Thomas was personally acceptable to Henry; see p. 70.

had heard it said' that Thomas 'returned his seal to the king on a certain occasion when the king ordered him to seal a letter which Thomas thought should not be sealed'.[35]

The constitution of June 1264 followed the Provisions of Oxford in requiring officials to swear that they would take 'no reward, beyond food and drink commonly brought to the table'.[36] Cantilupe zealously upheld this oath, judging from an incident which Richard de Swinfield personally witnessed in 1265. Some monks, having business to transact at the king's court, offered Thomas a precious jewel. He refused the gift civilly but rebuked the monks for offering it, 'as if they thought him pliable and corruptible'.[37] Cantilupe's stand against 'rewards' may explain the question of his salary. The Provisions of Oxford made clear that the purpose of a salary was to prevent the acceptance of 'presents'. 'It is right that the king should pay . . . his servants sufficiently so that they have no need to accept anything from anyone else'.[38] On 26 March, 1265 Cantilupe was granted 500 marks p.a. for the upkeep of himself and his staff. Since 1261, when a salary was first introduced, chancellors had probably only received 400 marks p.a. Perhaps the extra 100 marks was granted to Cantilupe because he took a more rigid view of gifts than his predecessors. His concern to demonstrate his honesty is seen in the matter of the salary itself. A memorandum noted that the king had caused the writ, which granted the 500 marks, to be sealed in his presence and that of various ministers. It also stated that Henry had folded the writ with his own hands—an action otherwise unrecorded in his reign. Thus Cantilupe showed, in the plainest way possible, that he had not authorised his own increase in salary.[39]

According to the complaints of December 1263 one consequence of the failure—*defectum*—of chancellors before 1258 was the concession of writs 'against right and the customary forms of the chancery'.[40] The inference was that the chancellor should watch over the letters he issued, and resist those he considered irregular. That Cantilupe took this view is suggested by a statement of disavowal, without parallel in the reign of

35 *AA.SS*, 547. William's story does not fit the circumstances of Thomas' departure from court on 7 May when there is no evidence of any disagreement, and he handed the seal to Ralph of Sandwich, not the king; *CR* 1264-8, 54; see p. 68. Presumably on the occasion mentioned by William the king gave away and Thomas recovered the seal. It may be, of course, that William's details are inaccurate, and that in fact Thomas' argument was with the councillors rather than the king.

36 *DBM*, 106-9, 296-7.

37 *AA.SS*, 547, 607; from the canonization proceedings.

38 *DBM*, 68-9.

39 *CPR 1258-66*, 416; *Cal. Liberate Rolls 1260-7*, 169; L. B. Dibben, 'Chancellor and Keeper of the Seal under Henry III', *Eng. Hist. Rev.*, XXVIII (1911), 48.

40 *DBM*, 260-3.

Henry III, which was added to a writ of 7 March, 1265 enrolled on the patent rolls. This writ was *per,* that is authorised by, the justiciar (Hugh Despencer), Peter de Montfort, Adam of Newmarket and Giles de Argentan, all members of the council of nine. The record of authorisation then continues *tamen magister Thomas de Cantelupo cancellarius non consensit illi litterae;* 'however the chancellor did not consent to that letter'.[41] The root of Thomas' objection is not easy to uncover. He did not, perhaps, consider the matter to be of prime importance, otherwise he would presumably have resigned. The letter stated that the citizens of Lincoln had complained to the king that whereas they had been accustomed to pay a toll of 6s 8d p.a. at Boston fair, over the last seven years, the lords of the vill (Peter of Savoy and John de Vaux) had extorted £10 p.a. The king, therefore, 'wishing to be more fully informed of the truth of these matters', commissioned two judges to inquire into them. The writs 'against right and the customary forms of the chancery' complained about in December 1263 were probably those which initiated new and *ad hoc* legal procedures. The writ of 7 March was not of this type since it only ordered an inquiry. Perhaps Cantilupe had reservations because the investigation affected, in his absence and while his lands were in the king's hands, the rights of the queen's uncle, Peter of Savoy. Perhaps Cantilupe thought the writ should have been authorised by the whole council rather than four members of it. The next entry on the patent rolls ordered an inquiry into a complaint of the prior and canons of Noketon park. This writ was authorised by all the council, *per totum concilium.*[42]

'Excessive and unreasonable grants' by the king were another result of the failure of chancellors before 1258, according to the complaints of December 1263.[43] Many of these grants had been made by royal charters; the most solemn instruments which the chancery issued, since they conferred rights in perpetuity. Cantilupe consequently may have felt a special responsibility regarding the concession of charters, and perhaps this explains why they were sometimes 'given' by him as chancellor, rather than being 'given' by the king as was normal, or being left without a 'giving' clause at all. Between 1227, when Henry III began to issue charters, and 1238, when he deprived his chancellor, Ralph de Neville, of the seal, nearly all charters were 'given' by the chancellor, that is they ended with a clause which stated that they were *data per manum,* 'given by the hand', of the chancellor at a specified place and date. After Neville lost the seal in 1238, charters were 'given' by the king himself—*data per manum nostrum.* Apart from a few charters issued in 1243 and 1261 no

41 PRO C/ 66/ 83, m.21d; *CPR 1258-66,* 481-2.

42 *ibid.,* I would like to thank Dr Paul Brand for discussing this writ with me. The responsibility for the interpretation, however, is my own.

43 *DBM,* 260-3.

other 'giver' appears until Cantilupe's appointment in 1265.[44] On the charter roll for 49 Henry III, before Thomas received the seal, charters were either 'given' by the king, or ended with a highly unusual clause which stated that they had been 'witnessed' by the king. The latter form appears on the first two charters of Cantilupe's keepership, which are dated 27 February, and on charters of 5 March and 14 April. The other four charters belonging to Thomas' term were all 'given by the hand of master Thomas de Cantilupe, chancellor of the king'.[45] Thus Cantilupe indicated that he had authorised, or had in some way taken responsibility for these grants.[46] His successor as keeper did not shoulder the same responsibility. After Thomas left court on 7 May the king resumed as 'giver'.[47]

Under the Provisions of Oxford the chancellor was to hold office for a year, and answer for his term before the king and council. These regulations are not found in the constitution of June 1264, but the chancellor, like other officials, was to be appointed by the council of nine. If officials 'behaved badly' the council could dismiss them.[48] Cantilupe, unlike his predecessor, was appointed by the nine and perhaps he felt answerable to them. Conceivably, a marked feature of Cantilupe's chancellorship—the sharp increase in notes which indicated on whose authority

44 Dibben, *op. cit.,* 50, 43. The charters of 1261 were the last issued during the chancellorship of Nicholas of Ely.

45 *ibid.,* 50; PRO C/ 53/ 54, ms. 6, 4-3. On the charter roll the charters of 27 February; 5 March; and 14 April (a duplicate with different witnesses of one 'given' by Cantilupe on 1 March) end *T*[*este*] *R*[*ege.*]. This form, which the present writer has discovered only once outside the roll for 49 Henry III, appears on several charters before Cantilupe's appointment, and on one after Evesham, that of 18 October. The form implies that the original charters ended *Teste me ipso,* the usual conclusion for royal letters but not for charters. However it is impossible to be certain how the originals ended since none survive. The question is made the more puzzling by a fourteenth-century copy of an otherwise unknown charter which is dated 3 March and is 'given' by Cantilupe. In its text and witnesses this charter is identical with the enrolled charter of 5 March which ends *Teste Rege;* PRO C/ 53/ 133, m.3. The original of the enrolled charter of 20 March (to Montfort) 'given' by Cantilupe, survives in Bibliothèque Nationale, Paris, Clairambault (1188, f. 79. (The second grant to Simon de Montfort on 20 March is by letter not charter).

46 For discussion of the 'giving' clause, J. B. Edwards, 'The English Royal Chamber and Chancery in the Reign of John' (unpublished Cambridge Univ. D.Phil. thesis, 1974), 118-32; see also C. R. Cheney, *English Bishops' Chanceries* (Manchester, 1950), 81-90; Chaplais, *op. cit.,* 14-15.

47 One might wonder whether one reason for Cantilupe taking over the 'giving' of charters was that Henry III was making difficulties over doing it. Is this the explanation for the appearance of the *Teste Rege* clause (note 45 above)? Henry must have resented the charter of 20 March which gave the honour of Chester to Simon de Montfort. However, other charters 'given' by Cantilupe seem no more important than ones which Henry 'gave' after Thomas' departure. The king 'gives' all seven charters between Thomas' departure and Evesham, save the last which is merely 'given at Hereford'.

48 *DBM,* 106-7, 296-7.

royal letters were issued— should be seen against this background. The increase coincides exactly with Cantilupe's assumption of the seal and thus was probably ordered by him. If Cantilupe felt accountable for his term it was sensible to record on whose orders he had acted, the more especially as the political outlook was uncertain. Cantilupe received the seal on 25 February, 1265. In the close roll of October 1264-October 1265 about 200 letters were issued before his appointment, of which twenty-three were authorised. Of about 170 letters for which Thomas was responsible between 25 February and 7 May authorisations were appended to 108.[49] Before Cantilupe's appointment no letter on the face of the roll had been authorised since 12 February, leaving ten unauthorised letters. After Cantilupe received the seal there was a run of twenty-seven letters until 9 March of which only two were unauthorised.[50]. A similar pattern can be seen on the fine rolls. In the roll of October 1264-October 1265 not a single letter was authorised before Cantilupe's appointment. After 25 February authorisations began at once.[51] There was also an increase in authorisations on the patent and liberate rolls.[52]

A final indication of Thomas' sense of the chancellor's responsibilities may be discovered in the regulations which were issued on 7 May, 1265 for the use of the seal while he was away from court. Since it is, on balance, unlikely that Thomas' departure on 7 May was connected with any challenge to his authority as chancellor, he probably played a large part in devising these rules. Normally, when the chancellor left court, the name of the keeper of the seal in his absence was recorded in the briefest of notes on the chancery rolls.[55] On this occasion, by contrast, it was laid down that, until Thomas' return, Ralph of Sandwich was to keep the seal in the king's wardrobe under the seal of Peter de Montfort, or Roger de St John, or Giles de Argentan, all members of the council. Ralph could

49 *CR 1264-8,* 1-54, 78-116.

50 *ibid.*, 22-41. The colour of the ink and the shape of the hand suggests that the first eight authorisations were added later than the entries to which they belonged. It seems that the clerk initially continued with his old practices, and then was pulled up; PRO C/ 54/ 82, m.9.

51 PRO C/ 60/ 62, m.7.

52 During Cantilupe's term, in the patent rolls *circa* 1 in 7, and in the liberate rolls *circa* 1 in 5.5 letters were authorised, as against *circa* 1 in 13 and 1 in 8 respectively between 28 October-25 February, 1265; *CPR 1258-66,* 385-423; 473-86; *Cal. Liberate Rolls 1260-7,* 145-74. After Thomas' departure, in all the rolls, there is a gradual falling off in the rate of authorisations. In Henry III's reign generally there are great fluctuations in the frequency with which letters were authorised. The whole subject needs further study.

55 *e.g. CR 1256-9,* 220, 225, 342, 368, 403.

only seal writs, other than those which were routine, in the presence and with the consent of one of these three councillors. Cantilupe, it seems, was determined to prevent irresponsible use of the seal during his absence.[56]

Thomas Cantilupe, therefore, gives every appearance of having been an active and conscientious chancellor. Why did he hand over the seal on 7 May? The court at this time was at Gloucester, engaged in abortive negotiations through Walter de Cantilupe and others for a settlement with Gilbert de Clare. T. F. Tout wondered whether Thomas departed because he was 'weakening in his support for the revolutionary government'.[57] Evidence could be brought to support this case. According to the story of Cantilupe's nephew, Thomas had clashed once with Henry III and had returned the seal to him. He had certainly disagreed with councillors over the Boston fair inquiry. Perhaps such episodes left Cantilupe disillusioned with conciliar rule. Hence his reconciliation with Henry III after the battle of Evesham. A somewhat different theory might be that Cantilupe's colleagues had become frustrated by difficulties which he had made over the issue of letters, and he was 'advised to leave', as Sir Maurice Powicke put it, because the Council wished to be 'more certain' about the use of the seal.[58]

There are, however, problems with such hypotheses. Thomas' career after Evesham can only throw uncertain light on his attitudes in April and May 1265.[59] More concretely, there is no evidence of a breach between Thomas and his colleagues at the time of his departure on 7 May. Cantilupe was no place man. A well-attested story tells how he sought leave to retire from the council of Edward I when he was opposed to one of the king's decisions. Yet in May 1265 he did not resign as chancellor, and Sandwich was to hold the seal merely till his return. On 7 May itself Thomas joined with Hugh Despencer and Peter de Montfort in authorising a royal letter. On 30 May when the court was at Hereford a letter was sent which ordered officials to collect a tallage on the Jews and to 'do it with master Thomas de Cantilupe our chancellor if he is still staying in London'.[60] Clearly Thomas was still recognised as chancellor and considered a loyal member of the government. References to Thomas' return seem more than a polite fiction. The conditions for Ralph of Sandwich's use of the seal tied one of three councillors permanently to court. No arrangements were made for replacements or deputies. These conditions cannot have been intended to endure for long. In the event the political situation soon made Thomas' return impossible. On 28 May the Lord

56 *CPR 1258-66*, 423; *CR 1264-8*, 54. There were precedents both for the seal being kept in the wardrobe, and for its keeper being a layman, as was Ralph of Sandwich; Tout., *op. cit.*, 287-8; compare *Ann. Mon.*, IV, 168.

57 Tout., *op. cit.*, 311, n. 2.

58 Powicke, *op. cit.* (1947), II, 492, n. 5.

59 This point is discussed below.

60 *CR 1264-8*, 55, 62.

Edward escaped from custody. He quickly formed an alliance with the earl of Gloucester. In June the two broke down the bridges over the river Severn, and Montfort and the court became trapped on the Welsh side of the river. Thomas, who had been staying in London, was powerless to rejoin his friends.

If, then, there was no cleavage between Cantilupe and the Montfortians, why did he depart? It was not uncommon for chancellors to hand over the seal and spend time away from court. May 1265, however, seems an unlikely time for a vacation. Perhaps Thomas left to perform some special mission. The fact that he went to London, and that the court knew this, are pointers in that direction.[61]

If Cantilupe had hopes of resuming as chancellor, they were crushed by Montfort's defeat and death at the battle of Evesham on 4 August, 1265. Cantilupe returned to academic life until his election to the bishopric of Hereford in 1275. According to one story, impossible to authenticate, Walter de Cantilupe confessed on his death bed that he had erred in favouring Montfort's party.[62] There is no clear indication from his career after 1265 that Thomas took this view. Evesham had killed the cause of the great earl. Cantilupe could not avoid the new world. He had soon to act in it as his uncle's executor. How far Thomas' past conduct as chancellor affected his position after Evesham is difficult to say. Personally, at the time of his appointment, he may have been acceptable to the king; in some ways he had treated his monarch with respect. On the other hand, there had probably been disagreements over individual letters and charters. Within three weeks of Evesham Thomas was granted letters of safe conduct to go where he wished in England; but he did not have a clean bill of political health, and in February 1266, as 'sometime chancellor', he obtained a writ which admitted him to grace, and forgave, in the conventional words of the time, the king's 'rancour and indignation'.[63] By the following year he had apparently fully recovered or acquired a place in the king's esteem, since he is found with the style 'king's clerk' (August

61 A badly damaged letter to king Henry from '. . . Cantilup . . .', who was in London, may have been written by Thomas at this time; PRO SC/ 1/ 3/ 3; *PRO Lists and Indexes,* LX (1968), 36. It was chiefly concerned with a request which the king had made to the Dean and chapter of St. Paul's. However, it refers to 'when I will come to you'. It also states that 'it is believed that the messengers of the king of France in a short time are about to come to England'. Louis IX's messengers were eagerly awaited by Montfort in May 1265, and one wonders whether Cantilupe was sent to meet them and conduct them to court. There are, however, problems with this hypothesis; see *CR 1264-8,* 120-1.

62 *Flores Historiarum,* ed. H. R. Luard (Rolls Series, 1890); III, 9.

63 The admission to grace was on 10 February, 1266, only two days before Walter de Cantilupe's death; *CPR 1258-66,* 443, 549, 596. Another member of the council of nine, Giles de Argentan, who was captured at Evesham, was admitted to grace in the same month.

1267).[64] Perhaps their common piety had always been a bond between the two men. There was nothing inconsistant about Thomas becoming a 'king's clerk'. He thereby acknowledged a personal association with Henry. He did not necessarily condone his government. The title was probably honorary, and there is no evidence that Thomas was active in the king's service. In 1267 or 1268 he left England for the university of Paris.[65] The accession in 1272 of Edward I, a far abler and wiser man than his father, must have made schemes for conciliar rule seem irrelevant. Cantilupe was one of many former Montfortians to rise high in Edward's service. Nonetheless the memory of the great earl may have been cherished in Thomas' circle. Both Thomas' steward and hawk were said to have been cured of illness through the earl's miraculous intervention. The compilers of Cantilupe's own miracles were happy to preserve the statement that Thomas was 'as much a saint as Simon de Montfort who is buried at Evesham'.[66]

The second phase of Thomas' career outside the schools confirms the impression of a strong and vigorous personality given by the first. He returned to the king's council not simply because he was bishop of Hereford. Edward would never have chosen him, had he not thought highly of his abilities and wanted him as a councillor. In 1279 Thomas was appointed one of the regents during the king's absence from the kingdom —a position that his father had held in 1242.[67] The one substantial story preserved of Cantilupe as an Edwardian councillor seems utterly characteristic of a man who in 1265 had refused to consent to a royal letter. When Edward proposed to give a converted Jew the right to bear witness against Christian forgers, Thomas rose up in tears and sought leave to withdraw from the council. The king gave way.[68]

Thomas Cantilupe was bishop of Hereford for a comparatively short time—seven years. He was chancellor of Henry III for only a few months. Yet he made a significant impression in both offices. In 1265 Thomas may well have been fired by the desire to run the chancery in the

64 *CR 1264-8*, 326, 332; *CPR 1266-72*, 300.

65 Emden, *op. cit.*, I, 347-8.

66 *Chronicle of Rishanger*, 70-1; *AA.SS*, 671. It has been suggested that, whilst bishop of Hereford, Thomas' former politics influenced him in his proceedings against the relatives of his predecessor, Bishop Peter de Aqua Blanca (1240-68), the hated foreign minister of Henry III; N. Yates, 'Bishop Peter de Aqua Blanca', *Journal of Ecclesiastical History*, XXII (1971), 314. However, Cantilupe's register does not suggest any particular hostility to the family; nor does it show he had a 'dislike of foreigners'; *Reg. Cantilupe*, 13, 135, 188, 192, 247, 195, 294, 197, 199, 214-5, 233-4, 248-50.

67 Thomas was on the council by February 1276; *Cal. Close Rolls 1272-9*, 288; *CPR 1272-81*, 309.

68 *AA.SS*, 547-8. The judge Ralph of Hengham witnessed this scene.

spirit of the reforms which the Provisions of Oxford had brought to England. He rejected bribes; he refused consent to a royal letter; he recovered the 'giving' of royal charters from the king; he increased the notes of authorisation to writs. As bishop of Hereford, Cantilupe's 'zeal and love for his church and for the conservation of its rights' made him a conscientious diocesan, and plunged him into law suits against the mightiest in the land.[69] Thomas had a fertile and ordered mind. It is no accident that two of the most unusual entries in the chancery rolls in the thirteenth century belong to his period as chancellor—the statement that the king folded a writ with his own hand, and the rules laid down for the use of the seal in his absence. The same type of mind is seen at work in Thomas' episcopal register; for example, in the detailed instructions Cantilupe issued to his steward.[70] Probably the greatest influence on Cantilupe's political career was his uncle Walter. The two made similar bishops. Both were personally austere. Both worked hard in their dioceses in the cause of reform. Both were also political bishops, and sat on the king's council. Robert Grosseteste perhaps would have worried whether such activity was compatible with diocesan duties. The Cantilupes might have replied that it helped them defend the interests of their sees and the rights of the church. They may also have rejected any narrow distinction between affairs of church and state. Prelates who contributed as councillors and diplomats to their country's peace and well-being surely helped the cure of souls.[71] Bishops like the Cantilupes, active at court and in the diocese, were an important 'hinge upon which the social order turned'.[72] The more one studies Thomas Cantilupe's career as an academic, as a chancellor of Henry III, and as bishop of Hereford, the more the impact which he made on contemporaries becomes explicable. In the discharge of his duties, Thomas instructed his steward to display 'an open heart and a vigilant mind'—*cor directum et animum vigilantem.*[73] It was these which Cantilupe brought to every field of his activity.

69 *Reg. Cantilupe,* 215.
70 *ibid.,* 108-11.
71 Grosseteste would have acknowledged the force of this point; see his letter to Walter de Cantilupe, *Roberti Grosseteste Epistolae,* ed. H. R. Luard (Rolls Series, 1861), 302-4. See also *Robert Grosseteste,* ed. Callus, 181.
72 *ibid.,* 182; Powicke, *op. cit.* (1947), II, 716.
73 *Reg. Cantilupe,* 110.

VIPERS AND GARDENS OF BALSAM: ST THOMAS AND THE VIRTUES OF PURITY AND PRUDENCE

by Barbara Ross

Until a century ago, the only life of St Thomas of Hereford available to those who wished to know more of the saint was one written in 1674.[1] Its author was Richard Strange, a Jesuit who was head of the English Province of his Society from 1674 to 1677. He is described by a recent Jesuit historian as a simple man, easily frightened by the intrigue of his times, and mild and ineffective as a Provincial, although something of a scholar.[2] His admiration for the last Englishman canonized before the break with Rome was such that he wrote a biography as an example for his own 'unfortunate age'. Its shape was dictated by the records of the canonization process, but the emphasis on various aspects is his own. He dwelt on all the saint's virtues, but particularly on his austerity and purity of life. There is indeed ample evidence of these qualities in St Thomas; but it also seems that, like a Tacitus berating his contemporaries with the praise of Germanic virtues, Strange dwelt on such qualities because he had sadly observed they were no longer to be found in the court of Charles II. Furthermore, his seventeenth century misunderstanding of thirteenth century attitudes, unless recognised, serves to confuse rather than assist a twentieth century reader. An instance of this is the great emphasis on the supposed personal oversight of Thomas' education by his parents when he recounts how the infant was nourished by a 'devout, noble and holy matron' and had pious teachers from the age of seven. Courts are places of infamy and vice, where virtue is laughed out of countenance, although the court of Henry III was different and might be termed 'a sanctuary of piety and virtue'. Nevertheless, Thomas' parents were ever mindful that 'Vipers creep into gardens of balsome', and took care to banish all folly and vanity from the sight of those innocent eyes!

1 *The Life and Gests of S. Thomas Cantilupe, Bishop of Hereford and some time before L. Chancellor of England. Extracted out of the authentique Records of his Canonization as to the maine part, Anonymus, Matt. Paris, Capgrave, Harpsfeld, and others.* Collected by R.S.S.I., (Ghent, 1674. Reprinted Burns and Oates, London, 1879). The quotations in this article are from the 1674 edition, chapters III, XXIV and XXV.

2 See Bernard Bassett, *The English Jesuits from Campion to Martindale,* (London, 1967), 244: 'at the peak of the Popish Plot, Fr Peter Hamerton made heroic and successful efforts to move the terrified ex-Provincial to safety in the North'. 'Mr Strange', writes Hamerton, 'resolved I should not leave him and to take him with me was a hard task for his looks, words and the fright he was in spoke what he was'. *See* H. Foley, *Records of the English Province of the Society of Jesus,* 7 vols., (1877-88), V, 624. His interest in English saints is also shown by documents in connection with the transference of some relics of St Chad to Flanders in 1669, *ibid.,* II, 232. A brief outline of Strange's life by Thompson Cooper is in the *Dictionary of National Biography.*

Strange's tender solicitude for childhood and his praise of conjugal affection and concern should not make us forget that in the thirteenth century these virtues were not widely accepted or practised. Children of the nobility spent long periods away from their parents who attended separately to the masculine and feminine duties of their stations. The likelihood of children, even royal ones, being totally reared at court was slight, since the king, his retinue and officials were constantly on the move. Similarly, baronial households journeyed from manor to manor, although an estate reputed to have a healthy situation might be chosen as a more permanent residence for young children and their nurses. Possibly, Hambleden in Buckinghamshire, where Thomas was born, was such a place for the Cantilupe children. Mothers of the baronial class normally handed over their children to wetnurses, preferably ones with the superior qualities which attached to those who had borne sons. It could, however, be argued that the nameless 'noble matron' who nourished, or brought up, Thomas was more a governess than a wetnurse, if 'noble' refers to social position and not moral qualities, since ladies did not undertake the latter role. Such highly-born children as Thomas normally each had their own nurse/supervisor who was not automatically the nurse of their babyhood, and the existence of this person does not necessarily mean that Thomas' mother died whilst he was an infant as has occasionally been claimed.

In a period so hazardous for the health of children, William de Cantilupe and his wife, Millicent, widow of Amauri de Montfort, Count of Evreux, were extremely fortunate that eight of their children survived to adulthood. It is difficult for both general and specific reasons to visualise the life *en famille* of the Cantilupe children. Evidence of the treatment of children and their place in society still has to be garnered from many sources and placed in a genuine medieval perspective; as regards the Cantilupe children we cannot even definitely place them in order of birth. William, who succeeded his father, and Hugh, the companion of Thomas' university studies and later archdeacon of Gloucester, were older than Thomas (who definitely was not the first fruit of his parents' marriage as stated by Strange). But the order of the sisters' births cannot be deduced. Possibly Juliana, the sister who is named in episodes of Thomas' life, was nearest him in age and a childhood companion, but it is just as possible that she features because she married the Marcher lord, Robert de Tregoz, and so, when Thomas resided nearby as the bishop of Hereford, she had more occasion to see him. By the age of seven, children of the baronial class were normally launched on their respective, individual paths, and the very number of Cantilupe children means that the older ones may not have had a close acquaintance with the younger. Ties of family membership were strongly maintained at this period, but they were not necessarily reinforced by bonds of affection and shared childhood memories.

The general pattern of education for children of the nobility seems to be that the boy who was to be a knight went to live in another noble family, the boy destined for the Church started his education in some suitable clerical setting, the girl destined for marriage either went to another noble household or travelled with her mother's establishment, while the girl who was to be a nun would enter as a novice as soon as practicable in her adolescence. This transference of the young to other households was declared to be for the learning of manners, but it also ensured an early start to the task of constructing the essential framework of friends, affinity and influence on which their future life would rest.

Strange makes covert reference to the striving of the nobility for preferment at the Stuart court saying the Cantilupe family 'were not so solicitous to propagate as to illustrate their family, and that familes, like individuals, are mortal and cannot come to a better end than to die in the bed of honour with integrity of fame and virtue'. Such remarks again show the basic lack of understanding on Strange's part of the nature of a thirteenth century baron's life in England. The maintenance of interests and estates, by judicious marriages, by appointment in the ranks of the royal bureaucracy and by the acquisition of ecclesiastical positions, was carried on in an atmosphere of royal or factional favour-seeking and favour-bestowal that was even more complex and all-enveloping for a thirteenth century baron than for a Restoration courtier.

The Cantilupe family is an excellent example of children distributed in marriage or in lay and ecclesiastical openings to the best advantage of the family in a very status and power conscious world. Thomas, contrary to his childhood desire to be a soldier, was placed under the guidance and protection of his influential uncle, Walter de Cantilupe, bishop of Worcester, as was his brother, Hugh. This ensured a continuance of family interests through the considerable pressure and patronage exercised by the Church. An appreciation of these aspects of thirteenth century life does not detract from Thomas' sanctity; it serves all the more to emphasise his subsequent personal humility and his responsible exercise of the authority which was inevitably attached to his position.

A convention of medieval hagiography was that, where relevant, the nobility of saints' origins should be stressed. Such emphasis is to be found in all the works, medieval or modern, dealing with St Thomas. In his case, however, as a true assessment of his social position, it became a relevant and significant consideration, since it is in the perspective of ideas current in the baronial milieu as well as of Church doctrine that the existing evidence of Thomas' views on virginity and womanhood should be placed. To my mind, all the recounted incidents have the ring of truth about them, even two which, it must be admitted, could be read as the normal set pieces found in nearly every medieval life of a male saint.

One of these is his special devotion to the Virgin Mary. This information is, however, circumstantially reinforced by the details that he fasted on all her feast days and chose that of her Nativity for his consecration as a bishop. The second case, a temptation episode, also has circumstantial details, being recounted by Eadmund de Aimar, a friar preacher who lived in Paris in the house opposite Thomas' lodgings. Paris, where even university lecture rooms were jumbled alongside houses of ill-fame, was well known for the temptations it presented to a young man's virtue. Thomas had to visit a burgher's house outside the city to change his English money and the money-changer's wife, a beautiful woman, pressed him to stay in the house, since it was late and the city gates would be closed. Thomas, persuaded by his companions, agreed and spent the night in a comfortable bed in a pleasant room. During the night the woman entered his room by a secret door and got into his bed, but Thomas was only pretending to sleep and rolled away from her out of bed on to the floor, whereupon she went away. In the morning she asked him how he had slept and, refraining from any personal condemnation, he merely said 'very badly, for he had been tempted by the Devil.' She then asked him to tell the truth and she also would tell the truth, asking whether he had been asleep or awake. He said 'awake', so she then admitted that she was the 'devil' who had tempted him. But then she promised to lead a decent life in future and is believed to have kept that promise.

Other incidents related concerning women should be regarded as inevitable products of Thomas' time. To capture the underlying assumptions which resulted in the opinions expressed on women and virginity in the medieval period presents particular problems. Bewilderment caused by the gulf between ideals and images, on one hand, and the reality of day-to-day living, on the other, is one such problem; lack of a female perspective is another. It should be noticed that no women gave evidence to the canonization hearing except in relation to the miracles performed by Thomas. Indeed, for Thomas, the reality was that women were excluded from his daily life, except insofar as they were encountered in his priestly duties to his people. This exclusion was his deliberate intention and the accepted custom. Like that of his successor, Richard Swinfield, Thomas' episcopal household ran entirely on male servants; even the brewing and laundry, usually women's work, was placed out.[3]

His own sisters were, like other women, excluded as overnight guests in spite of hospitality being both a christian and an aristocratic imperative; he would, however, take an occasional meal with his kin. One incident related by two canonization witnesses relates to his refusal to kiss his sister, Juliana de Tregoz, when she visited him at Bosbury to congratulate

3 *A Roll of household expenses of Richard de Swinfield, 1289-1290,* ed. John Webb, Camden Society, LXII, 1855, xxxix, xl.

him on his bishopric. It was the custom among the English for prelates to kiss their kin, and he had apparently kissed her before. But now he held out his hand for her to kiss, thereby emphasising his episcopal authority rather than their kinship. When bystanders, presumably English, remonstrated with him, saying there would be no harm, he still would not agree. (It is worth recollecting here that in France the clerical kissing of relatives was frowned upon. St Bernard, abbot of Clairvaux, when he framed the Code governing the Templars, had forbidden them to kiss widow, virgin, mother, sister, aunt or any other woman; they should shun feminine kisses through which men are brought to danger). Family affection which may or may not have survived the separation in youth is not in question here. The incident only reflects the formal clerical attitude to members of that sex which had occasioned so much mischief to mankind, and whose light and wayward nature could only command serious consideration when the spiritual direction of their lives required attention.

Thomas, although of aristocratic origin, would have rejected the values of the kind of courtly world which gave rise to the literature of *amour courtois,* of allegory, lyric and romance, a literature dominated by women, or more accurately, preoccupied with new aspects of male/female relationships which men were trying to resolve.[4] Thomas, French-speaking and with so many connections with France through his parentage and his education in Paris and Orleans, would have been aware of this blossoming of European literature which also became part of the English tradition. Its depiction of woman, however, as a force of love which awakens man to higher aspirations was never one approved by the theologians; the only manifestation of such love which was at all acceptable was the development of devotion to the Virgin Mary. Dante fell in love with Beatrice at a place and time relatively close to the scene of Thomas' death near Orvieto in 1282, fused the tradition of courtly love and religious mysticism in his *Divine comedy* in a way which, it is surely safe to hypothesize, would have been shocking to Thomas.

In putting Thomas' views on womanhood into perspective, it must be recalled that there were traditional ingrained ideas on the subject which stretched back over centuries to their origins in Hebrew, Greek or Roman thought.[5] These ideas contained two elements: first, a definition of maleness which resulted in femaleness being defined as opposite or inferior;

4 See J. M. Ferrante, *Women as image in medieval literature from the twelfth century to Dante,* (Columbia University Press, New York, 1975), and *In pursuit of perfection: courtly love in medieval literature,* ed. J. M. Ferrante and G. D. Economou, (Kennikat Press, New York, 1975).

5 See Raoul Mortley, *Womenhood: the feminine in ancient hellenism, gnosticism, Christianity and Islam* (Delacroix, Sydney, 1981).

second, an attempt to understand the reasons for the creation of, or necessity for, the female half of humanity. Beneath these philosophical matters, however, lies the farrago of the accepted contemporaneous physiological basis of procreation and reproduction. Views on these subjects reveal, apart from sheer ignorance, deep suspicion of and prejudice against women. In the doctrine of 'humours', a woman was held to be more prone to the sin of lust than a man because her humours were more cold and wet than a man's. This humidity causes desire, but since the cold prevents blood from being digested as it should be, female blood requires the purging provided by coitus. The exact contribution of women to the reproduction of the species was a matter of debate, but the female part was usually found to be of lesser importance. The question was whether the female contributed matter and the male spirit, or whether she contributed part spirit and male both spirit and matter, or whether she was solely an incubating repository for the male seed. Other views may be said to have a pseudo-psychological basis. By defining the masculine variously as active, rational, logical, strong, political, free, intellectual, complete and spiritual, the feminine, as the opposite, was clearly passive, emotional, impulsive, weak, domestic, servile, sensual, defective and carnal.

Medieval theologians were naturally aware of such view when they addressed themselves to discovering the reasons for the creation of woman.[6] The Genesis account of creation quite clearly provided the explanation of the primacy of the male in the order of creation and the purpose of the female as companion and procreator for the male. Thomas Aquinas, who was a near contemporary of Thomas of Hereford, makes clear, following Augustine, that for any purpose other than the reproduction of the species a second man would have been more suitable. The views of Aquinas, however, given this initial assessment of the female, were less extreme than the misogynists of the period who placed squarely on women, in a particularly harsh manner, the responsibility for the existence of evil and death in the world as well as the blame for the individual incidents of wickedness and corruption experienced in daily life. Eve's part in the temptation of Adam and the expulsion from the Garden of Eden are, of course, the basic reason for this antagonistic attitude to women. Eve's transgression was that of all womenkind. Tertullian had centuries earlier summed up her collective guilt when he said:

> You are the Devil's gateway. You are the unsealer of that forbidden tree. You are the first deserter of the divine law. You are she who persuaded him whom the Devil was not valiant to attack. You destroyed so easily God's image, man. On account of your desert which is death, even the Son of God had to die!

6 See Rosemary R. Reuther, ed., ***Religion and sexism: images of women in Jewish and Christian traditions,*** (Simon and Schuster, New York, 1974), especially articles by R. R. Reuther, B. Prusak, and E. C. McLaughlin.

In short, as a professor of religious studies has recently put it, 'Evil, women and knowledge are a package deal'.[7]

These clearly identifiable attitudes and traditions do not, however, go far in explaining the importance of the ideal of virginity in the medieval church. Virginity, it hardly needs to be said, was an ideal for both men and women and its origin is to be found in an interpretation of Creation as expounded in Genesis 1.27. This clearly states that 'God created men in his own image: in the image of God he created him; male and female he created them'. It was difficult to comprehend how this could be since God is wholly spiritual and non-corporal and could not have male and female characteristics. The nature of God and of His life which is shared by the Blessed in Heaven, demanded and received contemplation and analysis in the light of every scrap of evidence and symbolism which could be gleaned from Holy Writ and tradition. This deep attention resulted in the conviction that 'Virginity is the most essential attribute of the christian, for it is the true image of the Divine nature'.[8] The unitary nature of God was either viewed as non-sexual monism, in which case bisexual characteristics of created humanity were relegated to a lower corporeal order, or it was viewed as monism which assimilated maleness, thus leaving femaleness to the lower order. Virginity, taken to be the state of unfallen human nature, mirrored the monistic nature of God, *una et simplex.*

The thirteenth century inherited a vast literature on virginity which cannot be traversed here. But it is only through an understanding of the importance attached at the time to virginity that Thomas' attitudes can be understood. Thomas valued bashfulness, the *verecundia virginalis,* a quality not possessed by a loved nephew whom he had had schooled at Oxford. During his last journey to Rome he was asked why this nephew did not accompany him. 'These young men, sayd he, are not now adays so bashful and modest as heertofore: for when I was such a one, if a handsome woman had looked me in the face, I should presently have bin putt to the blush, turned my eyes from her, or pulld my hatt over them, that eyther I should not have seen her or shee mee'. It was advisable to remove oneself from the unnecessary advances and presence of women, even relatives. When, however, women also aspired to this same ideal of virginity, they entered, as it were, a different category. Like the Virgin Mary, they were obliterating the sin of Eve. They were also treading the same spiritual path as many men. Thomas, therefore, did not shun women when they came into the sphere of his spiritual governance. His tour of inspection of the house of nuns at Limebrook, who lived as canon-

7 *ibid.,* (B. P. Prusak), 91.
8 J. Bugge, *Virginitas: an essay in the history of a medieval ideal.* International Archives of the History of Ideas, Series Minor, no. 17, (Martinus Nijhoff, The Hague, 1975), 37.

esses under the Augustinian rule, resulted in a letter which shows he had given them his full attention, even though probably weighty diocesan matters were pressing on him. It has been suggested that this letter reveals the possibility that on the visit Thomas was shown a copy of *Ancrene Wisse,* the Rule for English women religious which has so many intriguing connections with Herefordshire, and repeats the gist of part of this when he speaks of the need to guard the gates of the senses.[9] His enquiries have revealed that the nuns chattered, were indiscreet, did not keep their vow of poverty and travelled unnecessarily; his letter, however, is one of advice and encouragement as much as reproof. 'Truly the zeal for a good religious life and the unity in charity which we at our visitation found to be so flourishing among you gives me great joy in Christ', he says. He stresses the high calling of the sisters and the positive aspects of their way of life. He was even thoughtful enough to direct the letter be read in whichever language, English or French, the nuns best understood.

There can be no doubt that women and their very different world presented problems to one in Thomas' important social and ecclesiastical position; it was only prudent of him, being so placed, to remove himself from their world, except on those occasions when he was needed. It was reported that he said the conversation of women was foolishness and, probably, to one of his background, their talk would seem decidedly lightweight; women had no part in the academic, political, ecclesiastical and administrative worlds in which he lived and worked. But over all, on the evidence which survives, one cannot help but assess his attitude as kindly, just and sensible, free from the obsessive fear and fanaticism which so many of his contemporaries felt towards women. Two small incidents reveal a genuine consideration for women as individuals. He could not allow his widowed sister-in-law to have any horses from the estate since her husband's will had given no specific directions, but if she wanted some horses he offered her his own. Also, on one occasion when he was sitting at table with his brother-in-law, Robert de Tregoz, Thomas rebuked him for insulting a young woman by implying she was trying to attract the attention of the men.

Richard Strange devotes a whole chapter to Thomas' purity of life, describing it in seventeenth, rather than thirteenth, century terms. It was 'a wonderful innocency of life by which he is thought to have preserved the baptismal garment of his soule pure and unspotted all his life long, a privilege not granted to many'. It is a 'cleanes of heart to which our Blessed Saviour affixed a beatitude and in its beams our Blessed Saint saw God so present in all his actions that he was ashamed as well as reverentially afrayd to offend him'. 'Such a chaste body was fitt to be the consort of so pure a soule to make up one Angelicall compound'. Strange's life of St Thomas ends with a fine peroration on the necessity for prud-

9 L. J. Dobson, *The origin of Ancrene Wisse,* (Oxford, 1976), 272-3.

ence, a quality which is perhaps more apparent in the spiritual than the political aspects of Thomas' life. Prudence is 'the Science of the Saints, without which the greatest learning is ignorance and wisdome folly'. There follows a legal metaphor concerning the acquisition of eternal life which a lawyer like Thomas would have appreciated. 'If we must quitt eyther a lease for life or an inheritance, it would be deemed madness to part with the latter to secure the former'. Then, somewhat unexpectedly, especially given the views he had expressed on princely courts, Strange affixed a dedication to Cosmo de Medici, Duke of Tuscany. The very slight grounds for this dedication were that besides Thomas Cantilupe, another English saint, Richard, father of the saints Willibald, Winnebald and Walburga, had died in Tuscany in 741. Also, the Duke had shown a special interest in England by his recent visit to that country. Pepys, who saw the Duke partially hidden in a coach in Branford, said that he seemed 'a very jolly, good and comely man' and 'comes into England only to spend money and see our country'.[10] It is not known what the reaction of the Duke was to this enthusiastic, naive and frequently anachronistic work. But for us in the twentieth century, it remains a study of charm and interest, still capable of leading us to explore one thirteenth century 'garden of balsome'.

10 Diary of Samuel Pepys, entry on 5 April, 1669.

THOMAS CANTILUPE'S REGISTER: THE ADMINISTRATION OF THE DIOCESE OF HEREFORD 1275-1282

by David M. Smith

By the close of the thirteenth century all English bishops were keeping registers in which to record those administrative acts considered of particular importance for the efficient functioning of the machinery of diocesan government. Beginning in the Lincoln diocese in the early years of the century and modelled on royal and papal precedents, the practice of formal registration gradually spread to all other English bishoprics within a few decades. The contents and range of these registers understandably vary from diocese to diocese and from episcopate to episcopate. Ideally they should contain entries concerning the appointment of clergy to livings and related matters, the ordination of clergy to holy orders, business affecting the monastic orders and religious houses, entries touching on church fabric, property, and rights, episcopal visitations of the diocese, a record of commissions, licences, dispensations, indulgences and other memoranda, details of financial and estate administration, and copies of royal and papal letters and other important incoming correspondence. Needless to say, very few registers are so comprehensive in their scope.[1]

Thomas Cantilupe's register is the earliest to survive for the Hereford diocese and it seems likely that to Cantilupe, or at the very least to his registrar and household clerks, goes the distinction of introducing the bishop's register to Hereford. It is a relatively slim volume of just over seventy parchment folios, with an average measurement of 11½ by 6¾ inches, and bound in hide-covered wooden boards, sewn on four raised cords. There is a little rodent damage on the later folios of the register, and the binding has been repaired. It is the product of several episcopal clerks (there are various changes of handwriting) and is clearly a working record. Neatness is not always maintained in the arrangement. There are occasional erasures and cancellations of entries and some insertion of

1 For details of bishops' registers in general see D. M. Smith, *Guide to bishops' registers of England and Wales: a survey from the middle ages to the abolition of episcopacy in 1646,* Royal Historical Society, (1981); for the Hereford section see 95-104. The Hereford registers have also been discussed by D. Walker, 'The Bishops' registers of the diocese of Hereford, 1275-1539', *Transactions of the Woolhope Naturalists' Field Club,* XXXVI (1958-60), 291-7. Thomas Cantilupe's register, which is kept in the Diocesan Registry, St Peter Street, Hereford, was transcribed by R. G. Griffiths and published with an introduction by Canon W. W. Capes in the Cantilupe Society series in 1906 (hereafter *Reg. Cantilupe*). For a facsimile of a folio from the bishop's register see plate III.

loose parchment sheets. Spaces at first left blank are sometimes filled in with later material out of sequence. Often the scribes failed to note marginal headings to entries. The form of these entries varies: sometimes they are complete transcripts of letters, at other times a brief résumé of the episcopal act. The ink changes confirm that batches of entries were registered at regular intervals, and these delays account for some of the chronological confusion. A representation of a pointing finger is used to indicate what the scribes considered to be the more noteworthy entries, and documents of an earlier date were copied into the volume when they touched upon current business or were particularly needed for reference. Sometimes 'short cuts' were taken or omissions remedied by the insertion of extraneous material—for instance, ordinations of clergy are not always copied out in full in the proper sequence but on occasion the original list of names on a separate sheet of parchment (presumably drawn up at the time of the ceremony) is sewn into the register. There is also some indication of a change in registrational method soon after the register was begun, perhaps further emphasizing its experimental nature as the first of a series. The first folio bears the heading *Registrum de spiritualibus anno domini m^o^ cc^o^ lxx^o^ quinto* and this would suggest (as happened in other dioceses such as York) that it was the original intention to subdivide the register entries in a rather basic form, distinguishing the bishop's acts as a spiritual lord from those matters relating to the temporalities and estates of the see. The annual headings continue for Cantilupe's second and third pontifical years (1276 and 1277) but are then abandoned and it is quite clear that if the original plan had indeed been to segregate spiritual business from temporal business, it was very soon discarded. In common with several other dioceses the method of registration adopted by Cantilupe's clerks resulted in a single general register in approximate chronological order. Often, for ease of consultation, diocesan registrars evolved a system of registration based on category and territorial (usually archdeaconry) subdivisions, but it was not until the time of Bishop Thomas Charlton (1327-44) that the Hereford registers underwent such a modification and were divided into several category sections. All in all, Thomas Cantilupe's register is a simple, workmanlike record and although it cannot compare with the more sophisticated productions compiled by the registrars of his contemporaries on the episcopal bench, Pecham of Canterbury, Sutton of Lincoln, and Wickwane of York, it clearly served its primary purpose as an aid to the more efficient administration of the diocese.

Important as the contents of this register obviously are for any evaluation of Cantilupe's administrative abilities, by itself it is an imperfect record of his episcopate. In the first place it should be remembered that the register was never meant to be a complete record of the bishop's administration. Even within categories of business normally selected for registration there are many omissions: gaps exist in the list of clerical

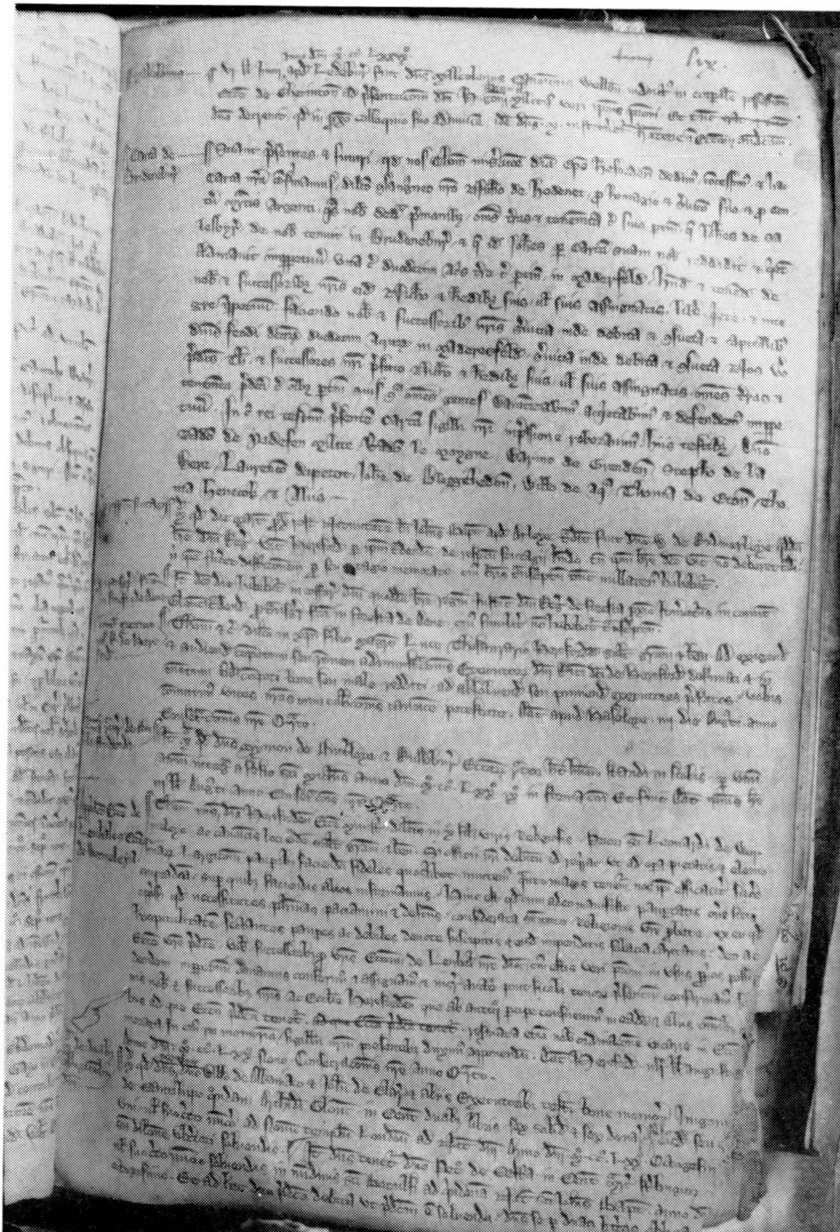

III. Registrum Thome de Cantilupo, episcopi Herefordensis, fo. 59r.

ordinations and the series of institutions to benefices;[2] and important legal documents concerning the Pecham/Cantilupe disputes failed to be registered until much later when they were copied into the register of Thomas's successor, Bishop Richard Swinfield (1283-1317).[3] Even discounting these scribal lapses, the fact remains that the bulk of the episcopal archives of the time has long since disappeared. Any thirteenth-century bishop would possess a large quantity of records acquired by natural accumulation —firstly, a variety of incoming correspondence, much of which would be considered worthy of retention and preservation—letters from popes and kings, magnates, episcopal colleagues, and a host of ecclesiastical dignitaries and subordinates, parish clergy, patrons of livings, and laymen. There would also be important confirmations of rights and privileges which needed to be carefully preserved. Private charters, agreements and the like would often be lodged with the bishop for safekeeping, and in addition to these there would be a not inconsiderable collection of records created by the bishop's own subordinates—accounts, rentals, surveys, court rolls and other memoranda relating to the running of the episcopal estates and finances, detailed records of legal proceedings and the course of visitations, and information on benefices and clergy in the diocese, supplementing the register. Much of this material would need to be kept permanently. Clearly, considering that a bishop was constantly on the move round his diocese or much further afield, he could not contemplate carrying around with him on his travels this great mass of records. Archivally speaking, he would travel relatively light, his household clerks probably taking with them the register and the more useful or current records. Items of particular importance or legal value could be stored in the cathedral church or in an episcopal residence, as could other material that did not require to be consulted with any frequency.

A few stray references exist to these episcopal archives and archive-keeping in Cantilupe's time. Visitation rolls of the bishop are known to have survived until at least the middle of the fourteenth century.[4] In 1276 charters and legal documents relating to a lawsuit of Thomas's predecessor, Bishop John le Breton, were kept in a chest in the cathedral chapter-house, under Cantilupe's seal.[5] Other records and financial tallies belonging to Cantilupe were placed in a leather bag and stored in a chest

2 For example, the testimony of Roger de Hunneden, subprior of the Austin friars in London, indicates that he was ordained by Cantilupe at Leominster (*Acta Sanctorum* (Antwerp-Brussels, 1643, sqq.), Octobris, I, (hereafter *AA.SS*), 556b-557a); his name does not feature in the surviving ordination lists. For an institution to Stoke Lacy not recorded in the bishop's register see *Historia et cartularium monasterii sancti Petri Gloucestriae,* ed. W. H. Hart, Rolls Series, 3 vols., (1863-7), II, 289.

3 *Registrum Ricardi de Swinfield, episcopi Herefordensis,* ed. W. W. Capes, Canterbury and York Society, VI, (London, 1909) (hereafter *Reg. Swinfield*), 32, 36.

4 *Registrum Johannis de Trillek, episcopi Herefordensis,* ed. J. H. Parry, Cantilupe Society, VI, (1910), 222, 237.

5 *Reg. Cantilupe,* 40-1.

behind the high altar of St Paul's cathedral in London;[6] on another occasion it was noted that various records concerning Peter Eymer, a canon of Hereford, had been kept in the episcopal coffers,[7] while in 1279 the acknowledgements of certain debts were strung on a file attached to the episcopal register.[8] Such then is the archival background to any study of episcopal administration.

In the later middle ages the diocese of Hereford contained within its borders Herefordshire (except for the Ewyas district in the south-west of the county which was in the diocese of St David's), the south-western portion of Shropshire, the district of Erging (Archenfield) around Monmouth, Gloucestershire west of the river Severn (the deanery of the Forest), several parishes in the west of Worcestershire which formed part of the rural deanery of Burford, a few parishes in Radnorshire and some on the eastern edge of Montgomeryshire. But at the time that Thomas Cantilupe was called upon to administer the diocese in 1275 its boundaries were not so rigidly defined, at least as far as the Welsh border territories were concerned. Shortly after he had become bishop, Cantilupe had to contest a claim to the Gordwr district of Montgomeryshire by Anian Sais, bishop of St Asaph. The dispute dragged on for years at the papal curia and was finally settled by compromise agreement in the time of Bishop Swinfield.[9] In the south of the diocese Cantilupe also came into conflict with Bishop Thomas Bek of St David's over the consecration of the new abbey church of Dore, which the latter claimed was in his jurisdiction—a conflict which according to evidence given at the canonization process almost came to blows. This St David's claim was raised once more after Cantilupe's death and was equally fiercely rejected by his successor.[10]

The sexennial tenth imposed on the English Church by Pope Nicholas IV just nine years after Cantilupe's death resulted in an assessment which, apart from its intrinsic financial importance, is additionally valuable for the information it provides on the diocesan organisation of the time.[11] The Hereford diocese was divided into two archdeaconries, Hereford in the south, Shropshire in the north; the former was subdivided into eight rural deaneries (Archenfield, Forest, Frome, Hereford, Leominster, Ross, Weobley, and Weston), the latter into six (Burford, Clun, Ludlow, Pontesbury, Stottesden, and Wenlock). Certain parishes were not under the

6 *ibid.*, 182-3. 7 *ibid.*, 198, *cf.* also 211. 8 *ibid.*, 213.

9 *ibid.*, 197, 209-10, 214-15, 229-30, 232-3, 236-7, 255-6, 279, 281-3, 286; *Reg. Swinfield*, 67-8, 204-12, 219-20; D. L. Douie, *Archbishop Pecham*, (Oxford, 1952), (hereafter Douie), 193-4.

10 *AA.SS*, 566b-567a; Vat. Cod. Lat. 4015, fo. 47r; *Reg. Swinfield*, 58-61.

11 *Taxatio ecclesiastica Angliae et Walliae auctoritate P. Nicholai IV, circa A.D. 1291*, Record Commission, (1802), (hereafter *Taxatio*), 157-74.

bishop's immediate control but formed the peculiar jurisdiction of the dean and other members of the cathedral chapter. For the whole of Cantilupe's episcopate the archdeaconry of Hereford was held by William de Conflans, a future bishop of Geneva, who received a licence for non-residence as soon as Cantilupe entered upon the bishopric;[12] the Shropshire archdeaconry had a more disturbed history in this period. The Savoyard archdeacon James Aquablanca or de Vitri was cited in 1277 to answer charges of illegal plurality of livings and non-residence and after protracted proceedings he was deprived in 1280. The immediate collation of the archdeaconry to Richard Swinfield was not effective, and Adam de Fileby subsequently became archdeacon.[13]

But it was not the archdeacons who were the most important administrative subordinates of the bishop; in fact Cantilupe gathered together into his household or *familia* a group of clerks well-versed in canon law and administration to form a kind of episcopal secretariat, and it was from their number that he appointed his officers, chief among them being the official, who presided over the bishop's court and carried out other administrative duties, and the vicar-general, the bishop's general administrative deputy when he was absent from the diocese. Clearly, a bishop had to depend a great deal on his household clerks and his choice was crucial for the effective government of the diocese—like St Hugh, bishop of Lincoln a century earlier, who 'thought, and indeed was completely convinced that without the assistance of highly trained men he could not really be of much use to the clergy and people under his authority.'[14] Canon Capes has abstracted lists of episcopal officials, both spiritual and temporal, and the names of clerks, chaplains, lawyers and officers of the household, from the register and further details are forthcoming from depositions in the canonization process and later diocesan evidence.[15] Prominent among the household were several university *magistri,* Luke de Bré, Roger of Sevenoaks, Robert of Gloucester, and William de Montfort. Luke de Bré became Cantilupe's official in 1275 and four years later was one of the two vicars-general appointed by the bishop during his absence. Among his preferments he held a canonry of Hereford and became treasurer of the cathedral. After the bishop's death he was commissioned by Archbishop Pecham, along with Robert of Gloucester, to receive the ordinands of the Hereford diocese in the vacancy, and by a curious irony became a trusted clerk of Cantilupe's adversary and rose to be the archbishop's

12 *Reg. Cantilupe,* 7-8.

13 *ibid.*, 63, 125-6, 137, 150, 160-2, 197-9, 241-2, 245-6, 253; *AA.SS*, 562b.

14 *Magna Vita Sancti Hugonis,* ed. D. L. Douie & H. Farmer, 2 vols., (London, 1961-2), I, 110.

15 *Reg. Cantilupe,* lxix-lxxi; *Reg. Swinfield,* 234, where Swinfield records that he was a chaplain of Cantilupe for about 18 years. (It is a salutary note about sources that Swinfield never appears in Cantilupe's register as an episcopal chaplain).

chancellor, serving as an executor of his will after his death.[16] Roger of Sevenoaks, who succeeded Luke as official, was rector of Sevenoaks in Kent, but in addition received rewards in the Hereford diocese from Cantilupe and Swinfield in the form of a prebend of Bromyard, a canonry at Hereford, and later the treasurership of the cathedral.[17] Robert of Gloucester, otherwise known as le Wyse, was appointed official in 1280 and remained in office until Cantilupe's death. A doctor of canon law, he was at Oxford University when Cantilupe was there and became a member of the bishop's household soon after Thomas's elevation to Hereford. He played a key role in the disputes between his diocesan and Archbishop Pecham and in the opinion of one recent historian was 'a loyal but somewhat hot-headed and unscrupulous subordinate'.[18] Whatever his personal qualities may have been, however, his obvious abilities were certainly recognised by Cantilupe and others and, after Thomas's death, he acted as the official of Bishop Richard Swinfield and later on became chancellor to Pecham's successor at Canterbury, Archbishop Robert Winchelsey. Needless to say, these offices brought with them the expected rewards in ecclesiastical preferment, among which were a canonry and the chancellorship of Hereford cathedral.[19] William de Montfort, a kinsman of Cantilupe, incepted under Thomas at Oxford University and later became its chancellor. He was given a canonry and the precentorship of the cathedral by Cantilupe in 1277 and acted jointly with Luke de Bré as vicar-general in 1279 and alone in the following year. He was co-executor of the bishop's will with Walter of Redmarley, another canon of Hereford, and these two were also joint guardians of the temporalities of the see at the time of the bishop's absence.[20]

While the choice of competent assistants would ensure the continued efficient administration of the diocese when the bishop was obliged to be absent from it, the officials themselves were not canonically able to carry out all the episcopal duties. Included among the sacramental functions

16 *Reg. Cantilupe,* 1, 112-16, 120-1, 151, 221-3, 291; *Reg. Swinfield,* 230, 274, 334-5; Hereford cathedral archives, 1066-7, 2285; Douie, 60, 62, 73; *The Register of John Pecham, Archbishop of Canterbury, 1279-1292,* ed. D. L. Douie, F. N. Davis & others, Canterbury and York Society, LXIV, LXV, (1908-69), (hereafter *Reg. Pecham*), II, 13, 61-2. It is also of interest to note that one of Cantilupe's proctors at the Roman curia, John of Beccles, eventually became Pecham's registrar. (Douie, 60, 224, 322; *Reg. Cantilupe,* 105-7, 209-10, 279-82).

17 *Reg. Cantilupe,* 63, 221-2, 245-6; *Reg. Swinfield,* 142, 154, 212-13, 315, 328; *Reg. Pecham,* II, 63, 88; *Taxatio,* 160, 169; Hereford cathedral archive, 1052.

18 Douie, 194.

19 *Reg. Cantilupe,* 224, 244, 250, 252-9, 268; A. B. Emden, *A Biographical register of the University of Oxford to A.D. 1500,* (Oxford, 1957-9), (hereafter Emden), II, 773-4; *Registrum Roberti Winchelsey Cantuariensis Archiepiscopi,* ed. R. Graham, Canterbury and York Society, LI, LII, (1952-6), I, 455, 473; II, 975, 981.

20 *Reg. Cantilupe,* 111, 119, 122, 221-2, 246, 248-50, 252-3, 256-7, 271; *Reg. Swinfield,* 70-1, 98, 101, 159, 204, 263; Emden, II, 1297-8; *AA.SS,* 555a, 700a.

of a bishop were the confirmation of children,[21] the ordination of the clergy, and the consecration of altars, churches and churchyards. These duties could only be performed by someone in episcopal orders, so that when Cantilupe was absent abroad, it was necessary for him to procure the services of fellow-bishops to undertake these responsibilities. In 1280 when already in France he commissioned the Welsh diocesans, Anian of Bangor and William de Breuse of Llandaff, to exercise the episcopal office in his diocese when requested by his vicar-general or official.[22] Understandably, he did not employ the other two Welsh diocesans of St Asaph and St David's, with whom he had jurisdictional disagreements.

As I have already remarked, a medieval diocesan bishop's life was peripatetic. When in his diocese he would spend his time, as Cantilupe's itinerary reveals,[23] travelling round from episcopal residence to episcopal residence or occasionally seeking hospitality at religious houses. Even the hazards of travel in the winter months do not seem to have curtailed Cantilupe's perambulations. In addition to residences within the confines of the diocese (of which Bosbury, Stretton Sugwas, and Bishop's Castle seem to have been popular with Cantilupe), the bishop had a London house, Montalt, purchased by Bishop Richard Maidstone earlier in the century for use when royal or ecclesiastical business brought him to the capital.[24] At other times he would be in attendance on the king in various parts of the country or his presence would be required at provincial church councils. It was in fact on one such royal occasion in 1277 that the famous incident occurred when Cantilupe was displaced from the lodgings at Powick, originally assigned to him, in favour of the earl of Gloucester. The bishop successfully petitioned Edward I to have them re-assigned to him, a fact solemnly recorded in the register.[25]

It is difficult to gain any clear idea of the bishop's personality or daily life from the available archives. Unfortunately no detailed household accounts survive, such as exist for his successor Richard Swinfield,[26] and although the depositions of witnesses in the canonization process

21 No records of confirmations of children were kept but the canonization evidence notes with approval that Cantilupe travelled about his diocese, wearing his stole ready to baptise and confirm, and that whenever anyone brought children to him for confirmation, he would dismount from his horse to perform the ceremony (Vat. Cod. Lat. 4015, fo. 59rv). For a similar story about St Hugh of Lincoln see *Magna Vita Sancti Hugonis,* I, 128.

22 *Reg. Cantilupe,* 253, *cf.* 221-2.

23 *ibid.,* lxv-lxviii.

24 For medieval residences of the bishops of Hereford see J. W. Tonkin, 'The Palaces of the Bishop of Hereford', *Transactions of the Woolhope Naturalists' Field Club,* XLII, (1976), 53-64.

25 *Reg. Cantilupe,* 123-4.

26 *A roll of the household expenses of Richard de Swinfield, bishop of Hereford, during part of the years 1289 and 1290,* ed. J. Webb, Camden Society, old series, LIX, LXII, (1854, 55).

throw much valuable incidental light on his character and the manner of his daily life, in sum total there is very little information. The register is a routine business record and the forms of the documents copied into it are for the most part governed by precedent and allow virtually no scope for any detail which might give insight into the bishop's character. Only rarely is there personal information or a 'vignette' portraying an aspect of life in the episcopal entourage. In 1279 there are two allusions to the ill-health of the bishop[27] (otherwise nothing is known of his physical state), and in the same year in the course of his dispute with the bishop of St Asaph, Cantilupe had a document of appeal drawn up while staying at his manor-house of Bosbury. The scribe notes that the bishop was in his hall before the mid-day meal when this was done and first read out the document to the assembled witnesses in Latin and then explained it to them in French.[28] Incidentally, further evidence about the linguistic problems Cantilupe experienced in his dealings with the local inhabitants of his diocese is contained in the testimony of Walter de Knulle, a Franciscan friar, at the time of the canonization inquiry. Walter records that because Cantilupe's vulgar tongue was Norman-French rather than English, he used to take with him for preaching purposes on his travels round the diocese his confessor, the Franciscan Henry de Bellington, who 'was an excellent preacher in the English tongue'.[29]

The task of administering a diocese presented formidable problems to any bishop intent on exercising an effective spiritual and paternal supervision over the ecclesiastical and lay population of his see. Not unnaturally, a great deal of any diocesan's business was concerned with the state of the clergy, secular and regular—their standards and credentials, the abuse of non-residence, the necessity for adequate provision for the cure of souls in the parishes, and the need to ensure that the beneficed clergy undertook their responsibilities as well as enjoying the revenues of their livings. These were all duties which Thomas Cantilupe tackled from the outset with considerable energy.

The problem of the holding of livings with cure of souls in plurality, and the resultant evils arising from clerical absenteeism and the frequent lack of pastoral provision for parishioners, was not a new one in the thirteenth century. Successive popes of church councils had tried to combat the growing abuse but without real success.[30] Theoretically the holding of two benefices with cure of souls was forbidden, but exceptions had been allowed by papal decrees and episcopal laxity. The constitution *De multa providentia* of the 1215 Lateran Council had confirmed the

27 *Reg. Cantilupe,* 224; PRO, *Ancient correspondence,* 15/154.
28 *Reg. Cantilupe,* 197. 29 Vat. Cod. Lat. 4015, fo 78r.
30 For a general study of the problems of pluralism and the legislation see *Associated Architectural Societies' Reports and Papers,* XXXIII (1915), 35-73.

papal power of dispensation affecting 'noble and lettered persons' (*circa sublimes tamen et literatas personas*) who ought to be honoured with larger benefices. In England various archiepiscopal statutes and the enactments of the papal legates Otto (in 1237) and Ottobuono (in 1268) had further inveighed against the practice. The canon *Christianae Religionis* issued by the Cardinal Ottobuono was particularly far-reaching and severe. By it he ordered the English bishops to hold inquiries in their dioceses about pluralism and non-residence, and that unauthorised pluralists so discovered should resign all their livings except the last one they had received. The problem was to be combatted in the future by presentees to benefices, who already possessed livings elsewhere, being obliged to show their valid dispensations before admission. (It must be said that this 1268 legatine constitution was not rigidly enforced by the majority of diocesan bishops.) Finally, just a year before Cantilupe's election as bishop, the second Council of Lyons, presided over by Pope Gregory X, had promulgated the constitution *Ordinarii locorum* which again laid down that all dispensations for plurality were to be examined. Cantilupe is known to have attended this Council[31] and was quite obviously much influenced by the various legislation. As soon as he became bishop he seems to have tackled this problem in his new diocese with considerable energy, and in his attacks he was certainly no respecter of persons.

An unfortunate legacy from his Savoyard predecessor Peter of Aquablanca (1240-68) was the presence of a veritable horde of Aquablanca relatives and associates still holding many dignities and wealthier benefices in the diocese. Cantilupe had already clashed with this foreign element in the days of Bishop John le Breton (1269-75) when the latter had deprived one of their number, Peter de Langon, of his cathedral prebend and had conferred it upon Thomas. Langon refused to accept the sentence of deprivation and appealed to Rome, and the case was still in progress at the time Thomas became bishop. (Indeed it was not finally concluded, in Langon's favour, until long after Thomas was dead).[32] Cantilupe, whose antipathy to foreign clergy being beneficed in his diocese is clearly stated in one of his letters,[33] soon began his onslaught on this Aquablanca clan. James of Aquablanca, a great-nephew of Bishop Peter, archdeacon of Shropshire and a portionist of Ledbury, two other great-nephews, Peter and Pons, portionists of Bromyard, and Hugh de Tournon, rector of Whitbourne, were cited to answer charges of pluralism and non-residence.[34] James, as mentioned earlier, was eventually deprived,

31 *AA.SS*, 549a-b.

32 *Reg. Cantilupe*, 12, 18-19, 187, 209-10, 213-14, 233, 250, 277; *Reg. Swinfield*, 68, 70-2, 98-9, 219, 258-73.

33 *Reg. Cantilupe*, 249.

34 *Reg. Cantilupe*, 135, 137-9, 141-2, 150, 162, 184, 188, 192-3, 247-8; A. T. Bannister, *The Cathedral Church of Hereford*, (London, 1924), 141-5.

although the proceedings against Peter and Pons were stayed through the intervention of their uncle, Emery, chancellor of Hereford, and other powerful protectors, and Pons at least survived to cause Bishop Swinfield considerable trouble.[35] Royal clerks also did not escape and Edward I had to intervene personally to stop the proceedings against one of them, Stephen of St George, portionist of Bromyard.[36] The copying into Cantilupe's register of a bull of Pope Nicholas III asking for inquiries to be made about the alleged loss in London during disturbances of various dispensations for plurality in favour of Geoffrey de Aspale, Queen Eleanor's chancellor, is also possibly a result of earlier episcopal investigations into Aspale's preferment.[37] Another prominent ecclesiastic, Hervey of Boreham, dean of St Paul's, London, found himself summoned to answer charges that he was holding the precentorship of Hereford without dispensation. As no dispensations were produced, the office was declared vacant and conferred on another.[38] Finally, Richard Gravesend, archdeacon of Northampton and a member of another important ecclesiastical dynasty, had obtained the church of Ross on Wye without suitable dispensation and subsequently suffered deprivation.[39] Further evidence exists in the register indicating that Cantilupe's investigations into non-residence and pluralism were pursued with determination.[40] The outcome of several of these cases remains unknown and some obviously dragged on inconclusively for years, but what information does survive would suggest that they were the result of a systematic episcopal inquiry (possibly at a visitation), not haphazard prosecutions.

In the matter of pluralism, Cantilupe's actions have occasionally been attacked by critics who have pointed out that before he became a bishop he was a most noted pluralist himself. That he possessed many benefices is quite true, but it is also clear that he possessed valid dispensations and took especial care, if we credit the canonization evidence, to make adequate provision for the cure of souls in his many livings.[41] The so-called 'reforming' bishops of the period, among whom we must number Cantilupe, were not primarily concerned with the total extirpation of pluralism *per se*—the holding of several benefices by royal 'civil servants'

35 *Reg. Cantilupe,* 135, 192-3; *Reg. Swinfield,* 244-5, 248-9.

36 *Reg. Cantilupe,* 141, 169-70.

37 *ibid.,* 203-4.

38 *ibid.,* 78-9, 88, 111, 121; *AA.SS,* 562b. As it turned out, although the bishop had obviously not received the news, Hervey was already dead by the time this happened (John Le Neve, *Fasti Ecclesiae Anglicanae 1066-1300,* (London, 1968), I, 8).

39 *AA.SS,* 562b.

40 e.g. *Reg. Cantilupe,* 127, 131, 136-9, 145-6, 151-2, 159-60, 162-3, 183-4, 188-90, 192-3.

41 For Cantilupe's preferment see Emden, I, 347-9; for his activities in these parishes see *AA.SS,* 549b-550b.

and ecclesiastical notables was a tacitly accepted feature of church life—rather, they were attacking unauthorised plurality of benefices and absenteeism. Pluralism and non-residence for canonically valid reasons were to be sanctioned by dispensation and licence, but care was to be taken to ensure that there was adequate pastoral provision for the cure of souls in the affected parishes.

If unlawful pluralism and absenteeism were to be relentlessly attacked, there was still canonical provision made, dependent upon episcopal licence, for the authorised absence of those clergy who wished to pursue their studies or go on a pilgrimage or crusade, or enter the service of a higher ecclesiastic or lay lord. The register is full of such licences granted by Cantilupe for between one and five years. Most of them are for educational purposes: Robert de Shepe, rector of Munslow, had permission to study theology or canon law for one year in England or for two years in France;[42] Edmund de Ba, rector of Westbury, was allowed to pursue his studies at Paris for two years;[43] and the rector of Clun was absent at Oxford for one year.[44] Master Caturmus, the rector of Eastnor, was given five years' leave of absence to go on a crusade,[45] and the vicar of Lydney was given similar permission in accordance, as the register entry states, with the indult granted to crusaders at the Council of Lyons.[46] In all such cases, and those concerning the farming of the revenues of benefices, special care was taken so that the cure of souls should not be neglected in the parishes of these absentee clergy. The crusading rector of Eastnor was allowed to farm the fruits and revenues of his church provided that in his absence he appointed a suitable vicar. Furthermore the rector was to give half a mark of silver each year to the poor of his parish while he was away. The licence for non-residence granted to the rector of Montgomery in 1278 was dependent upon his spending two marks a year on the repair of the books and vestments of the church and an additional two marks a year in alms to poor parishioners.[47] By a different kind of arrangement master John de Scheldesleye was given custody of the church of Burford for three years and he was to allow six marks a year to the non-resident incumbent, Geoffrey of Burford, while he was at his studies.[48] In all these instances and many others recorded in the register, Cantilupe's chief concern seems to have been that suitable provision for serving the benefices should be made out of their revenues.

In his initial efforts to control pluralism and absenteeism Cantilupe had for the most part been dealing with clergy appointed to benefices by his immediate episcopal predecessors, Peter of Aquablanca and John le Breton. By virtue of his office he was of course personally responsible for the ordination of the clergy of the diocese and for the institution of new

42 *Reg. Cantilupe,* 41-2.
43 *ibid.,* 45.
44 *ibid.*
45 *ibid.,* 6-7.
46 *ibid.,* 290.
47 *ibid.,* 168-9.
48 *ibid.,* 101-2.

presentees to livings, and it is in the performance of these functions, once he had been consecrated, that we should expect to see clear evidence of Cantilupe's desire to ensure the well-being of the religious life of the diocese. As far as they go, the records of his ordinations (though incomplete) and the appointment of new incumbents, confirm what contemporary witnesses tell us of his anxiety to maintain adequate standards and discipline among the diocesan clergy, and to provide pastoral care in the parishes.

Before ordaining clergy to minor or major orders it was necessary to ensure that the candidates had attained the canonical requirements of age, birth (proof that they were not illegitimate or of servile status), good character, education, and title (or means of support). While the times of the ordination ceremonies were fixed to the four Ember seasons, they were conducted wherever the bishop happened to be on his travels—in Cantilupe's case, Ledbury, Leominster, Ludlow, Newent, Whitbourne, and once outside the diocese at Tottenham.[49] The normal procedure seems to have been to give advance notice of the time and venue of an ordination ceremony and summon likely candidates to appear for examination beforehand. It is worth noting that Cantilupe's official was ordered to pay no regard to rank when he cited candidates to appear.[50] Although there is no evidence in the bishop's register of the examination of would-be ordinands, I think it can be safely assumed that, like contemporary bishops, Cantilupe would have employed commissaries, for example, learned members of his household, to conduct examinations into the qualifications of the candidates. What we cannot know is the thoroughness of the examination or the educational standards required.

In addition to candidates voluntarily presenting themselves for orders, there would of course be others, already beneficed but with inadequate orders, who had been commanded by the bishop to attend. From a long list of nearly one hundred beneficed clergy who did not attend the Leominster ordinations in 1277 (appended to the names of those who were actually ordained), it would seem probable that Cantilupe had conducted an inquiry into the orders held by incumbents in his diocese.[51] Certainly, the rectors of Thornbury, Blaisdon, Stanford, and Brampton Bryan suffered sequestration of their benefices for failing to appear at ordination ceremonies to which they had been summoned.[52]

Dispensations for illegitimacy enabling the recipients to proceed to orders could be obtained on papal authority and here again the evidence suggests that the bishop was careful to inquire into the character and attainments of petitioners. In 1277 Peter of Llanrothal presented a letter

49 For Cantilupe's ordinations see *ibid.*, 299-312.
50 *ibid.*, 25. 51 *ibid.*, 302-3. 52 *ibid.*, 30-1, 177, 194, 235-6, 240.

from Pope John XXI directing Cantilupe to grant him a dispensation for holy orders, if found suitable, notwithstanding he was illegitimate. Upon examination Cantilupe ordered him to study singing for a year, and some eighteen months later the dispensation was issued, Peter presumably having satisfied the bishop in the meantime.[53]

Whereas it was the rule that clergy should be ordained by the bishop of their native diocese, this arrangement would obviously not always be convenient or practical, and the issue of letter dimissory by their diocesan made it possible for the candidates to be ordained by another bishop. Occasionally ordinands omitted to obtain letters dimissory and once detected they required a dispensation to absolve them from this irregularity.[54]

The ordination lists in the register record the major orders of subdeacon, deacon, and priest, and generally also acolytes. The numbers ordained vary—in September 1277 the figures were 35 subdeacons, and 27 priests; in March 1279 the totals were 23 acolytes, 20 subdeacons, 21 deacons, and 8 priests. Care is taken to record the titles of the ordinands—the means of support until they found preferment. (If a bishop ordained anyone without sufficient title he was in theory obliged to maintain him at his own expense until he should be provided for). Unlike the practice which virtually became the norm from the fourteenth century, there is little evidence in Cantilupe's lists of religious houses providing titles (in fact only ten instances have been found). A few men in religious orders were ordained and in a couple of cases ordinands swore that they would enter religion within two years—one to become a monk at Monmouth priory, the other to be a knight hospitaller.[55] While a few candidates received titles from parochial incumbents, chantries, or the cathedral chapter, the vast majority were ordained to the title of patrimony, in other words, sufficient means of their own in money or land, the validity and amount of which they confirmed by letter or sworn testimony. The values are given in a few cases and they vary—forty, fifty, or sixty shillings; thirty acres of land and half a mill. One or two candidates were absolved the production of a title, and occasionally no titles are recorded at all. Cantilupe was understandably very careful to protect himself against any future liability for maintenance in such circumstances; in 1278 one Simon Franc of the Lincoln diocese, whom he had ordained deacon, swore an oath that he would not claim support from the bishop by reason of his ordination.[56]

With the institution of clergy to parochial benefices, Cantilupe seems to have taken as much care as with ordinations. The formal procedure has changed very little to this day. The patron of the living—be it layman,

53 *ibid.*, 124, 191, 308. 54 *ibid.*, 161-2, 231. 55 *ibid.*, 305-6.
56 *ibid.*, 303.

cathedral chapter, monastic corporation etc.—would present a clerk to the bishop for institution and if, after due inquiry into the cause of vacancy, the rights of patronage, and the credentials of the presentee, the bishop was satisfied, he would institute him and order his induction into corporal possession of the benefice. Any divisions of responsibilities or revenues, or liability for pensions or other payments, or the obligation of personal residence for vicars and so on would be specified at the time of institution. On several occasions it is noted that the institution was in accordance with the Council of Lyons, that is to say, with the decree of the 1274 Council obliging clergy to take priest's orders within a year of their institution or suffer deprivation.[57] Naturally enough the majority of institutions followed the routine course without problems, but from time to time doubts arose as to the exercise of patronage or the suitability of the presentee and further action was necessary. With clergy the chief causes of episcopal concern seem to have been their youth, inadequate orders, or lack of educational attainments. Henry de Upavene, instituted to Hopesay in 1280, was instructed to learn plain-song, and the bishop deferred a decision about the admission of Hugh Burnell to the church of Chetton because he was under age and absent.[58] In the same year, 1278, Roger de Hengham was given custody of the church of Hope Bowdler on condition that he was ordained at the next ordination ceremony.[59] Custody, or commendation, for a limited period was one way of dealing with presentees who did not come up to required standards. At the end of the allotted period they could be examined again pending formal institution. In patronage disputes the diocesan bishop was usually called by the king's justices to provide evidence, and not infrequently he could be directly involved in such a conflict. In 1278 the advowson of Much Marcle was disputed in the king's court between Walter de Balon and the abbot of Lyre, and Cantilupe appointed commissaries to make local enquiry about the right of presentation;[60] in an earlier dispute over the church of Ludlow the bishop was summoned to appear before the royal justices at Shrewsbury to answer a charge of impeding the rights of Theobald de Verdun as patron, and Theobald appears to have won his case.[61] On another occasion Cantilupe is found acting as arbitrator in a benefice dispute, at the request of Godfrey Giffard, the bishop of Worcester. Institution to the church of Wichenford was contested by two claimants, and Cantilupe eventually decided in favour of the local candidate but specified that an annual pension should be paid to the unsuccessful rival, a papal chaplain.[62] As well as legal wrangles over patronage and disputed presentations, some patrons just neglected to exercise their rights within the specified six months and in such cases the appointment or collation of the benefice devolved upon the bishop.

57 *ibid.*, 36, 82, 124, 243, 254.
58 *ibid.*, 243; 164 respectively.
59 *ibid.*, 185.
60 *ibid.*, 143-4.
61 *ibid.*, 140-1, 158.
62 *ibid.*, 99-100.

In addition to these powers of collation by lapse through the negligence of patrons, the bishop acted as patron in his own right of several parochial benefices, but certainly of much more significance were his powers of collation in respect of the prebends and dignities (saving the deanery) of his cathedral church. We have already seen how Thomas, as to be expected, gave some of these offices and canonries to the chief members of his household, but on the whole what little evidence survives in the register about his dealings with his chapter emphasizes the judicial and disciplinary aspects of their relationship—at one moment harassing members of the chapter for pluralism, at the next defending the rights and privileges of the cathedral against the violations of the citizens of Hereford, at another arbitrating between the chapter and the Dominican priory in the city.[63] Not that the bishop can be held solely responsible for this state of affairs seemingly dominated by litigation. It is true that he had his own differences over the prebend of Preston with Peter de Langon, to which I have made allusion earlier, but apart from this, the deanery itself, the treasurership, and the prebend of Inkberrow were all the subject of disputes during his relatively brief episcopate.[64] Long before he became bishop the deanery was being hotly contested at the Roman curia between Giles of Avenbury and John of Aquablanca, yet another member of Bishop Peter's influential family. By 1275 both candidates had appointed rival subdeans to administer the decanal jurisdiction and Cantilupe was soon involved in attempts to make temporary but more suitable arrangements for the exercise of the dean's authority pending a judicial decision. In fact, it was not until the year of the bishop's death that the deanery was finally adjudged to Aquablanca, who held it undisturbed for another thirty-eight years.

The diocese of Hereford was not particularly well supplied with religious houses (in comparison with other parts of the country) and of those that existed several had relatively meagre endowments and understandably were beset with financial difficulties as a result of this. Leominster priory was so deeply in debt in 1275 that Edward I took it under his protection and entrusted the administration of its estates to a knight, Roland de Harley, instructing him to provide from the revenues for the needs of the priory in food and clothing and for the poor.[65] Monmouth priory was evidently in similar straits some four years later when Cantilupe

63 *ibid.*, 5-6, 141, 186, 197-8, 232 (further proceedings against non-residence and pluralism are cited above).

64 *ibid.*, 2-4, 112-16, 118, 234-5; *Reg. Swinfield*, 321-6; John Le Neve: *Fasti Ecclesiae Anglicanae 1300-1541*, (London, 1962), II, 3-4 (deanery); *Reg. Cantilupe*, 32-3 (treasurer); *ibid.*, 84-7 (Inkberrow).

65 *Reg. Cantilupe*, 37-8.

issued an indulgence in its favour,[66] and the finances of the Augustinian priories of Wormsley and Chirbury were such that the bishop forbade them to admit any more canons without his express consent.[67]

The three main areas of contact between a bishop and the regular clergy of his diocese arose out of the institution and resignation of heads of non-exempt houses, the episcopal visitation of such communities, and the parochial responsibilities of these monastic corporations. Isolated entries in the register deal with the bishop receiving the profession of obedience from a newly-elected abbot,[68] appointing a coadjutor for a prior of Chirbury who had become infirm,[69] and nominating and confirming a prioress of Aconbury, whose previous election had been quashed on account of canonical irregularities.[70] Errors in the form of elections were a common occurrence and unless the candidate was manifestly unsuitable, the diocesan bishop usually provided him or her to the rule of the house by his own authority.

The appropriation of parish churches to monasteries and other ecclesiastical corporations obliged the diocesan bishop to ensure that the church would be adequately served in the future. Although by Cantilupe's time a large number of churches had already been appropriated, the practice continued during his episcopate. By such a grant of appropriation, the monastery or other body became rector of the church and received all or most of the benefice income subject to the reservation of a part of these endowments for the episcopal ordination of a vicarage, that is, revenues sufficient to maintain a priest who would exercise the cure of souls. Early in his episcopate Cantilupe ordained a vicarage in the church of Aymestrey, appropriated to Wigmore abbey, going into considerable detail about the land, tithes, and offerings reserved to the vicar, and the latter's obligations and duties.[71] He also gave permission for the prior and canons of Wormsley to appropriate Lyonshall church and the dean of Hereford cathedral to appropriate the church of Kingstone.[72] He personally received papal authorisation from Innocent V to appropriate the churches of Ledbury and Bosbury at the next vacancy to the charges of the episcopal *mensa* (that is, the revenues to go towards the bishop's expenses).[73]

66 F. G. Cowley, *The Monastic order in South Wales 1066-1349,* (Cardiff, 1977), 229, citing PRO E210/D4610 (not recorded in Cantilupe's register). For mention of two visitations of Monmouth priory by Cantilupe see *Registrum Johannis de Trillek, episcopi Herefordensis,* Canterbury and York Society, 222.

67 *Reg. Cantilupe,* 144-5, 147-8.

68 *ibid.,* 157. 69 *ibid.,* 228. 70 *ibid.,* 292. 71 *ibid.,* 44-5.

72 *ibid.,* 212-13; Hereford cathedral archive (hereafter HCA) 2160, printed by W. W. Capes in *Charters and records of Hereford cathedral,* (1908), 144-5.

73 *Reg. Cantilupe,* 126-7.

Inquiry seems also to have been made at times of visitation about appropriated churches. Leominster priory, on such an occasion, was asked to produce documentary evidence for the appropriation to them of Eye church, and at Churcham, which was appropriated to Gloucester abbey, the bishop enjoined that a site should be provided for a vicarage, or else the vicar should be entertained in the abbey's manor-house, since at the time he was living some distance away.[74]

Some evidence survives for the visitation of religious houses—in fact much more than for parochial visitations. Leominster is particularly well documented if only because of the apparent reluctance of the community to obey Cantilupe's instructions. On 11 January 1277 the bishop, with an impressive entourage, came to Leominster and after a sermon preached in the chapter-house, the visitation proper began.[75] Cantilupe personally examined the prior and subprior but delegated the examination of other monks to the official and certain household clerks. What was of particular importance at the visitation was the difficulties over the rights of parishioners having access to the church, since the monks had reserved a door leading to the church for their own use, and the monks' failure to ring the bells (provided by the parishioners) at times of service. The bishop ordered that these and other irregularities should be corrected and that the offending door be removed (an injunction the monks were slow to heed and which was eventually reversed by Cantilupe's old adversary, Archbishop Pecham, when he visited the Hereford diocese after the bishop's death).[76] Towards the close of Thomas's episcopate, the absent bishop and his official, Robert of Gloucester, were once again involved in difficulties with Leominster and its mother-house, Reading abbey, which led to the sequestration of the priory's property and the deposition of the prior.[77]

The bishop's injunctions to the nuns of Limebrook, the canons of Wormsley and those of Chirbury mostly deal with problems of general discipline, and the faults in these cases are not usually of a very serious nature.[78]. The rule of silence must be better observed; access of lay persons to the house must be strictly controlled, and at Chirbury any necessary business with laymen was to be conducted in the parish church

74 *ibid.*, 229, 237-9.

75 *ibid.*, 46-9, 79-80, 87-9, 95, 116-17; PRO, *Ancient correspondence*, 15/152; *AA.SS*, 562a, 606a; C. R. Cheney, *Episcopal visitation of monasteries in the thirteenth century* (Manchester, 1931), 69, 96.

76 *Registrum epistolarum Fratris Johannis Peckham, archiepiscopi Cantuariensis*, ed. C. T. Martin, Rolls Series, 3 vols., (1882-5), II, 505-7.

77 *Reg. Cantilupe*, 269-72, 289, 296; PRO, *Ancient correspondence*, 10/8; Douie, 198. For the case of the subprior of Leominster and his alleged immorality with a nun of Limebrook and other women see *Reg. Cantilupe*, 265-7; *AA.SS*, 562a; Douie, 199.

78 *Reg. Cantilupe*, 144-5, 147-8, 200-2. For Cantilupe's visitations of Bromfield priory and some comments on its condition see *Reg. Trillek*, 237.

or the cemetery. The canons of Chirbury were also ordered to enclose their conventual buildings since grave scandals had arisen from the frequenting of lay men and women. Those canons who had been defamed in this regard were to be punished by the prior. The prior himself was enjoined not to absent himself from the cloister, refectory, and dormitory, as he wont to do. No women were to stay within the walls of Wormsley priory, and at Limebrook the nuns were advised to choose their servants with care, so that their conduct and behaviour would not be a corrupting influence.

It has already been remarked that the bishop's visitation rolls have disappeared, and if it is dangerous to make any generalisations about the state of the regular clergy in the diocese based on the few surviving records, it is quite pointless to comment on the bishop's visitations of the clergy and laity in the parishes. As it is, a few references exist in the register which show that the bishop was conducting visitations in person or else deputing the official in his absences.[79] Several incumbents are cited for non-appearnce, others are prosecuted for immorality and for not paying procurations; a lord of the manor removing church goods is excommunicated, as is an adulterous burgess of Hereford who eventually suffers imprisonment by the royal authorities at the bishop's behest.[80] In sum total, the evidence—while a useful indicator of the bishop's activity—is too scanty for any judgements to be made. Similarly, because of other archival losses virtually nothing survives about the daily workings of the bishop's consistory court, or the exercise of testamentary jurisdiction over the clergy and laity, ironically both causes of famous disputes with his metropolitan, Archbishop John Pecham, as will be related elsewhere in this volume.

This paper has naturally enough concentrated so far on the spiritual administration of the diocese, but it must not be forgotten that the bishop of Hereford was also an important temporal lord. Bishop Richard Swinfield once described his see as 'one of the least valuable bishoprics in England'. If the circumstances in which this statement was made (refusing a request for preferment) caution us not to immediately accept it at face value, other evidence certainly confirms that Hereford was not a wealthy bishopric by English standards.[81] Cantilupe's register is remarkably full of business relating to the temporalities, much of it of course of a routine or expected nature—the appointment of stewards, bailiffs, and other officers, the confirmation of grants and rights, financial and auditing memoranda, instructions about game, stock and crops, proceedings against poachers and so forth. But here again emphasis is often laid solely on Cantilupe's

79 *Reg. Cantilupe,* 219 (for official).
80 *AA.SS,* 561b; *Reg. Cantilupe,* 145-6.
81 *Reg. Swinfield,* 2, *cf. Taxatio,* 168.

quarrels and legal wrangles over the episcopal possessions—his claims to certain Montgomeryshire estates occupied by Prince Llewelyn,[82] his successful dispute with Gilbert de Clare, earl of Gloucester, over the episcopal chase in the Malvern Hills,[83] and the fixing of the boundaries, long contested, between the bishopric lands and those of the powerful border family, the Corbets.[84] Indicative though these examples are of Cantilupe's prevailing concern to reclaim lost or disputed property and rights of the see, another important aspect of the bishop's activity is to be seen in the anxiety shown for the efficient administration of the temporalities. In instructions to his steward about the appointment of bailiffs at Whitbourne and Ross and the defence of the Marches in 1276, he appends detailed rules for the management of the estates and the financial accounting, so that the mismanagement and arrears of previous years might be prevented in the future.[85]

This study of Thomas Cantilupe as bishop of Hereford, of necessity brief and selective, will have undoubtedly indicated that the bishop took his diocesan responsibilities very seriously indeed, and his efforts in all aspects of his pastoral work, though not always successful, reveal something of the vigour and energy that he put into the administration of his diocese. The accusations of litigiousness often levelled against him must, I think, be viewed in the light of the bishop as a temporary custodian and guardian of the rights and possessions of his spiritual spouse, the church of Hereford. To modern eyes, Cantilupe, and indeed many fellow-bishops of the time, seem over-anxious to resort to legal action at the slightest provocation. Yet, the bishops no doubt felt that it was the prime responsibility of the episcopal incumbent *pro tempore* to safeguard and defend the rights of the see, and to pass them on to a successor without diminution. No doubt such a sentiment governed Cantilupe's actions as a bishop; it was a characteristic that brought forth nothing but admiration from his former household clerks when they gave evidence, years later, to the papal commissioners enquiring into their late master's life and acts.

82 *Reg. Cantilupe,* 9-11, 29-32, 42, 103-4.

83 *ibid.,* 23, 34, 36, 52-6, 59-62, 84, 104-5, 227-8; Vat. Cod. Lat. 4015, witnesses nos. 1, 5, 47, etc.

84 *Reg. Cantilupe,* 67-73; Vat. Cod. Lat. 4015, fo. 94v.

85 *Reg. Cantilupe,* 108-11; for an account of feudal service rendered by Cantilupe in the Welsh wars see *Reg. Swinfield,* 76-7.

THE CANTILUPE-PECHAM CONTROVERSY

by R. C. Finucane

The conflict between the Bishop of Hereford and Archbishop John Pecham is of interest since it illustrates some of the tensions that complicated thirteenth-century church governance and reveals something of the underlying clash of personalities. Though the issues were not new, the uncompromising attitudes of both men threw them into high relief. As Irene Churchill wrote, the story is fairly well known.[1] To state the case in briefest terms, the quarrel concerned jurisdiction: could a bishop's subjects appeal directly to the provincial Court of Arches without the bishop's cognizance; secondly, could the archbishop as of right adjudicate in testamentary matters where the deceased left goods in more than one diocese? Pecham would have said yes to both points.

The root of the problem was the Franciscan archbishop's enhanced vision of his own powers both as metropolitan and as apostolic legate, which he exercised by extending Canterbury jurisdiction (including tuitorial appeals) at the expense of his suffragans, and through his enthusiastic approach to diocesan visitations. This, and his sometimes overbearing manner, eventually provoked many of his bishops, especially the aristocratic and equally stubborn Cantilupe. The present essay draws upon printed materials and an unpublished Vatican manuscript, the 1307 inquiry into Thomas' 'excommunication', which fills in some of the gaps and illuminates unnoticed aspects of this sometimes unedifying confronta-

1 Irene Churchill, *Canterbury administration,* 2 vols., (1933), esp. 1, 472-5, and *c.f.* I, 153-7, 380-4, 462-9; Decima L. Douie, *Archbishop Pecham,* (1952), (hereafter Douie), 192-234, on the archbishop's conflicts with suffragans; see also *Registrum Johannis Pecham,* ed. D. L. Douie, N. L. Davis and others, (Canterbury and York Society, LXIV, LXV, (1969, 1968), (herefater *Reg. Pecham,* C&Y.), LXV, 51-4 for the archbishop's point of view; introduction by W. W. Capes in *Registrum Thome de Cantilupo,* Canterbury and York Society, II, (1907), (hereafter Reg. Cantilupe), esp. xlvi-lv; for an earlier thirteenth-century example of suffragans uniting, *cf.* M. M. Morgan, 'The Excommunication of Grosseteste in 1243', *English Historical Review,* LVII, (1942), 244-50; F. M. Powicke, *The Thirteenth century,* (second ed., 1962), 445-509, esp. 488-90: the two prelates 'were like oil and water'.

tion.[2] Evidence from sources not particularly favourable to Thomas suggests that his avowed partisans did not seriously compromise themselves in presenting their versions of the conflict in 1307, though some elaboration is to be expected.

While Thomas was in Normandy in 1280-81, his Official, Robert of Gloucester, received various prejudicial mandates against which he appealed to the Apostolic See. After Thomas came back and was subjected to similar orders, he too decided to turn to the papacy. On 12 October, 1281 Cantilupe formulated an appeal at Bermonsey[3] and, following receipt of another of Pecham's mandates, appealed again on 27 December at Ledbury. This was notified to Pecham in South Malling on 15 January, 1282 by Thomas' cleric Robert Wych, accompanied by the notary Hildebrand, and Robert of Gloucester's appeal was further announced by Wych in the Court of Arches two days later.[4] As a result, Pecham warned his curial proctors in Italy to watch Cantilupe's people and he also requested assistance from various cardinals;[5] on 26 January he issued a blanket excommunication of any disturbers of the rights and privileges of his church of Canterbury.[6]

After further attacks and rebuttals the two prelates collided head-on in London. Pecham had called his bishops together on 5 February, 1282 to discuss the problem of freeing Amaury de Montfort. Thomas was there and seems to have participated in the general discussion. But, as

2 Vat. Cod. Lat. 4016, of 147 folios, contains descriptions or copies of about sixty documents relating to the dispute, only about half of which are found in published registers. In addition, there is sworn testimony from more than three dozen men who lived through the debate of the 1280s. The manuscript also contains information on records and record-keeping in 1307, about which the writer plans to publish further articles. The advantage of this source over printed materials are evident in the following comparisons. *Registrum Ricardi de Swinfield,* Canterbury and York Society, VI, (1909), (hereafter *Reg. Swinfield*), 42, lines 2 and 3, *ut metropolitanus seu primas, nec ut legatus* is *ut metropolitanus scribitis non ut legatus,* (fo. 27v); 41, line 4, *dominum papam et me* is *dominum meum et me* (fo. 27v); 42, line 4 from bottom *transmittentes eciam pape* is *timentes eciam propter,* (fo. 28r). Though Vat. Cod. Lat. 4015, the canonization inquiry excerpted in *Acta Sanctorum* is also used in this article, all folio references are to Vat. Cod. Lat. 4016 unless otherwise indicated. The edition of the *Acta Sanctorum* used is chiefly that of 1643 sqq. The entry for Cantilupe under his feast of 2 October was published in 1765. The revised edition (1866) has also been used. The editions are distinguished by the date after the abbreviation *AA.SS.*

3 fos. 48v-49r.

4 fos. 23v-24r, 38rv, 6v, 28r (margin), 42v-43r. *cf.* fo. 19r. *Registrum epistolarum Fratris Johannis Peckham,* Rolls Series, (hereafter *Reg. Peckham* RS.), I, 278-9; for Hildebrand, see C. R. Cheney, *Notaries public in England in the thirteenth and fourteenth centuries,* (Oxford, 1972), 24-5, and fo. 51r. Robert Wych is not to be confused with Robert 'le Wyse' (of Gloucester).

5 *Reg. Peckham,* RS., I, 278-9, 282-3, (19 Jan.), 276, n. 1.

6 fo. 52v.

the archbishop later reported to his curial proctors, in the course of the conference he learned that some letters had been brought from the curia for Cantilupe though the bishop of Hereford, being present, denied any knowledge of such letters.[7] This would undoubtedly have raised the archbishop's suspicions. On the 7th the simmering hostility at last erupted. Though that winter Saturday was some twenty-five years in the past, the commissioners of 1307 obtained testimony from half-a-dozen people who had been present. Of course memories fade and are distorted by prejudice, and in addition it seems that the occasion in 1282 was itself tumultuous and confused. The following reconstruction is based upon a comparison of the written and oral evidence collected in 1307, as well as Pecham's printed register.

The archbishop and bishop, each with his group of advisers, met on 7 February in the great hall at Lambeth Palace. The parties were seated at a bench beneath the south-facing window of the hall, opposite the fireplace.[8] Many statements passed between the two sides, with authorities quoted back and forth.[9] It may have been during these preliminary stages that Pecham again presented Thomas with a written order to excommunicate Robert of Gloucester.[10] In any case, eventually the arguments must have risen to boiling point since all at once (*statim*) Pecham left the room and went into a little chamber adjoining the hall to confer with his counsellors.[11] These advisers, according to Richard de Lacy who testified in 1307, had much to do with the excommunication of Thomas. Surrounded by his *familia* in the little room the archbishop dictated the sentence there and then, the notary Beccles writing it on a small piece of parchment.[12] One eyewitness (John de Lewes) testified that Pecham wept as he ordered this to be read to Cantilupe.[13]

The next step is confused. Robert de Lacy read the excommunication, assisted by John de Lewes. In 1307 these two claimed that Lacy came from the small room into the hall, sat at a bench with his back to the fireplace as he faced Cantilupe and his people seated under the window, then read the sentence to them. After this he and Lewes left their desk or bench and rejoined Pecham in the small room, closing the door behind them. Cantilupe then came to the door and read an appeal against the archbishop.[14]

In 1307 these events were described in very different terms by the people who had been with Cantilupe on that February day. According to

7 *Reg. Peckham*, RS., I, 306-10; *cf.* Douie, 200.
8 fos. 45r, 70v.
9 fo. 6v.
10 *Reg. Peckham*, RS., I, 290.
11 fos. 6v, 37r-v, 49v; for their names *cf.*
12 fo. 44v.
13 fo. 71v, fos. 44v, 70v, and *Reg. Peckham*, RS., I, 300.
14 fos. 44r-45v, 70v.

them, after Pecham had retired into the small room Robert de Lacy opened the door and, still standing on the threshold, read something from a small piece of parchment (*cedulam parvam*) in a low voice that could not be heard above the noise of the people milling about the hall. One of Thomas' clerks, Robert de Radeswell, who moved very near so that he could hear him, discovered Lacy announcing some sort of excommunication of the bishop of Hereford. Lacy gave no indication of his authority for this, or even whose words he was reading, nor did he exhibit any copies. Having finished his reading he immediately re-entered the small room.[15] Confusion at once: out in the great hall some said that the document was an excommunication of Thomas, others that it was not a direct excommunication but an inhibition under penalty of excommunication.[16] According to one of Cantilupe's people the statement ran 'Lord Bishop, *moneo vos ne vos infringatis libertates ecclesie Xri cantuariens adhuc scdo ego moneo et adhuc tertio ego moneo qd si monitionibus meis non parueritis, in vos excois sentenciam profero'*.[17] The 1307 commission asked Lacy if the sentence could be found in Pecham's register. He answered that it could, though 'he did not know where the registers were' but probably at Canterbury.[18] In fact Pecham's printed register does supply the archbishop's version of the excommunication: *Quod si monitis nostris non parueritis, exnunc vos in hiis scriptis excommunicamus.*[19] In either case Pecham seems to be warning as well as bringing the sentence into effect; the archbishop always appears to have believed that this combination of condition and disposition was a valid sentence. The objections raised by Cantilupe's people, however, about how it was delivered, exactly where Lacy stood—he himself on cross-examination could not remember the details elicited in 1307,[20]—how loudly he spoke, the authority behind its public promulgation: all suggest that the papal commissioners were probing for reasons to explain why Cantilupe and his advisers subsequently ignored this 'excommunication'.[21]

After the document was read, one of Thomas' men or possibly the bishop himself went to the door and loudly demanded a copy of anything that may have been read which was prejudicial to the bishop and the see of Hereford, 'frequently repeating loudly, we request a copy, a copy, a

15 fos. 6v-7r.

16 fo. 37r.

17 fo. 7r: 'Lord bishop, I warn you not to infringe the privileges of Christ Church, Canterbury, and a second and a third time I warn you, that if you do not obey my warnings I am bringing sentence of excommunication against you.'

18 fo. 45v.

19 *Reg. Peckham*, RS., I, 300, 'That if you do not obey our warnings, henceforth we excommunicate you in these writings'.

20 fo. 73v.

21 For the 1307 summary of these points, *cf.* fo. 140r. I am grateful here, as on other points, for suggestions made by Dr. Patrick Daly.

copy'.[22] Whoever it was that demanded a copy of this mysterious document—and in 1307 Robert de Lacy again conveniently forgot whether a copy had been requested[23]—no copy, not even a verbal reply, issued from the small chamber. After Cantilupe and his counsellors had waited some three hours,[24] Thomas approached the door 'and striking it said these words in a loud, angry voice easily heard by those in the large and the small rooms,

> Lord Archbishop, I wish to appeal from you to the Apostolic See, and out of reverence for that See, you should listen to me'.[25]

Thomas' notary Hildebrand recorded that the bishop went to the door saying that he proposed to submit (*interponere intendebat*) an appeal to the Pope, which Pecham should hear. The door, which had meanwhile been partly re-opened, was then slammed in Thomas' face, which he asked everyone present to note.[26] Robert Wych, probably embroidering the episode, says Thomas' foot was caught in the door when it slammed, causing him to limp back to his advisers in the great hall.[27] The upshot of this undignified rebuff was the formal recitation, at the closed door, of Cantilupe's appeal to the Pope and the handing over of a copy to the archbishop's clerics, who eventually came out. When this appeal (which does not appear to have been registered) is compared with the earlier appeal of 12 October, 1281 (also unregistered), it is clear that Thomas no longer accused the archbishop's Official but the archbishop himself, as is evident from the very first words of the statement, *Cum vos pater*. The appeal may be summarized as follows:

> Since you, reverend father, and your officials have ordered our subjects [named] to appear before you without our consent, ignoring our jurisdiction, in cases over which you have no jurisdiction, and since you have been asked to repeal these unjust burdens and to desist totally from this usurpation of our jurisdiction and to order your ministers to desist in future from these usurpations (*ab huius gravaminibus et usurpacionibus desisterent*), but this, against justice, you have not done, therefore, fearing further injustice we appeal to the Apostolic See in these writings; we appeal lest you attempt any harm to us or our goods or people through suspension, excommunication, interdict or any other way, and we ask the Apostolic See for protection and tuition (*proteccioni et tuitioni*). We intend to seek justice at a superior tribunal; we do not intend to shrink from our appeal or earlier appeals.[28]

22 *'iterando frequenter et clamando, copiam, copiam, copiam petimus'*, fo. 7v, where Robert Wych is said to demand a copy. But he himself admits that he was absent when the 'excommunication' was read (fo. 50r), so he would probably not have demanded a copy. Robert of Gloucester says (fo. 24r) that Thomas went to the door, saying 'Lord archbishop, have a copy made for me.' When Pecham issued a similar conditional excommunication of his suffragans in 1288, he again refused to provide them with a copy, (see Douie, 224-25).

23 fo. 45v. 24 fos. 11v, 24r. 25 fo. 37r.

26 fo. 50r. Hildebrand's son, also present, testified that the door was shut *ante oculos* of Thomas (fo. 36r).

27 fo. 50v. 28 fos. 41v-42r, 50r, 37v, 70v.

His appeal having been read and delivered, Cantilupe and his counsellors decamped, left Lambeth, crossed the Thames and entered the bishop's London house. Many learned men gathered there that afternoon and evening.[29] Thomas asked them to give him good advice: should he proceed in this matter or not? If it were not a good cause he wished to desist—presumably fully aware that Pecham now meant business—but if it were a just action he would manfully (*viriliter*) follow up his appeals unto death (*usque ad mortem*). His advisers told him that he should go ahead, to which Cantilupe agreed. Robert de Ros, who reported this scene, heard Thomas say 'to the death', a prophetic statement that would eventually be widely talked about in England (*notorium in Anglia*).[30]

After committing himself to battle Thomas began his campaign at once. It is probable that on that very evening of 7 February he and his advisers decided that he himself should go to the Roman curia, for within the week King Edward I had been approached and on the 15th of February he sent a letter from Sherborne on Thomas' behalf to Matthew Rosso Orsini, Cardinal Deacon of St Mary in Porticu: Thomas, *de consilio nostro,* noble and learned bishop of Hereford whose church is threatened (as it is said), has appealed to the Apostolic See *ab audencia venerabilis patris Joannis Cant Arepi* and has proposed to follow up that appeal *personaliter* in the Roman Curia; Edward asks for special attention to be paid on Thomas' behalf.[31] Two days later the king granted Thomas letters of protection and safe-conduct to the court of Rome.[32] Before leaving England, however, Thomas realized that he must do as much as possible to fortify his position: he must make certain that Pecham was indisputably notified that he took exception to the events of 7 February, he must prepare his case to be presented to the curia, and he must try to gain as much support as he could from his fellow-suffragans.

To carry out his first objective he quickly dispatched Robert Wych to read an appeal, this time—if possible—before the archbishop himself. After the unpleasant scenes of 7 February, Pecham had withdrawn from Lambeth and set out for Mortlake. On the 9th he left Mortlake for Guildford, but broke his journey at the priory of Newark. As the archbishop's party were leaving the priory after their rest, Robert Wych caught up with them on the road. The description of what happened comes from the testimony of a 'Pecham man', William Russell (in 1307 *custos* of the registers, books and cartularies of the archiepiscopal Court of Arches).[33] Wych announced himself as Cantilupe's proctor, then began to read an appeal on Thomas' behalf. 'But the said archbishop, unwilling

29 fo. 42r. 30 fo. 37v, 42r. 31 fo. 19v.

32 PRO., *Calendar of Patent Rolls,* Edw. I, Vol. II, 12, entry for 17 Feb., 1282. On 20 Feb. the king confirmed two attorneys for the bishop.

33 fo. 74v. *Cf.* Churchill, *op. cit.,* I, 454 and II, 195; Winchelsey appointed him in Sept. 1306

to listen, rode on and, exasperated (*turbatus*), he ordered his *familia* in attendance on him to get rid of this rascal (*quod repellerent illum Ribaldum*) because he was excommunicated.' The archbishop's retainers violently seized Robert 'and threw him into a pit or ditch that was at the side of the road'. The witness believed that the ditch was to the left and that there was water in it.[34] Nevertheless Robert followed the archbishop's party to Guildford (probably at a safe distance) and next day, 10 February, 1282, he had better luck. He was still not allowed into Pecham's presence but the archbishop relented enough to allow him to meet with some of his *familia* in Guildford parish church. There an appeal in public form in Hildebrand's hand was notified to the archbishop through his representatives and a copy presented.[35] In it Robert set out the events of 7 February, beginning by stating that Thomas, along with his adviser Ardicio of Milan (see below) and Thomas (Ingelthorp), Dean of St Pauls, who wished to help conciliate the two prelates, met peacefully with the archbishop at Lambeth. Robert then described the subsequent violent scenes, ending with the bishop's appeal being read and handed over to Master Peter, Pecham's official. After that the archbishop had savagely excluded Thomas from further communication at Lambeth, against all of which Robert Wych now appeals on Thomas' behalf.[36] Whatever Pecham himself had in mind on 7 February, he would no doubt have construed this appeal by Thomas at Guildford as continued refusal to acknowledge Canterbury's superiority. Henceforth the archbishop behaved as if Thomas' excommunication were not conditional but a matter of fact.

As for Thomas' other immediate objectives, the preparation of his curial brief and the securing of co-operation from other English bishops, he relied heavily upon one of his Hereford canons, Master Ardicio de Comite,[37] papal collector and chaplain, *nuncius in Anglia,* whose knowledge of the curia and of canon law was now put at the bishop's service. Ardicio had witnessed the Lambeth conflict of 7 February and within a week he was writing to Thomas about the Roman appeal. On 13 February he assured Cantilupe that he would advise the bishop's agent en route to the curia of the best policies to follow there. He also asked Thomas that a copy of Pecham's document read at Lambeth (if and when the archbishop supplied one) be sent to him at once so that *appellatio legitima* could be formulated to Rome. Meanwhile Ardicio would discuss the situation with his advisers.[38] A week later (20 February) he wrote again to Thomas. He had seen the bishop's appeals in a document shown to

34 fo. 76r-v. In 1307 Robert Wych modestly said that the prelate's *familiares . . . impediebant eum ne legeret,* a milder version, (fo. 49v).

35 fos. 49v, 53v.

36 fos. 15f-16r; *cf.* fo. 24r.

37 Ardizzone Conti, *cf.* Cheney, *op. cit.,* 21.

38 fos. 18v-19r.

him by Thomas' clerk Robert. They should be sent to the curia, where Thomas' canon Philip[39] could discuss them with the Hereford proctors. Ardicio advised further that if Thomas received a copy of Pecham's Lambeth statement and it contained any sentence of excommunication, interdict or suspension, the bishop should make an appeal including statements to the following effect: the sentence was unjust since appeals had already been made; it was levied without proper warning; the archbishop should have been more temperate but was moved by rancour of spirit.[40]

Meanwhile Pecham was busy too, writing to the bishop of London and other suffragans on 17 February. Since Thomas, because of his behaviour towards Canterbury, deserved to be excommunicated (*suis demeritis exigentibus sententiam excommunicationis majoris meruit innodari*) and since a sentence is of no efficacy unless it is published, Pecham ordered the publication of the excommunication, and confirmation of publication, before 17 May.[41] This mandate was brought to Ardicio's attention by some of the bishop of London's men.[42] After conferring with them Ardicio wrote to the London bishop Richard Gravesend (d. 1303) explaining that the whole issue arose from Pecham's claim to be legate in England and the consequent extension of Canterbury jurisdiction to the subjects of all of his suffragans. Hence Thomas appealed. Ardicio, citing various canons, claimed that any sentence levied while Thomas' appeals were pending was unjust. London, therefore, should ignore Pecham's mandate, whose execution would in effect be an injury to the Apostolic See. In addition, not only did Thomas' appeals precede the 'excommunication', but no copy of any such sentence had been provided; furthermore canon law suggested that bishops should be barred from exercising their episcopal duties prior to any excommunication, which clearly was not the case with Cantilupe. Ardicio ended by remarking that much more could be written against this unjust process. On 28 February he wrote to Thomas, enclosing a copy of this letter to the bishop of London. He advised Cantilupe of Pecham's order to publish the excommunication, then told him that he should speedily (*velociter*) take a copy of his appeal first to the bishop of London and then to the other bishops, exhorting them to disregard the mandate from Pecham, 'from whose jurisdiction after legitimate appeals you are *de jure* exempt'. Ardicio closed by noting that Philip had crossed *mare Anglicanum* and was on his way to the papal curia.[43] At about the same time, no doubt, a courier was carrying Pecham's version of the events of 7 February and afterwards, to Canterbury's proctors in Italy.[44]

39 Presumably Philip de Comite, Hereford prebendary and nephew of Ardicio. See *Reg. Cantilupe,* 248-9.
40 fo. 18v.
41 *Reg. Peckham,* RS., I, 299-300.
42 fo. 17r.
43 fo. 17r-v.
44 *E.g.,* letter of 26 Feb. in *Reg. Peckham,* RS., I, 306-10.

Thomas next turned to the task of securing the co-operation or at least the neutrality of his fellow bishops. He had to convince them of the justice of his cause before leaving England, when he would be unable to counteract Pecham's influence. Although he already enjoyed the confidence of some of the suffragans as in a sense the representative of their common resistance to the archbishop, more positive steps were required. These steps were taken during the first week of March, 1282. After renewing his appeal at Gloucester on 3 March,[45] next day Thomas issued formal letters procuratorial for Robert Wych.[46] Apparently the bishop had decided to put Ardicio's advice into effect: Wych was to undertake the strenuous task of notifying Cantilupe's fellow-bishops of the dispute and the wrongfulness of Pecham's actions, then to ask for their co-operation. Between 6 March and 16 April, Robert Wych—with Hildebrand in tow—visited eleven bishops, starting with London, as Ardicio had advised.[47] Fortunately the text of Wych's statement as delivered before the bishop of Worcester on 27th March, 1282 was copied into the record of 1307; presumably the same format was followed for the other bishops.

Wych began by setting out Pecham's mid-February letter ordering the publication of Thomas' excommunication.[48] He then went on to note that this is amazing since the bishop had done nothing deserving of such treatment. Furthermore, Thomas had asked for a copy of any charges, but

> no copy has been seen or received; but 'now, as if settling into ambush preparing to slay the innocent, he [Pecham] does not fear to send you an injurious, defamatory and malicious letter'. This letter, requesting publication of excommunication, is null and void in the first place because legitimate appeals were already pending. Secondly it is against ecclesiastical law since proper warning of excommunication was not provided; 'but the archbishop, proceeding irregularly and with animosity wrongly observed the converse order' (*animose et prepostere procedens conversum ordinem perperam observavit*) and promulgated the said sentence, if such it was, injuriously to pontifical dignity, the archbishop seeking his own ends and seeking to tyrannize over his subjects rather than to consult their interests.

After reviewing the events of 7 February, Wych then claimed that Thomas was only protecting his church, as he was sworn to do. 'The archbishop, falsely trying shamefully to slander my lord's reputation, blows into the dust and raises dirt into his own eyes.' The defamation of a brother bishop injures the Church of Rome. Pecham, rather than scorning them, ought to protect those appealing to the Holy See. Wych advises the

45 Robert of Gloucester also renewed his appeal against Pecham's excommunication; nothing was said about such a sentence in Thomas' appeal. See *Register of Bishop Godfrey Giffard,* ed. J. W. Willis Bund, Worcester Historical Society, (1898-1902), (hereafter *Reg. Giffard*), II, 145.

46 fo. 43v.

47 fo. 41r-v. The others, in order, were Salisbury, Bath and Wells, Exeter, Worcester, Coventry and Lichfield, Lincoln, Ely, Norwich, Chichester, and Rochester.

48 *Reg. Peckham,* RS., I, 299-300

bishop to disregard Pecham's letter since the archbishop, being prejudiced, should not be believed. The bishop is also reminded that this quarrel over jurisdiction applies to him as well; if he allows Pecham's claims he is prejudicing his own situation. The statement ends with a warning that an appeal to the pope would be lodged against anyone complying with Pecham's letter.[49]

Probably something similar to the above had first been read before the bishop of London on 6 March. Before leaving the area the intrepid Robert Wych attempted to beard the lion by reading another version of Thomas' appeal in the Court of Arches, on 9 March. The confrontation of that Monday has come down from two eyewitnesses: Hildebrand, whose contemporary protocol recorded the events the notary saw, and Richard de Kimberley, who had served Thomas in various capacities since about 1273.[50] Wych's statement was to be presented, Kimberley explained, before the Dean of Arches 'where the general court of the archbishop is held as for his whole province'. Robert approached the dean and said,

> 'Master, I wish to read something before you.'

The dean replied,

> 'Read, in the name of the Lord.'

Wych began reading quickly (*festinanter*). When the dean realized that it concerned Thomas' appeal he interrupted, saying,

> 'Friend, we have a great deal to do. Do not hamper us and this consistory, but go, along with Hildebrand the notary who is with you, into some corner of the church and there read and propose whatever you wish to read or propose or do before us.'

But Wych was not to be so easily put off. He replied,

> 'Lord Dean, I wish to read this document in this consistory (*in hoc consistorio*) before you.'

He then continued reading, even more quickly (*velociter*). At this the dean, Mgr. Roger de Rowell (Rothwell)[51] was flabbergasted (*mirabiliter est turbatus*). He ordered his men to expel the proctor Wych, so Ralph the cleric, William Bedellus and Mgr. William, *examinator* of the consistory,[52] seized the proctor's arms and struggled to expel him, but Kimberley and others with him defended Wych while he continued to read. Finally the dean, very upset, ordered that none of the advocates, proctors and

49 fos. 28v-30r. It is also possible that Wych's statement to Giffard was presented in a way that emphasized Giffard's own problems with Pecham.
50 Vat. Cod. Lat. 4015, fo. 33r. He gave testimony to the commissioners in May, 1307, Vat. Cod. Lat. 4016, fos. 38v, 43v; apparently Richard has conflated the Arches appeal of 17 Jan. with the later one of 9 March.
51 Rothwell; *cf.* Churchill, *op. cit.*, I, 64, and II, 17.
52 Churchill, *op. cit*, II, 240 and Index, 294, as well as I, 436-457 for personnel of Court of Arches.

others standing about were to listen to Robert Wych, under penalty of excommunication and suspension. They all left immediately and Robert finished his reading before an empty court.[53]

Pecham responded within a week of this contretemps in Arches. On 15 March he again ordered his 'right hand' the bishop of London to excommunicate Thomas throughout the diocese by 30 March, in this cause for which he, Pecham, was prepared to die.[54] On the same day he wrote to the Dean of Arches that since the bishop of London was remiss in this matter, the dean was to publish the sentence throughout London and its churches by 30 March.[55] Obviously Pecham was having difficulty getting the so-called excommunication published.[56]

Thomas, meanwhile, having seen Robert Wych undertake his tour of the bishops, had left England towards the end of the first week, or during the second week, of March.[57] While enroute through northern France he must have received a further mandate from the Canterbury Official Peter 'de Sco Mario' (Seymour) since on 18 March, 1282 at St. Riquier, a Benedictine abbey some ten kilometres east of Abbeville, Thomas lodged another appeal citing the Official's continued harassment.[58] On the 23rd Cantilupe wrote to the bishop of London from Paris to persuade him to ignore Pecham's order about publishing the excommunication. Thomas also spoke of certain papal letters he had received prior to any such excommunication.[59] He is sending the document (*lram papalem bullatam*) to the bishop of London as evidence of this, to be discussed, he suggests, at the forthcoming Easter council.[60]

Robert Wych continued to tour England on his propaganda mission. He found himself before the bishop of Exeter on 22 March.[61] The next day, since Pecham was also in Exeter on visitation,[62] the undaunted proctor once again approached the archbishop. According to Hildebrand's written account submitted in 1307, Wych went into the cathedral and asked the archbishop to listen to an appeal against him on Thomas' behalf, in the terms found in the document he held. When he began reading this the prelate said wrathfully (*irato animo*) 'We will not hear you because we excommunicated you at Lambeth; get away from us (*recede a nobis*).'

53 fo. 38v, 43v; appeal copied on fo. 42r-v.
54 *Reg. Peckham,* R.S. I, 315-6. For the special relationship between Canterbury and London, cf., e.g. Churchill, *op. cit.,* I, 112, 355, 474.
55 *Reg. Pecham,* C & Y., LXV, 142-3; fo. 74v.
56 Douie, 200-201.
57 *cf.,* fos. 7v 42v. Thomas left before Pecham prohibited papal judges-delegate from hearing the case, not, as Douie suggests (205), afterwards, in consequence of the prohibition.
58 fo. 18r-v.
59 *cf.* Pecham's remarks in *Reg. Peckham,* RS., I, 270.
60 fos. 17v-18r.
61 fo. 41r.
62 Pecham's *Itinerarium,* fo. 52v; *cf.* Douie, 206, Churchill, *op. cit.,* I, 297.

But Robert went on reading, which so angered Pecham that he ordered his men to throw him out. They seized his arms and clothing at once, dragging him by force through most of the cathedral—in the archbishop's presence—until Robert, at last cracking under the strain, shouted 'Harrow! Harrow, on the archbishop and his men who are maltreating me!'[63] At this Pecham ordered his people to release him, then turned on his heel and disappeared into the chapter house. Robert tried to follow but the way was blocked by door-keepers and Pecham's men. He contented himself with reading out his statement and appeal at the door, word for word. He was then approached by Roger, archdeacon of Leicester, and Robert de Lacy, who came up to him in the church and said 'We are here on behalf of our lord the archbishop of Canterbury. Read and recite here, before us, whatsoever you wish and we will listen to you', which, presumably, was done.[64]

There is another eyewitness description of a confrontation between Wych and Pecham, by William Russell, a member of Pecham's entourage when Robert landed in the ditch near Guildford. His testimony probably refers to an incident at Lambeth. He claimed (in 1307) that Pecham had finished Mass and was leaving the chancel when Wych approached but, seeing him, 'the said archbishop, with his hands raised, flew at the said Master Robert as if he wished to seize and attack him *'et idem areps levatis manibus cucurrit contra dcm mgm Robm ac si vellet eum apprehendere et invadere*). When the archbishop's men surrounded him to expel him, Wych was shouted at by the prelate, *clamavit alta voce,* 'I excommunicated you, and still I excommunicate you.' Not to be outdone, Robert replied, 'And I appealed and still appeal' after which he shouted Harrow! It was said that Robert would have been badly treated if certain agents of Earl Gilbert of Gloucester, who had accompanied him, had not been there.[65]

A week after the Exeter incident, Pecham—predictably—was writing again to his curial proctors explaining how Thomas had appealed after being excommunicated, and warning of rumours that he was en route to the curia. If he had actually gone, the proctors were to withstand him strenuously when he arrived.[66] About the same time, the end of March, the archbishop announced the formal excommunication of Robert Wych, and prohibited anyone listening to the charges he was bringing; whoever received a copy of his *libellus famosus* should destroy it.[67]

During the next month, while Thomas was moving south into Italy, hostilities appeared to lessen in England. Pecham and his suffragans seemed to reach agreement about respective spheres of jurisdiction at the

63 fo. 50v; *harou, harou sur larcevesq e sur sa gent qu mal me fount.*
64 fo. 50v.
65 fo. 76v.
66 *Reg. Peckham,* RS., I, 318-20, (31 March).
67 *ibid.*, I, 320-22.

1) TO CRY HARROW ON ANYONE: to denounce a person's doings.
2) In law of Normandy & Channel Islands (haro) a call repeated thrice, and followed by action in the court, in cases of trespass OR ENCROACHMENT.

London council held after Easter.[68] On 27 April the bishop of Norwich asked Thomas to return, claiming that Pecham was now affably disposed and any action against Thomas suspended.[69] Unfortunately this was not the case. As events were to show, the archbishop was to continue to clash with his bishops long after 1282. One of those prelates, Godfrey Giffard of Worcester, sensed this even in the midst of discussions about the *gravamina.* On April 20, Godfrey complained that Pecham was interfering in a certain divorce case and had sent prejudicial mandates to his ministers. Furthermore, although the archbishop had ordered him to publish the excommunication of Cantilupe, Godfrey, considering the objections of the bishop of Hereford to be similar to his own, appealed to the Apostolic See —in effect formally joining his cause to Cantilupe's. Robert Wych was among those present when this appeal was announced; the certificate of appeal was drawn up by Hildebrand.[70] Godfrey wrote to Cantilupe at the end of April urging him to fight on against Pecham, and about 3 May sent Robert Wych, as his own (as well as Thomas') proctor, to Italy; he carried Godfrey's letter to Thomas and further instructions concerning the bishop of Worcester's appeal.[71]

Thomas had reached Italy by mid-May. He fell ill at Florence and sent Robert de Radeswell ahead, with John de Kempsey and a layman (Richard Cissor) to the papal curia at Orvieto.[72] When they arrived they found that Pecham's proctors Reynerius of Florence and Philip of Cornwall had already started rumours that Thomas, an excommunicate, was unfit to approach the curia.[73] Radeswell procured the services of learned men such as Dom. Angelus, as well as enlisting the help of Thomas' proctors John of Bitterley and 'the most notorious of late thirteenth-century English curial proctors, Adam of Fileby'.[74] Radeswell and his group then called upon the cardinals at their Orvieto lodgings; though they met with sympathetic responses, they were advised to go to the pope himself.[75] Some time about the third week of May, after they addressed *quandam peticionem* to the pope, *auditores* were appointed to hear the matter. These were cardinal Benedict Gaetani (later Boniface VIII) and (probably)

68 *cf. Reg. Giffard,* II, 146-7; *Reg. Swinfield,* 32; Douie, 207-13, Wilkins, *Concilia,* II, 75-6; *Reg. Peckham,* RS., I, 334-7, Churchill, I, 427-30.

69 *Reg. Swinfield,* 36.

70 *Reg. Giffard,* II, 148-9; Douie, 201-2, 213-15.

71 *Reg. Giffard,* II, 147-8, (30 April).

72 fo. 74v. Martin IV, (1281-85) never entered Rome as pope but ruled from Orvieto and then Perugia; *cf.* D. Waley, *Papal State in the thirteenth century,* (1961), 202-3.

73 *cf. Reg. Peckham,* RS., I, 276, 306r etc. for Reynerius; fos. 31v, 7v-8r.

74 R. Brentano, *Two Churches; England and Italy in the thirteenth century*, (1968), 46; *cf.* 41-8 for these two proctors.

75 fos. 8r. 31v: *de cardinali ad cardinalem.*

3) a cry of distress or alarm: a call for succour.

cardinal John Chioletti.[76] They were assisted by others, such as the English cardinal Hugh of Evesham, during their meetings in the hall of the papal palace.[77]

After the cardinals had cited both sides and examined their letters of authorization, Gaetani—so Radeswell testified in 1307—said to Pecham's proctor Reynerius,

> 'You, who have spread it about that the bishop of Hereford is not a man of fit and proper condition (*integri status*), have you anything for us to establish that this is so?'[78]

Reynerius answered affirmatively, at which Thomas' people asked that such evidence be produced by a specified time, avoiding delay (one of the functions of such hearings); the auditors agreed. When in a few days they met again, Reynerius presented a letter from the archbishop stating that Thomas 'deserved to be bound by sentence of excommunication'.[79] Then one of the assisting cardinals—Matthew Rosso, to whom King Edward had written in mid-February—said smiling (*subridendo*), 'Have you any other letter or other form of sentence apart from this one?' Reynerius said yes, though this letter ought to be sufficient. To this Matthew replied, 'I believe that many of us deserve to be bound, yet are not bound; though one deserves it, it does not follow that he is bound' by such a sentence.[80] After this Gaetani asked what else the proctor could produce. Reynerius submitted apostolic letters appointing judges-delegate in the matter of Thomas' being unjustly cxcommunicated, which, as far as Reynerius was concerned, raised a *prima facie* doubt about the bishop's actual status. Two objections were brought against this line of argument, firstly (by Master Angelus) that since the *audiencia,* in which such letters were obtained, was not a judicial venue but only *praeparatorius* to obtaining judgements, the wording of such documents did not constitute a judgement.[81] Secondly, Radeswell told the cardinals that in any event Thomas knew nothing of this so-called admission of a possible 'excommunication' nor about petitioning for papal letters mentioning such a sentence.[82] But where did this petition come from? In 1307 John de Bitterley admitted that, unaware that Thomas was coming to the curia, as his proctor he had petitioned for letters appointing judges-delegate to investigate Thomas'

76 fos. 31v, 144v; Chioletti, to whom Pecham himself had written asking for support on 19 Jan., *Reg. Peckham,* RS., I, 282-3.

77 fo. 8r-v; on Hugh *cf.* Brentano, *op. cit.,* 50-6.

78 fo. 8v, *Tu qui diffamasti Epm. Hereford quod non erat homo integri status, habesne aliquid ad informandum nos quod ita sit?*

79 *'Excommunicationis sentencia meruit innodari',* very similar to the expression used in Pecham's letter of 17 Feb. to the bishop of London, (*Reg. Peckham,* RS., I, 299), presumably the source for Reynerius.

80 fos. 8v-9r.

81 fos. 9r, 31v. *cf.* Jane Sayers, 'Canterbury proctors at the Court of "Audentia Litterarum Contradictarum" ', *Traditio,* XXII (1966), 311-31.

82 fo. 9r.

excommunication. Thomas knew nothing about this petition, nor were the letters ever used.[83] After considering the whole matter the cardinals declared, towards the end of the first week of June, that

> notwithstanding the things proposed by you [Reynerius] in the name of your lord the archbishop of Canterbury whose proctor you are, we pronounce that good man the bishop of Hereford to be a man of fit and proper status and, as such, he ought to be admitted

to the papal curia.[84]

Bitterley wrote to Thomas telling him the good news, which Radeswell took at once to the bishop, who had meanwhile moved south from Florence.[85] He and Radeswell met (probably on the 9th June) in a village outside Orvieto where they spent the night, Thomas listening to an account of events at the curia.[86] Next day[87] Cantilupe entered Orvieto, where he was cordially welcomed by the pope and cardinals. Martin IV sent him two capons in two large silver dishes with two vessels of wine; after the messenger had tasted these victuals and been given one-half mark, Thomas and his *familia* enjoyed their meal.[88] Within a week, having settled in, Thomas visited the pope hoping to complete the business that had brought him so far. Martin had him sit on his own bed, in Bitterley's and Radeswell's presence; they heard the pope say, 'Why have you not come to see us more often? We believed our doorkeepers (*hostiarii nostri*) did not allow you in.'[89] Ominously, Thomas replied, 'Holy Father, I have been worn out (*debilis*)—and still am.'[90]

Some time between 24 June and 10 July[91] Martin IV moved from Orvieto to nearby Montefiascone, seat of the Tuscan Patrimony in the Papal State.[92] Thomas procured cramped lodgings in Castrum Florenti (Ferento, now ruins) some ten kilometres away. From here he visited the curia two or three times a week. During July it seems that his petitions and appeals were being considered by the *auditor*, cardinal Gervasius.[93] Unfortunately, by August, before anything decisive could be done, Thomas fell seriously ill. Though he was still celebrating Mass on the 15th and 16th of August, on the 18th he received papal permission to make his will.[94] During the final week of his life, which he spent at Castrum Florenti attended by Robert Deynte, he confessed to, and was

83 fo. 31r-v. 84 fos. 32r, 35r, 9r. 85 fo. 32r.
86 fo. 9v. 87 Probably 10 June, fo. 35r. 88 fos. 9v, 22v, 32v.
89 One had to provide against such a possibility, *e.g.* in June, 1281 Thomas authorized 'gifts' for *hostiarius dom. pape,* (40 shillings), and the papal *cubicularius,* (10 marks), along with the customary payments to cardinals and other curial staff. See *Reg. Cantilupe,* 273-6.
90 fo. 32v; *cf.* 9v, which suggests that this conversation took place at Montesfiascone.
91 A. Potthast, *Regesta pontificum Romanorum,* II (1875), 1771.
92 Waley, *op. cit.,* 100, 251. 93 fo. 9v. 94 fos. 101v, 62v.

absolved by, the papal penitentiary.[95] Deynte, who had served him for fifteen years, knew his master more intimately than anyone: he used to wash the bishop's hairshirts, he slept near him in his chamber, he brought the candles whenever Thomas worked into the night, writing or composing *sermones,* sitting on his bed amidst his books. It was Deynte who held Thomas in his arms the night of 25 August when he uttered his last words, 'I commend my spirit'. Only two others were present, a layman in charge of the wardrobe and Nicholas, Thomas' chaplain. The rest of his *familia* were absent that Tuesday evening since no-one, *nec medici nec socii,* thought Cantilupe would die so suddenly.[96]

On 30 August, 1282, the flesh and viscera of Thomas were buried in the monastery of San Severo, then a house of Premonstratensian canons, outside Orvieto. According to eyewitnesses the site of interment was near the wall by the south doorway used by the canons to enter the church from the cloister.[97] Thomas' faithful followers were present at the funeral service, along with five cardinals. One of these, the Franciscan cardinal Jerome (who became Pope Nicholas IV in 1288) celebrated the Requiem Mass and delivered the eulogy. Hugh of Evesham was among the other cardinals.[98] One other follower of the dead bishop was there too. Robert Wych, who seems to have suffered so much for his master in England, had also arrived in Italy; he saw Thomas with the pope on 14 August. After Thomas' death Robert too paid his last respects at San Severo. Robert Wych had ample grounds to describe himself to the commissioners of 1307 as one who *pre multis aliis erat secretarius* of Thomas, one *nutritus ab eo ab infancia sua.*[99]

The will that Thomas made during the week before his death was already being honoured. No copy seems to have survived, but on 31 August, 1282 the same (probably Italian) notary who drew up the will recorded receipts of legacies already handed over to Thomas' *familia* who had come with him to Italy.[100] There are about two dozen individual legatees along with payments for funeral and household expenses for returning to England. The more important members of the *familia* received generous bequests of cash, horses or mules, and cloaks. Evidently John de Clare had been chosen by Thomas to carry on the running of the household, for he was allotted various amounts for present and future

95 *cf. AA.SS* (1765), Oct., I, 578-9, for summary.
96 Vat. Cod. Lat. 4015, fos. 108r-109v.
97 Vat. Cod. Lat. 4015, fos. 101r, 110r.
98 Vat. Cod. Lat. 4016, fos. 101v-102r, 22v, 10r, 51r; *cf. AA.SS* (1765), 580.
99 fo. 51v. In Douie, 218-22, the two Roberts are confused; her comments refer to Wych, not, as she states to Robert 'le Wyse' of Gloucester; Wych was at one time proctor for Robert of Gloucester, fo. 43r.
100 B. G. Charles and H. D. Emanuel, eds., *A Calendar of the earlier Hereford Cathedral Archives* (NRA), 3 Vol. (1955), II, 559-60, Hereford cathedral archives, (hereafter HCA.), 1414.

needs as well as receiving as a personal legacy a higher sum (40 marks) than anyone else, along with a mule and a piece of dark blue cloth.[101] Robert Wych was left 20 marks, a piece of white cloth, a furred cloak with hood and a horse called Assh, a legacy which compares favourably with the others of Thomas' immediate council. Among the household servants, ranging from John the cook (15 marks) to Walter the page (1 mark), old Robert Deynte was left the respectable sum of 20 marks and—fittingly —Cantilupe's bed and appurtenances. Eventually, months after the party had returned to England, Pecham approved formal administration of the will on 11 May, 1283 and appointed auditors to examine the accounts and close probate on 30th April, 1285.[102] Though there are indications of a few other legacies, there is one bequest that is of some interest: in October, 1283, Pecham acknowledged receipt of £20 in lieu of a palfrey and a ring bequeathed to him by Thomas, once bishop of Hereford.[103]

While the conflict was drawing to a close for Thomas in Italy, in England Pecham was continuing to implement his own policies. He wrote again to Reynerius his curial proctor on 23 July, 1282, to re-emphasize his version of events.[104] Pecham restated his case with greater clarity, then again claimed that Lacy promulgated the sentence at Lambeth in writing, after which Thomas immediately appealed to Rome. 'He says however that he had appealed earlier, which is unknown to me.' It is curious that Pecham could have written this in view of his own acknowledgement of the notification of appeal he had received on 15 January, to say nothing of earlier appeals on Thomas' behalf.[105] Pecham also comments that in any event he cannot see how the pope would entertain Cantilupe's case.

About the time that Thomas was found to be a fit person to approach the curia, cardinal Gaetani had written to Pecham, sending the letter with John of Pontoise, new bishop of Winchester, who would explain things more fully to the archbishop.[106] The cardinal besought Pecham to modify his anger, which discredited all parties. The archbishop replied on 1 August, 1282.[107] He was amazed and saddened to see that the cardinal had been taken in by Thomas. He spelled out his version for Gaetani but

101 John de Clare normally handled Thomas' financial affairs, *cf. Reg. Cantilupe*, 259-63, 293, etc.

102 *Reg. Pecham,* C & Y., LXIV, 197; *Calendar Heref. Archives* II, 572, HCA. 1416, Vat. Cod. Lat., 4016, fo. 62r.

103 *Cal. Heref. Archives,* II, 570, HCA. 1050; Vat. Cod. Lat. 4016, fos. 61v-62r.

104 *Reg. Peckham,* RS., I, 382-3.

105 Douie, (200), seems to believe that he was genuinely unaware of Thomas' appeal to Rome predating the 'excommunication', but Pecham refers to an appeal notified in mid-January in *Reg. Peckham,* RS., I, 278-9. Except for this acknowledgement, it may be that Pecham could have objected to the form of notification, or perhaps to a misunderstanding of who was in fact appealing.

106 fo. 19r-v.

107 *Reg. Peckham,* RS., II, 393-5; *cf.* Douie, 216.

here the controversy was considerably toned down. Pecham nearly bypassed the Lambeth excommunication with an oblique reference, but, instead, he stressed that though he, Pecham, agreed with his suffragans about their *gravamina,* Thomas was obstinately rejecting this peace offer. *Haec est veritas, pater sanctissime,* he claimed. While composing this letter Pecham would have been influenced by the bishop of Winchester, who no doubt informed him that all was not well at the curia, since Thomas was found to be eligible to approach and present his case. Hence Pecham seems to have dropped his usual line and emphasized another—himself as spurned peacemaker (at least for Gaetani's benefit). By the time the archbishop's reply to the cardinal would have reached the curia, however, Thomas had already died.

When he heard of Thomas' death, Pecham wasted no time in exacting his revenge.[108] On 30 September, 1282 he appointed Adam de Hales his Official for Hereford *sede vacante* and a week later, 6 October, he wrote to tell the Hereford dean and chapter that he would be arriving for a visitation on 15 October.[109] According to Pecham's own *Itinerarium* he entered Hereford cathedral in great procession on Thursday, 15 October, 1282. After a benediction he went into the chapter house where he preached on the theme *Religio munda et immaculata hec est visitare pupillas et viduas.* Following this he discussed his visitation rights with the dean and chapter.[110] Next day, Robert of Gloucester appeared before Pecham and humbly asked that the penalties brought against him by the archbishop should be revoked. The prelate agreed provided that Robert find 100 pounds sterling as surety for his obedience and undertake a pilgrimage to the Holy Land. In addition he was to go to Canterbury and present twenty pounds of wax or candles (in honour of the twenty patron saints of the church), as well as place a written promise of obedience on the altar of St Thomas Becket. Then, on his way back through London, he was publicly to proclaim his guilt and his promise never to harm the liberties of Canterbury, before the archbishop's Official or the Dean of Arches.[111] He was to carry out his penance before 25 November, 1282 and to obtain confirmatory sealed letters from Canterbury and the Court of Arches.[112]

108 Though the trip from Italy to England usually took 5 to 7 weeks, it could take as little as 25 or 29 days. George B. Parks, *The English Traveler to Italy,* I, (1954), 182-3.
109 *Reg. Pecham,* C & Y., LXV 60, 176; cf. Churchill, *op. cit.,* I, 237-8.
110 fo. 52v.
111 fos. 53r, 57r-58v. Beccles' copy of Pecham's *Itinerarium* says *centum* (53r) whereas Hildebrand's records mention *mille* (57r); the first figure is more probable than the second.
112 fos. 57v-58r. After this Pecham arranged for the release of the Bramfords, whose year-long imprisonment in the divorce case that helped precipitate the conflict had, unfortunately for them, become a matter of principle. On Saturday (probably 17 Oct., 1282, not—as Douie says, p. 197, summer of 1283) they were released and absolved, fo. 53v.

Objections about Pecham's proposed visitation of the diocese dragged on through November.[113] By early December, however, the archbishop prepared to go ahead as planned. He scheduled the visitation to begin on 5 December, but two days before this he once again encountered his old adversary, Cantilupe. On 3 December the Hereford precentor William de Montfort presented a document to Pecham at Leominster, a letter patent, dated Orvieto, 5 September, 1282, with the red seal of the Roman penitentiary. In it Galfridus de Sheppey stated that after confession Thomas received absolution and penance from him, which Pope Martin IV later confirmed. At Leominster, Alan of Beccles made a notarial exemplification of the document at Pecham's request.[114] This absolution was ignored by the archbishop, for on 10 December he warned the Hereford canons that under penalty of interdict they were in no way to attempt to bury Thomas' bones in their cathedral, or any holy ground, unless it could first be shown to him that Thomas had been absolved from the sentence of excommunication brought at Lambeth. Pecham said he would be quite willing to allow burial if anyone sought absolution from the sentence *forma iuris.*[115] Since to do so would have been to admit the validity of the excommunication, stalemate resulted.

Meanwhile, the bones, under the custody of John de Clare,[116] were according to Robert Wych kept for a while at the French port of Wissant;[117] news of Pecham's unwillingness to allow them into England may already have reached the homeward-bound *familia.* Here it may be appropriate to note that there is no evidence that Richard Swinfield, Cantilupe's successor, was in charge of the bones, nor indeed is there any evidence that he accompanied Thomas to Italy or, consequently, was present at his death and burial service, as is often claimed. Swinfield was carrying out his duties in England as archdeacon of London, which he held between September 1281 and July 1282; Pecham addressed mandates to the archdeacon of London in May and June of 1282.[118] To return to the remains of the bishop, it seems that when they were at last brought

113 *Reg. Peckham,* RS., II, 421, 430-431, 478, 484-6; *Reg. Pecham,* C & Y., LXV, 177; *Cal. Heref. Archives,* II, 562.

114 The document printed by Cheney in *Notaries Public,* op. cit., 166-67 and plate II, from HCA. 1414A; *cf. Calendar Heref. Archives,* II, 563-4. Another version in Vat. Cod. Lat. 4016, fos. 55v-56r. The document itself was submitted to the 1307 commission, fo. 61v.

115 fo. 53v.

116 Vat. Cod. Lat. 4015, fo. 83r.

117 Vat. Cod. Lat. 4016, fo. 51r.

118 Le Neve, *Fasti ecclesie Anglicanae,* rev. I, St Paul's, 1066-1300, 12. *Reg. Pecham,* C & Y., LXV, 45-6, 148. Swinfield is never among those subscribing documents during Thomas' Italian journey, nor is he ever mentioned by those who were present. Nor, in 1307, does he say that he went to Italy, (*AA.SS,* (1866), 541 *et seq.,* and (1765), 599, *et seq.*); in fact he says he has the details of Thomas' death, return of the bones to England, and eventual burial, at second hand, *dixit ex relatu . . . audivisse* (*AA.SS.* (1866), Oct. I, 548).

into England it was all done quickly before Pecham could react.[119] *Acta Sanctorum* records the claims that the persecuted bones bled during this journey and notes that the heart—thanks to Edmund Earl of Cornwall—was eventually enshrined at Ashridge. As for the bones, what was required was intermediation. About 20 January, 1283 at Northampton, where some sort of ecclesiastical as well as parliamentary gathering occurred,[120] one of the royal commissioners, Edmund of Cornwall as it happens, approached Pecham on this delicate issue.[121] There is some question about absolution, but this would seem to have been part of the arrangement.[122] In any event, according to John de Lewes, one of Pecham's notaries, Thomas' remains, in two caskets, were placed on the altar of the church of St Andrew at Northampton where they received the archbishop's approval for burial.[123] Thus, at last, Thomas returned to Hereford where, in early 1283, he was buried under a flat slab in the east end of the cathedral. When Bishop Swinfield translated the bones to the tomb/shrine in the north transept in 1287, Cantilupe's miraculous career began.[124]

Though Pecham allowed Thomas' burial in 1283, even though he may have granted an indulgence of twenty days for prayers for his soul in August, 1284, the old animosity continued. On March 28th, 1287, a woman claimed to have been cured at Thomas' grave at the east end of the cathedral, which was immediately publicised by Swinfield's almoner Gilbert de Cheveninge. It was said in 1307 that *istud fuit primum miraculum* publicly worked by the dead bishop. On the very next day Master Thomas de St. Omer, Hereford canon and Pecham's Official for Llandaff *sede vacante,* called Gilbert before him and rebuked him: 'He should not have done this without the authority of the lord archbishop on account of the dispute' going on at the Roman curia between Pecham and Thomas at the time of the latter's death. Furthermore, St Omer attributed the miracle to an earlier bishop of Hereford, Robert de Bethune (d. 1148), also buried in the cathedral. Cheveninge was suspended for a week.[126] In spite of this censure, after the translation of 3 April, 1287 miracles corus-

119 fo. 78v.

120 *cf.* G. O. Sayles, *The King's parliament of England* (1975), 90, 93; E. W. Kemp, *Counsel and Consent* (1961), 76-7; Wilkins, *Concilia,* II, 91-2; *Reg. Peckham, RS.,* II, 486-8, 501-2, 508-9; *Handbook of British Chronology* (1961), 508, 553. Robert Wych says *in parliamento,* fo. 51r.

121 fo. 104r; *cf.* Powicke, *op. cit.,* 506-7.

122 fos. 24v, 46r, 146v.

123 fo. 72r.

124 *cf.* R. Finucane, *Miracles and Pilgrims,* (London, 1977), chap. 10, 181 *et seq.;* there the date of original burial is mistakenly given as 1282.

125 fos. 62r, 10r.

126 Vat. Cod. Lat. 4015, fo. 212r, also in *AA.SS.*

cated and Cantilupe's cause seemed vindicated from beyond the grave. The still-unforgiving Pecham well understood the propaganda value of these thaumaturgic wonders.[127] He wrote to Robert de Lacy, then studying at Paris, 'Blessed God! That the Lord performs miracles for excommunicates these days!'[128]

By this time his troubles with Swinfield and other suffragans were increasing and he faced the same old battles—over many of the same issues.[129] Towards the end of his life Pecham's mind clouded, his associates went in fear of his irascible attacks upon anyone who disagreed with him.[130] His last illness of 1292 involved an ironic final confrontation between the old combatants. In October some of the archbishop's people, hoping for a miracle, sent a candle to Thomas' shrine on his behalf, but his appeal was unanswered; two months later he followed the bishop into eternity.[131] In 1307 the papal commissioners found that Thomas' 'excommunication' was illicit[132] and that therefore they could go ahead with the canonization inquiry, which ultimately resulted in the creation of another English saint.

127 *cf.* Douie, 338.
128 fo. 46r.
129 *cf.* Douie, 218 *et seq.*: *Reg. Swinfield,* 175-8, 182-4.
130 M. D. Knowles, 'Some aspects of the career of Archbishop Pecham', part II, *English Historical Review,* LVII (1942), 178-201 at 198-9.
131 Douie, 217-18; *AA.SS* (1866), Oct. I, 536, Vat. Cod. Lat. 4015, fo. 311v-312r; Vat. Cod. Lat. 4016, fo. 89v.
132 fos. 141r-142v, 144r.

THE PROCESS OF CANONIZATION IN THE THIRTEENTH AND EARLY FOURTEENTH CENTURIES [1]

by Patrick H. Daly

In the thirteenth and early fourteenth centuries, just as today, canonization entailed a definitive papal sentence whereby a given member of the faithful departed with a proven reputation for holiness of life and miracles was formally proclaimed a saint. By this papal proclamation a liturgical cult of the new saint was approved and extended to the universal church, his feast day was established, his veneration endorsed and the invocation of his intercession by the faithful encouraged.

For the first millenium of the church's history decisions regarding eventual canonization of a putative saint were simply taken by the local bishop or by a provincial synod.[2] Moreover, these decisions were arrived at after little or no formal inquiry into the saint's claims to veneration. Even the first generally acknowledged papal canonization, that of Bishop Ulrich of Augsburg by Pope John XV in 993, was effected following a most casual and summary perusal of the late bishop's *acta*.[3] As papal canonization became more frequent, however, the number of laws governing canonization increased correspondingly and a manner of procedure in the matter was specifically laid down. By the end of the thirteenth century the process whereby a saint won official papal recognition was a protracted exercise in litigation, the criteria by which any saint's merits were assessed were clearly established, and the role of each official and party involved was strictly circumscribed.

1 The present article is based on the author's doctoral dissertation, 'Thomas de Cantilupe, Bishop of Hereford c.1222-1282: the making of a medieval saint', 2 vols. Ph.D. thesis, Catholic University of Louvain, 1981.

2 The most important work on the relationship between ecclesiastical authorities and the evolving process of canonization is E. W. Kemp, *Canonization and authority in the Western Church* (Oxford, 1948). On the earlier period in the church's history see A. Amore, 'Culto e canonizzazione dei santi nell' antichita cristiana', *Antonianum,* 52 (1977), 38-80; H. Delehaye, *Sanctus: essai sur le culte des saints dans l'antiquité,* Subsidia hagiographica, 17 (Brussels, 1927). Important modern studies on the history of canonization are D. Blaher, *The Ordinary process in causes of beatification and canonization: a historical synopsis and commentary,* Catholic University of America Canon Law Studies, 268 (Washington D.C., 1949); L. Hertling, 'Material per la storia del processo di canonizzazione', *Gregorianum,* XVI (1935), 170-95.

3 On the establishment of the papal monopoly in matters of canonization, see S. Kuttner, 'La Réserve papale du droit de canonisation', *Revue historique du droit français et étranger,* 4th series, XVII (1938) 172-228. See also E. W. Kemp, 'Pope Alexander III and the canonization of saints', *Transactions of the Royal Historical Society,* XXVII (1945) 13-28.

It is the aim of the present chapter to sketch briefly how the canonization process operated in the thirteenth and early fourteenth centuries. By happy coincidence there is no case which can better illustrate the progress of a medieval saint's cause from its cautious inception to the definitive papal sentence than that of Thomas Cantilupe.[4] Thus by describing the system in general first and then by following the progress of Cantilupe's cause step by step it is hoped to sketch a clear picture of how the canonization machinery functioned in this period.[5]

1. Preliminary steps

Those who desired canonization for a putative saint and who initiated and furthered a canonization campaign were known as petitioners. The first step these petitioners took to set the legal process in motion was to send a letter known as a letter of postulation to the papal court formally requesting consideration of their saint's cause. They also recruited others to request the same on their behalf. Their supporters were usually bishops, religious communities, local nobility or sometimes even the sovereign, and from various case histories it emerges that the number of letters written mattered less than the prestige of their authors and the influence the latter enjoyed at the time. Letters of postulation, irrespective of their author, were all much the same where the contents were concerned. A general reference was usually made to how a new saint enhanced the Church, the merits and miracles of the particular candidate in question were elaborated upon, and finally the Pope was requested to inaugurate an inquiry into his cause. The similarity of these letters is in large measure explained by the manner in which those who wrote them were recruited and briefed by the petitioners or by a proctor appointed by them. A suggested text was usually circulated, the supporters added their name and seal plus the date and place of signature. Once these letters were assembled, they were sent in a batch and, sometimes accompanied by supplementary documents, were forwarded to Rome. One consignment was usually insufficient to persuade the Pope to take the preliminary steps the petitioners requested: he had to be formally approached several times. Indeed often the Pope was not the only recipient of these letters: by the end of the thirteenth century the influence of the cardinals had become so great that their help too was often solicited. The postulatory letters were delivered by a special messenger sent by the petitioners. Then often a proctor resident at the

4 A great wealth of primary source material survives from the Cantilupe case, chiefly the following manuscripts: Vatican City, Bibliotheca Apostolica Vaticana, Vat. Cod. Lat. 4015, 4016, 4017 and Vat. Otto. 2516; Rome, Bibliotheca Alexandrina, 99; Paris, Bibliothèque nationale, Lat. 5373 A; Oxford, Exeter College 158; and numerous miscellaneous manuscripts from Hereford cathedral archives.

5 A study similar in nature to our dissertation is Margaret Toynbee, *St. Louis of Toulouse and the process of canonization in the fourteenth century,* (Manchester, 1929).

papal court was specifically employed to keep reminding the Pope of a particular request regarding canonization and urge him to appoint a commission of inquiry.

The decision to appoint a commission of inquiry lay exclusively with the Pope, yet he never acted without consultation. By the mid-thirteenth century it had become normal practice for him to pass over to a cardinal or committee of cardinals documents—*vitae,* solemnly attested miracles, informal testimonials or postulatory letters—received on behalf of the candidate before setting up the inquiry.[6] In the case where the cardinals' advice to the Pope was positive he appointed commissioners, who had the status of judges-delegate, to investigate the so-called saints' *fama* and miracles.[7] As a rule this commission contained at least one bishop: often he was a compatriot of the putative saint but never someone who had a vested interest in an eventual canonization. By his specific mandate the Pope instructed the commissioners to inquire in depth into all aspects of the would-be saint's life and miracles according to specific instructions included by him in the bull of the appointment.[8] This bull was known as a remissorial letter and the inquiry they were to carry out at the local level (*in partibus*) was known as the informative inquiry.

The idea that Thomas Cantilupe might have been a saint occurred to his successor as bishop of Hereford, Richard Swinfield, as early as 1286,[9] yet it was only on 18 April, 1290 that he formally brought Cantilupe to the attention of the Pope in a letter of postulation. From a remark made by Pope Clement V when eventually appointing a commission of inquiry in 1305, it transpires that Swinfield's letter of 1290 was only one of a long series: letters had been received at the papal court from Edward I, the archbishop of York, fifteen bishops, seven abbots, eleven counts, as well as from numerous barons and nobles, all attesting to Cantilupe's virtues and miracles.[10] Of these many letters, seventeen survive. Textual comparison between letters sent by England's bishops in three batches in 1294, 1299 and 1305 demonstrate that there was a blue-print circulated by Swinfield

6 See R. G. E. Cole, 'Proceedings relative to the canonization of Robert Grosseteste, Bishop of Lincoln', *Associated Architectural Societies' Reports and Papers,* XXXIII, pt. 1 (1915), 8.

7 See James Gaetani-Stephaneschi, *Ordo Romanus XIV* in Jean Mabillon and Michel Germaine, *Museum Italicum, seu collectio veterum scriptorum ex bibliothecis Italicis* (Paris, 1687-89) 2, 418-19.

8 See *Ordo Romanus XIV,* 419.

9 On 7 October 1286 Swinfield wrote to his proctors at the papal court to inquire whether any miracles were occurring at the place where Cantilupe's *viscera* lay buried at San Severo, see *Registrum Ricardi de Swinfield, episcopi Herefordensis A.D. MCCLXXIII-MCCCXVII* (hereafter *Reg. Swinfield*), ed. W. W. Capes, Canterbury and York Society, VI, (London, 1909), 68.

10 *Acta Sanctorum,* 3rd ed., Bollandists (Paris/Rome, 1863/75), October, 1, 585, (hereafter *AA.SS*).

which they all copied.[11] Moreover, the tone struck by King Edward I in his postulatory letter was very similar to that of the bishops: he had requested help from Hereford in drafting his letter, help which two canons of Hereford hastened to London to supply on 8 September, 1305.[12]

Messengers were sent from Hereford to the papal court with each batch of letters and Clement V admitted that Hereford representatives had spoken to him of Cantilupe and expounded in his presence.[13] It was not only messengers specifically sent to visit the curia for that purpose who pleaded Cantilupe's cause: Hereford's bishop, dean and chapter had primed others to lobby for their candidate. Firstly, the English cleric John de Ross, a resident at the curia, had been made a canon of Hereford in 1306 and Swinfield profited from his nomination to urge him to work zealously for the late bishop's canonization.[14] Secondly, and rather remarkably, William Gainsborough, bishop of Worcester, spoke directly to Clement V about Cantilupe.[15] Thirdly, not wishing to rely on occasional delegations to the Apostolic See nor on well-disposed friends who happened to be at the curia, the Hereford authorities kept a permanent proctor on the spot to represent their interests. In 1291 they appointed one of their own canons, Alan de Creppinge, a doctor of civil law just fresh from studies in Bologna, as proctor with special responsibility for the promotion of Cantilupe's cause.[16] Unfortunately, a dispute arose between Creppinge and his employers, and the resulting tension may partly explain why it was some years before progress was made on the case.

It was the letters sent in 1305 which prompted the newly-elected Pope Clement V to act on Hereford's request for an inquiry. Yet, as was the custom, before he set up a commission he received advice from three cardinals to whom he had submitted whatever documents Hereford had sent for review. The cardinals were John Minus, cardinal-bishop of Porto, Thomas Jorz, cardinal-priest of St. Sabina, and William de Long, cardinal-deacon of St. Nicholas in Carcere Tuliano.[17] The advice given by this committee of cardinals to Clement V was positive for, on 23 August, 1306,

11 Most of the bishops' letters are unpublished and are to be found in Vat.Cod.Lat. 4015, fos. 260v-263r.
12 See *Reg. Swinfield,* 440-41, 420-21; Thomas Rymer, *Foedera, conventiones, literae et cujuscumque generis acta publica inter reges Angliae et alios imperatores,* 3rd ed. (The Hague, 1739-45) (hereafter *Foedera*) 1, pt. iv, 43.
13 AA.SS, October, 1, 585.
14 *Reg. Swinfield,* 428-29.
15 Vat. Cod. Lat. 4016, fo. 63v. What is remarkable about William of Gainsborough's warm support for canonization is that he and Pecham were the only Franciscans to become bishops in medieval England. The Franciscans who gave evidence in the London inquiry of 1307 were less than enthusiastic about Cantilupe's sanctity. The general attitude adopted by the Franciscans to Cantilupe is a topic the present author hopes to treat at length in a separate monograph.
16 See *Charters and Records of Hereford Cathedral,* ed. W. W. Capes (Hereford, 1908), 159-63, 171-72, 192.
17 AA.SS, October, 1, 585.

he appointed three commissioners to carry out an informative inquiry *in partibus* into the life and miracles of Thomas Cantilupe with a view to a possible canonization. These commissioners were William Durand, bishop of the southern French diocese of Mende, Richard Baldock, bishop of London, and William de Testa, then papal nuncio in England. The main burden of responsibility fell on Durand, a distinguished canonist and skilled judge-delegate and the most competent of the three in this domain,[18] since both Baldock and Testa were constantly distracted by other pre-occupations throughout the period of the inquiry.[19] There is no evidence to suggest that any of the commissioners were specifically requested by Hereford, yet the subsequent cooperative spirit demonstrated by them would indicate that they had no problems with the Pope's choice.

2. The Informative process

The basic aim of the local inquiry (*processus informativus*) such as that on which the commissioners embarked in 1307 was to assemble evidence regarding the putative saint's life and miracles on the basis of which a decision would later be reached by the Pope and cardinals regarding canonization. By coming to the focal point of a cult the intention of judges-delegate was, firstly, to interview those most intimately connected with a would-be saint, those who either knew him personally or were familiar with his popular reputation. Secondly, the aim was to receive statements from and examine those who claimed his miraculous intercession in their favour. These inquiries *in partibus* always took place in the city or place where the putative saint had lived and/or was buried, or in areas where he was well known.

Throughout the thirteenth century refinements were introduced into the canonization process on papal initiative to ensure that oral evidence given during the local inquiry should be coherent and reliable. Gradually a systematic method of cross-examining witnesses emerged and this led in turn to a corresponding logical order in the evidence presented. An actual scheme of interrogation was drawn up by the commissioners in consultation with the representative of the promoters of a putative saint's cause: each scheme contained rubrics or general headings of inquiry known as *articuli*, and a list of questions known as the *interrogatoria*. The *articuli* were general headings of universal application under which the most

18 On William Durand II, bishop of Mende, see T. de Morembert, 'Durand, Guillaume II', *Dictionnaire de biographie française*, ed. M. Prevost, R. D'Amat (Paris, 1933-) 12, 661-62; P. Viollet, 'Guillaume Durant le jeune, évêque de Mende', *Histoire littéraire de la France*, 35 (1921), 1-139.

19 On Ralph Baldock, see H. A. Tipping, 'Baldock, Ralph de (d. 1313)', *Dictionary of National Biography*, I, 948. On William de Testa, see W. E. Lunt, *Financial Relations of the Papacy with England to 1327* (Cambridge, Mass., 1939), 557-58, 585-86, 621; W. E. Lunt, 'William de Testa and the Parliament of Carlisle', *English Historical Review*, XLI (1926), 332-57.

important aspects of any potential confessor's life could be summarized. They usually numbered four or five and concerned the faith and life of the candidate, his reputation, his miracles and the devotion of the people to him. The *interrogatoria* were a series of very specific and detailed questions designed to elicit precise information concerning particular incidents or phenomena, usually miracles. The *interrogatoria* were normally furnished to the commissioners in a supplementary document accompanying the remissorial letter, while the *articuli* and sometimes more particular headings known as *capitula* containing details regarding a candidate's birth, family, career and virtues, were presented to the commissioners by the petitioners' representative.

It was the function of the judges-delegate to gather evidence rather than pass judgement on it. Obviously they did have to follow their scheme of interrogation closely, exercise discernment and sift at least some of the evidence, but they were aware that critical assessment of it was to be made by others elsewhere. If the commissioners' role could be conceived of as passive rather than active, the reverse however was true of the promoters' chief representative at the hearings who was known as the postulator. He was nominated by the petitioning party to prepare the case of the candidate for canonization and push his cause in the informative process.[20] His function was equivalent to that of the plaintiff's proctor in a normal ecclesiastical court,[21] and his commission was to see a cause through to its completion.

Hereford's postulator was Henry de Schorne, a canon of the cathedral and doctor of canon law, who was well suited and equally well prepared for the task that awaited him.[22] He had been particularly involved in pushing Cantilupe's cause for some time prior to the opening of the inquiry. He had been sent by Swinfield to brief Edward I on Cantilupe and help him draft his postulatory letter in September 1305,[23] and it was he who was dispatched to the curia in April 1306 specifically to promote Cantilupe's cause.[24]

William Durand arrived in England in February 1307,[25] but it was only in July that the three commissioners opened the informative process. This

20 For the history of the office of postulator in canonization causes, see A. Mitri, *De Figura juridica postulatoris in causis beatificationis et canonizationis* (Rome, 1962), 23-46; for the role of the postulator in the thirteenth and fourteenth centuries, see 43-46.

21 For the operation of the judge-delegate system in the normal ecclesiastical courts, see Jane E. Sayers, *Papal judges-delegate in the province of Canterbury, 1198-1254* (Oxford, 1971).

22 See A. B. Emden, *A Biographical register of the University of Oxford to A.D. 1500* (Oxford, 1957-59) 3, 1696.

23 *Reg. Swinfield,* 420-21.

24 *ibid.*, 420, 428-29.

25 See *Chronicles of the Reigns of Edward I and Edward II,* ed. W. Stubbs, Rolls Series (London, 1882-83), I, 150.

delay in starting was due to the fact that, following upon a subsequent papal mandate, the three had been requested to look into the matter of the suggested excommunication of Cantilupe by Archbishop Pecham of Canterbury in 1282. They held an inquiry into this latter matter in London between 15 April and 15 June, interviewed forty four witnesses, examined a considerable amount of documentation and held extensive consultations with legal experts only to reach the conclusion that Cantilupe had not been excommunicated, that the sentence issued by Pecham had been both null and illicit, and that there was no reason why they should not proceed with examining the late bishop's life and miracles.[26] The inaugural session of the informative inquiry took place in the chapter-house of St. Paul's cathedral, London, on Thursday, 13 July.[27]

Basically the inquiry consisted in interviewing witnesses who gave evidence regarding the life and reputation of Thomas Cantilupe, or attributed miracles. In all one hundred and eighty one witnesses made depositions, 152 being brought forward by Schorne, 29 being called by the commissioners on their own authority. Each witness swore to testify truly. Although the specific evidence given at the Cantilupe inquiry is outside the purview of the present chapter, a detailed breakdown of what was expected of the witnesses sheds major light on the information the inquiries *in partibus* aimed at acquiring. Each witness was expected to fully account for himself: he had to state his social rank, the extent of his education, whether he was rich or poor, whether or not he was a relative of Cantilupe's and, finally, his age. The body of the scheme of interrogation which Durand and his colleagues followed in examining witnesses was divided under four general headings (*articuli*). The first covered Cantilupe's life and virtues: they wanted biographical details, to know how he discharged his pastoral functions as bishop, and to discover whether he embodied the conventional series of virtues. The next article covered his *fama:* they asked whether it was generally believed that Cantilupe was a saint. In a remarkable concern that the witnesses provide reliable information, the commissioners checked and double-checked their sources. Regarding Cantilupe's *fama* they asked witnesses how they knew of it, when, from where and from whom; they checked to see that the original source was trustworthy by asking was their informant himself a good person, a special friend or blood relation of Cantilupe's, or someone who had benefited from the latter's intercession. As a final check they asked their interviewees to define their terms of reference: what did they mean by public reputation or common opinion? The third article covered the miracles and here questions were many and detailed. Briefly what the commissioners wished to ascertain was whether the claimed miracle was truly miraculous: they wished to establish in the case of a cure whether

26 The complete records of this extensive inquiry into Cantilupe's excommunication survives as Vat.Cod.Lat. 4016.
27 *AA.SS,* October, I, 587-88.

remedies other than spiritual had been applied, whether recovery had been immediate or gradual, and whether independent witnesses could testify to a noticeable improvement in the condition of the person claiming a cure. Under the fourth article witnesses were asked about popular devotion to the late bishop and how they knew of it.[28]

As has been mentioned, it was not up to the commissioners to pass a value judgement on the evidence, yet they did have to interpret it in the most literal sense. In the excommunication inquiry there had been no problem: since virtually all the witnesses were well-educated clerics, many with a legal background, they spoke Latin or French and were thus immediately understood by the commissioners and all others present.[29] The witnesses in the informative inquiry were far less homogeneous since, in fact, they were drawn from every stratum of medieval English society.[30] Most of the religious spoke Latin (*literaliter*), many of the secular clergy addressed the commissioners in French, virtually all the lay witnesses gave evidence in English, and there was even a handful from the Marches who spoke only Welsh. Interpretation was thus essential. In London the task was fulfilled by the notaries *"in Anglicana lingua experti interpretati"*[31] and later by local Dominicans *"in Anglicana locutione expertos"*.[32] At Hereford it was Franciscan friars who fulfilled the task, two of Welsh origin interpreting the witnesses from the border areas.[33] *

From its opening in the chapter-house of St. Paul's on Thursday 13 July, the London session of the informative process ran for a little over four weeks, until Saturday, 12 August. Unfortunately, Baldock and Testa were frequently absent. Nevertheless, each morning a number of witnesses were received, invited to make a deposition and then cross-examined, thus ensuring that the inquiry proceeded smoothly. Once the London inquiry closed, Durand and Baldock went west and arrived in Hereford on 28 August to remain in the city seventy-eight days.[34] On the morning of Thursday 29 August the bishops went to the cathedral to inspect Cantilupe's tomb, to make an inventory of the *ex-votos* surrounding it and in general to brief themselves on the situation in Hereford. In London witnesses testifying regarding Cantilupe's life and virtues were interspersed with those attesting to the miracles, but in Hereford all the witnesses *de vita* were examined first, between 29 August and 15 September, and those attesting to the miracles from 15 September until the closing day, Monday, 12 November. On the last day there were still many witnesses waiting to make statements regarding miracles attributed to Cantilupe so, under pressure from the Hereford authorities, the commissioners allowed

28 *ibid.*, 589-90.
29 *ibid.*, 596.
30 See R. M. Wilson, 'English and French in England, 110-1300', *History,* XXVIII (1943), 60.
31 Vat.Cod.Lat.4015, fo. 91^{v}.
32 *ibid.*, fo. 64^{r}.
33 *ibid.*, fos. 219^{v}-20^{r}.
34 *AA.SS,* October, I, 594-95.

* not just border areas but Gower - as William Cragh, the hanged man only spoke Welsh. See The Hanged Man Robert Bartlett.

a lengthy list of miracles to be read into the record of the process.[35] When Durand returned to London he sent a lengthy report on the preceding eight months' activity to Clement V: this acted as a covering letter for all the process records (ie. the records of both inquiries) dispatched to the papal court.

3. The Process at the curia

Cantilupe's informative process closed in November 1307, yet it was April 1320 before he was declared a saint. In many canonization processes it was this final phase which tended to be the most protracted. The major source for the curial phase of the canonization process in the high middle ages is, by happy coincidence, precisely contemporaneous with the final phase of Cantilupe's process: it is the *Ordo Romanus XIV* of Cardinal James Gaetani-Stephaneschi, a papal ceremonial written between 1304 and 1328, as well as copious notes taken by the cardinal in its preparation.[36]

In general the curial process began when the Pope committed the records of the informative process presented by the postulator, ie. the *procès-verbal,* to a group of chaplains of his court to be examined. They constituted what was known as the *Rota Auditorum.* These chaplains did not concern themselves with evaluating the documents nor with passing judgement on their contents: they simply drew up rubrics (general headings and summaries of contents) and imposed order on the documents. Once the *procès-verbal* had been returned to the Pope, he delegated three cardinals, one from each rank, to make a thorough examination of the rubrics, and indeed of all the documents, and report to him in solemn consistory.[37] The cardinals were known as the "examiners" and they were the first to actually evaluate a case, something not expected of the judges-delegate. By the fourteenth century cardinals had heavy demands on their time so there was sometimes a long delay before they reported to the Pope and their colleagues. When eventually their examination of the rubrics, the *procès-verbal* and other documents was completed, the three cardinals presented the Pope with their report known as the *relatio processus.* In this report the cardinals not only considered the contents of the documents and assessed their veracity but, under the rubrics, they placed extracts from the process which would highlight various aspects of a putative saint's career and miracles.[38] Sometimes all they furnished

35 *ibid.*, 595.
36 See L. H. Labande, 'Le Cérémonial de Jacques Cajétan. Les données historiques qu'il contient, *Bibliothèque de l'Ecole des Chartes,* 54 (1893), 45-74; B. Schimmelpfennig, *Die Zeremonienbücher der Romischen Kurie im Mittelalter* (Tubingen, 1973), 148-244; M. Dykmans, *Le Cérémonial papal de la fin du moyen âge à la renaissance,* 2 vols., Bibliothèque de l'Institute Historique Belge de Rome 24, 25 (Brussels/Rome, 1977, 1981).
37 *Ordo Romanus XIV,* II, 419.
38 For a fuller account of the preparation of the *relatio processus* from the process of Ivo of Kermartin (+ 1303; Canonized 1347), see *Monuments originaux de l'histoire de St. Yves,* ed. M. de la Bordiere (Saint-Brieuc, 1887), xxix-xlix.

was a summary of the candidate's life based on the evidence *de vita* and, in greater detail, the arguments for and against the selected miracles. The *relatio processus* was presented to the entire Sacred College of cardinals assembled in solemn but secret consistory. As a rule an immediate decision regarding canonization was arrived at. The rubrics *de vita* were read out and discussed by the Pope and cardinals, and the miracles were dealt with in like manner. After consultation it was decided whether or not each rubric and miracle was proved. Then the Pope asked whether canonization could be proceeded with. If the cardinals' verdict was positive the Pope called together all prelates then at the curia and sought final advice. Again, if the advice was still positive, he fixed a date for canonization, appointed seven or eight prelates to preach at the canonization ceremony and nominated two cardinals, expert in scripture, to prepare the day's liturgy.[39]

In the case of Cantilupe's process there was a slight delay in getting the *procès-verbal* to the cardinal-examiners because the notaries were at loggerheads with the Hereford authorities regarding default on payment for their work of transcription.[40] On 17 June, 1308 Henry de Schorne eventually presented the cardinals with the article of Cantilupe's excommunication plus six volumes copied from the original process.[41] The Pope had appointed as examiners the same three cardinals as had approved the setting up of an informative inquiry, yet they were never destined to present a *relatio processus*. The process was suspended at various stages during its curial phase so Hereford repeatedly had to exert pressure through further letters of postulation and personal delegations to the Apostolic See.[42] It was as a result of a fresh batch of letters that Clement V anew committed the Cantilupe dossier to a committee of cardinal-examiners in 1313. Record survives of the three first days of their proceedings (11-15 May, 1313) but they were still only itemizing the documents when the manuscript record breaks off.[43]

The text of the *relatio processus, summarium* or working document which the new Pope John XXII and the cardinals sitting in consistory used to make the final decision on Cantilupe's canonization survives in three separate manuscripts.[44] It is divided between a brief summary of the most important stages of the late bishop's career and a consideration, some of it in considerable depth, of 24 selected miracles attributed to him.[45] The date of this report's composition can be placed somewhere between 14 August,

39 See *Ordo Romanus XIV*, II, 418-24.
40 Hereford cathedral archives (hereafter HCA.), 1439, 1443, 2673.
41 HCA., 1443.
42 *Foedera,* II, pt. i, 14.
43 Vat. Cod. Otto 2516, fos. 44r-46v. See also Dykmans, *op. cit.*, II, 230-32.
44 Paris BN Lat. 5373 A; Exeter Coll. 158; Bibliotheca Alexandrina 99.
45 See A. Vauchez, *La Sainteté en occident aux derniers siècles du moyen âge d'après les procès de canonisation et les documents hagiographiques,* Bibliothèque des ècoles françaises d'Athenes et de Rome, 241 (Rome, 1981), 633-47.

1318 and March 1320 and its author was probably a junior curial cleric.[46] Not only has the text of the cardinals' reference document survived but, thanks to the note-taking of Cardinal Gaetani-Stephaneschi, an account also survives of the actual proceedings of the final consistories of the Cantilupe process which took place in the week preceding Holy Week 1320. In this forum the miracles were first discussed and approved, yet, despite the approval of the cardinals present, John XXII deferred a decision regarding canonization until absent prelates had been consulted. The latter were also to approve but it was only at a final public consistory held after Easter that the Pope finally gave positive indication that it was his intention to canonize Cantilupe.[47]

A canonization ceremony was one of great solemnity, usually attended by a large gathering of ecclesiastical and civic dignitaries. The ceremony opened in a church richly decorated with candles and tapestries with the solemn entrance of the Pope (all surviving accounts comment on the magnificence of his vestments). When seated on his throne the cardinals paid homage and then he began to preach. Once his sermon was over, the miracles attributed to the new saint were read out. The pontiff, addressing the congregation, then asked them to pray that God might preserve him from error in his decision. The *Veni Creator* was chanted and a series of prayers and genuflexions followed. The prayers over, the Pope made public his definition of sanctity. He ascribed the new saint to the catalogue of saints, fixed his feast and office, and extended both to the universal Church. When the Trinity and all the saints were duly praised the saint's feast was added to the calendar and a special indulgence was proclaimed. The cardinals intoned the *Te Deum* and liturgical prayers were directed to God through the new saint. A deacon commenced the *Confiteor* and the Pope proceeded to celebrate Mass in the saint's honour. Mass completed, the ceremony drew to a close.[48]

It was on the morning of Thursday, 17 April, 1320 that Pope John XXII went to the church of Notre Dame des Doms in Avignon and, with Gaetani-Stephaneschi and his brother Cardinal Napoleon as assistants to the pontifical throne, proceeded with the liturgy of canonization of the late bishop of Hereford. John preached on the text: 'He was tried and found perfect, and he shall be in glory' (Sirach 31 : 10). For the rest he proceeded strictly according to the rubrics: he canonized Cantilupe and then went on to celebrate the Mass of the new St Thomas.[49]

46 The date of the *relatio's* composition can be fixed at some stage between 14 August, 1318 and March 1320 since, at one stage Cardinal James Colonna is referred to as *bone memorie* and he died on the former date, while the plenary sessions considering Cantilupe's case had begun in mid-March 1320. See Paris BN Lat. 5373 A, fo. 68r.

47 See Schimmelpfennig, *op. cit.* 164-66.

48 See *Ordo Romanus XIV* II, 412-13, 418-24.

49 See Stephen Baluze, *Vitae paparum Avenioniensium,* ed. G. Mollat (Paris, 1914-21), I, 140-41, 160, 170, 174, 179.

CANTILUPE AS THAUMATURGE: PILGRIMS AND THEIR 'MIRACLES'

by R. C. Finucane

Several years before his canonization in 1320 Cantilupe had already attracted thousands of pilgrims who congregated in the north transept to pray at his tomb, offer money or votives and report or even undergo 'miraculous' cures under the eyes of one or two custodians.[1] Though most pilgrims had not come seeking, or giving thanks for, cures, the records of these miracles are virtually the only sources of information on individual pilgrims to the Hereford saint, aside from sporadic references to noble and royal visitors. It is probably not unrealistic to assume that pilgrims involved in miracles do vaguely represent the generality of all pilgrims—they are, if not a statistical cross-section of the crowd in the background, indicators of the sort of person one could expect to find in that crowd. The present paper concerns these special pilgrims, in particular those involved during the month of April, 1287, when pilgrimage began; we then consider with less detail subsequent stages during the thirteenth century, and conclude by analyzing more carefully the miracle-touched pilgrims of the fourteenth century. The changes noted among these different groups probably reflect generalized changes in the crowds of pilgrims as a whole, between the first miracle of 1287 and the last recorded wonder of 1312.[2]

The miraculous career of Thomas was launched on Thursday, 3 April, 1287 when, amidst the throngs arriving for Holy Week solemnities (Easter fell on 6 April), Bishop Swinfield moved the bones to the north transept; but there had been a preview a week earlier. Edith, wife of Robert the ironmonger of Hereford, began behaving strangely (someone suggested post-natal depression, Robert blamed alcoholism). Apparently she had bitten her mother's nose (or finger), attacked her husband, loudly reviled her neighbours and even blasphemed against God.[3] Finally Robert trussed up the *furiosa* and sent her to Hereford cathedral for a cure at the altar of the Holy Cross. After about a week, during which she was shifted, bound and screaming, between the chapel of the Holy Cross in the rood loft and the Virgin's chapel in the east end of the church—where Thomas' bones still lay—on 28 March she claimed to be cured through a vision of 'saint'

1 For this aspect of Thomas' cult see Finucane, *Miracles and Pilgrims* (1977), chap. 10 and, for 'miracles' generally, chap. 4 through 6.

2 The miracle of AD 1404 noted in Exeter Coll. MS 158, fo. 60r (foliated 61) is ignored here. The miracles are found in *Acta Sanctorum*, Octobris, I, in the 1765 (Antwerp) ed. 610 ff. (hereafter *AA.SS*). Better versions in Vat. Cod. Lat. 4015, and the Exeter College MS. (hereafter EC.) References to both these are to folio numbers.

3 *AA.SS*, 632-3, 636, 697-8; fuller accounts in Vat. Cod. Lat. 4015, fo. 211r-219v.

Thomas. There are several accounts of the cure, which naturally vary in detail, but the attribution to Thomas was a well-nigh unanimous opinion. Certainly Swinfield's almoner Gilbert de Cheveninge, present at least some of the time, quickly and publicly gave Thomas full credit, for which one of Archbishop Pecham's men immediately suspended him.[4] Cheveninge was to become one of the custodians of the tomb after the 3 April translation; even at the canonization inquiry of 1307, as Hereford proctor he was enthusiastically producing witnesses to Thomas' miracles, including Edith's. Though spiritual boon was perhaps premature as far as Swinfield's plans for the cult were concerned, as we shall see it helped to set the pilgrims in motion. It was generally believed to have been Thomas' first public miracle, celebrated with bell ringing and a *Te Deum*.[5]

Thomas' miraculous powers were fully released on Holy Thursday, 3 April, when the bones entered the new tomb. Although nearly 500 miracles were recorded by the tomb-custodians between 1287 and 1312, the peak occurred when enthusiasm was at its height at the start of the cult during April 1287, when some seventy-one miracles were listed. Some of these earliest cases illustrate the importance of suggestion in cult-building. For example, the cure of Edith the *furiosa* became so well-known that within a week it had encouraged at least two others not only to go to the tomb but to be cured there. The mother of Juliana heard about Edith's miracle and sent her crippled daughter, in a wicker basket, to the shrine for a cure. While lying on the floor on Good Friday morning (4 April) Juliana saw another similarly-afflicted suppliant, Gilbert the minstrel, get up from his stretcher and walk round the tomb. With some effort she rose up, went to the tomb, and told Cheveninge and his fellow *custos* that in a vision Thomas had commanded her to walk. The wonder was duly publicized with cathedral bells, a procession and *Te Deum*. When Juliana returned to her village near Sugwas her local parish priest extolled the miracle on Easter Sunday, boosting Thomas' notoriety even more.[6] Another pilgrim, the reeve of a local knight, was also drawn to the tomb/shrine after hearing about insane Edith's experience. On 7 April he was cured of a horrible growth on his neck which had troubled him for over ten years, as he claimed.[7]

Edith's example was followed by others, but interpersonal influence of another kind is illustrated in the cure of Milo Pychard, a well-known knight of the shire. After suffering for six years from the effects of injuries received in a tournament, Milo (having heard of cures on Thurs-

4 See Finucane, 'The Cantilupe-Pecham controversy' in the present volume.
5 Besides references in Edith's miracle, note 3 above, see Vat. Cod. Lat. 4015, fos. 85v, 88v, 110r. There are indications too of earlier miracles effected though Thomas' belt and cap.
6 *AA.SS,* 657, 622-24; EC., fo. 1r; Vat. Cod. Lat. 4015, fo. 169v.
7 *AA.SS,* 625, 628-9, 657-58; Vat. Cod. Lat. 4015, fo. 182v; EC., fos. 1v-2r.

day and Friday) arrived on Saturday and was healed at the tomb on Easter Sunday, 6 April. Bishop Swinfield had personally invited him to attend the ceremonies. Since, as the record puts it, he was *famosus et notus*—he was sheriff in Herefordshire from about 1299 to at least 1305—his miracle became widely known, *valde vulgatum,* and presumably influenced his social equals and inferiors to turn to Cantilupe.[8]

Pilgrims interacted with each other in many ways. Sometimes, those who had been cured were allowed by shrine-keepers to remain on hand as living proof of saintly powers. One of Thomas' pilgrims did even more than this: on Holy Saturday a certain Matilda was cured of dementia. She was still in the area next day, for when Julia of Hereford was struck blind in one eye as punishment for doubting Thomas' powers, Matilda herself took her to the tomb, where she was cured after confessing her errors.[9]

Official announcements in the cathedral and outlying parish churches, the example of local, sometimes influential, people cured by the saint, informal village gossip and speculation, all helped to expand the area of influence around the tomb. The news spread throughout the diocese and eventually began attracting pilgrims from more distant regions. During April, 1287, however, the cult still had a very local character. The seventy-one listed pilgrims came from fifty-four different sites, of which eight are unidentifiable. Of the remainder, one was Hereford city itself, supplying ten individuals cured at the tomb, all on or before 9 April at the very start of the cult. Hereford citizens will turn up in the miracle lists in later months and years, but never to such an extent. The average distance travelled by the rest of April's cured pilgrims,[10] calculated as a straight line to the cathedral, was twelve miles. Even such short journeys were difficult for the ill; one wonders about Milo Pychard's mood on his arrival, having rumbled along the springtime roads in his farm cart the relatively few miles from Strangford.[11] In any event, the local people represented in these pilgrims were probably accustomed to walking or riding into the cathedral city relatively often, so that reports about a new saint would quickly have been disseminated by, and amongst, them.

It is probable that in episcopal villages a bias already existed in favour of the dead bishop. This connection is illustrated in a miracle attributed in the thirteenth century to the saint of nearby Worcester. Waiting at Wulfstan's (d. 1095) shrine for a cure, a man from a village belonging to the monks of Worcester cathedral cried out, 'My lord, holy Wulfstan, am I not your villein, born and raised on the land of your church? Why do

8 *AA.SS,* 641; Vat. Cod. Lat. 4015, fo. 241r-v; see PRO, *List of Sheriffs* (1898), 59 and *Registrum Ricardi de Swinfield,* Canterbury & York Society VI, (1909), hereafter *Reg. Swinfield,* 386, 409.
9 *AA.SS,* 657, 649; EC., fo. 1v.
10 These came from forty-five villages, eight of them contributing two individuals.
11 For Milo, see note 8 above.

you despise me? Daily, as I watch, you cure foreigners and strangers and do not deign to consider me, your special servant.'[12] Perhaps something similar went through the minds of the villagers of Hereford episcopal estates when thinking of Cantilupe; for them a sense of identification with place of origin also entailed consciousness of specific overlordship—as in most medieval villages. Of the thirty Hereford episcopal estates separately listed in the late-thirteenth century 'Red Book',[13] eight supplied a cured pilgrim during April, 1287. On the first day (3 April), when five miracles occurred at the tomb, the very first of these involved Johannes de Masintone from Ledbury.[14] According to the 'Red Book' a certain Johannes de Masyntone held two virgates on the bishop's estate at Ledbury during the 1280s.[15] Next day two of the seven cured pilgrims had come from two other episcopal manors (one of the pilgrims, Juliana, had received alms from Cheveninge at one of those manors before her cure).[16] A week later one of these two manors supplied yet another pilgrim among the five cured that day (11 April).[17] Though there were many other obvious channels for the propagation of Thomas' cult which would have attracted the great majority of pilgrims, the foregoing suggests that—at least in the early stages—the tenants of episcopal manors felt, or may have been stimulated to feel, some special affinity with the dead bishop. Some villagers may have seen him, visiting his estates, before his fateful journey to Italy. It is likely, too, that as *he* perambulated, Swinfield more openly promoted devotion to Thomas among his manorial (and spiritual) subjects through the local clergy. Certainly in the years leading up to the cult (1285-86) he was encouraging his fellow-bishops to offer indulgences for prayers for Cantilupe's soul.[18]

Whatever had attracted them, the people healed during this first month were predominantly female (forty-five women to twenty-five men and one infant). The most commonly-reported miracles were cures of the crippled and blind, which accounted for fifty-eight of the seventy-one cases; the remainder involved other physical ailments. Summing up the characteristics of these pilgrims of April 1287, then, most of them were local, female, and claiming what may be termed 'traditional' miracles at

12 *Vita Wulfstani* of William of Malmesbury, ed. R. R. Darlington, Camden Soc. 3rd ser. XL (1928), 135.

13 'A Transcript of "The Red Book," a detailed account of the Hereford bishopric estates in the thirteenth century', ed. A. T. Bannister, Camden Soc., 3rd ser. XLI (*Camden Miscellany,* vol. XV, 1929), 1-36.

14 *AA.SS,* 649, 657 with wrong date; Vat. Cod. Lat. 4015, fo. 265r, EC., fo. 1r.

15 'Red Book' 18, and see vi for dates.

16 For Juliana see n. 6 above and 'Red Book' 8-9 for the estate; *AA.SS,* 650, 657; EC., fo. 1r; 'Red Book' 7-8. Unfortunately, the names of most tenants are omitted in Bannister's edition.

17 *AA.SS,* 649, 658; EC., fo. 2r; 'Red Book' 7-8.

18 See A Calendar of the earlier Hereford cathedral muniments, comp. B. G. Charles and H. D. Emmanuel, (National Library of Wales, 1955), (hereafter NLW), II, 571-73, 577; Vat. Cod. Lat. 4016, fo. 60r-61r, the 'excommunication' record.

Cantilupe's new tomb/shrine (though a few cures took place at the now-empty grave in the Virgin's chapel). Even before 1287 was over, however, this pattern began to alter, and in succeeding years the character of reported miracle-touched pilgrims changed unmistakably. This suggests modifications in the overall pattern of pilgrimage to Cantilupe's tomb.

Limitations of space necessitate a résumé of the subsequent 250-odd thirteenth-century miracles, i.e., from May 1287 through 1299. During this period pilgrims came from increasingly distant towns and villages, as news spread about the new thaumaturge. By the end of 1289 most recorded pilgrims lived some twenty-five to thirty-five miles from the tomb. During 1290 this figure jumped to about sixty miles, and for the next decade the average seldom dropped as low as forty miles. Possibly Swinfield's appeal to the pope for Thomas' canonization in 1290[19] and the joining of other bishops in this appeal during 1294 may account for this boost in notoriety. Another, related, alteration was a shift in the locale of the miracles themselves. At first—throughout most of 1287—most of the cures occurred at the tomb. Gradually, during 1288 and 1289, more and more people tended to experience their cures at home or elsewhere, afterwards going to Hereford to give thanks and an offering. From 1290 onwards, most miracles took place at sites other than the north transept of the cathedral. This outward movement, reflected in mileages and miracle venues, represents *inter alia* the migration of the idea that assistance, *suffragium,* could be obtained by calling on Thomas without being present at his tomb: his reputed 'sanctity' was now strong enough to be detached from the aura round his bones and to enter the expectant consciousness of those living outside this immediate region.

Concurrently, however, the number of miracles declined from the April peak; during May about thirty-eight were recorded and by December, 1287, only one. Overall, though, 1287 was to be the best year in the cult's history, with about 160 reported miracles. After that, year by year, the number of pilgrims reporting such wonders fell; during 1299 only ten were listed. Finally, as time passed the proportion of women reporting miracles steadily declined until, after 1288, most participants listed by shrine-registrars were male. Another change related to these alterations concerned the miracles themselves, which is best exemplified by the fourteenth-century pilgrims, below.

Though a decline in miracles before the turn of the century suggests a slowing down of incoming pilgrims generally and a natural cooling of popular enthusiasm, the cult gained momentum in other respects. A few bishops offered indulgences for pilgrimage to the tomb[20] while at the

19 *Reg. Swinfield,* 234-5.
20 NLW, II, 585, 588.

council of Westminster in September, 1294, Swinfield canvassed his fellow suffragans for letters of postulation to be sent to the pope,[21] as he did also at the May parliament of 1299.[22] Meanwhile pilgrims continued to deposit their coins, candles, wax images and silver models at the tomb; in 1290/91 the cathedral fabric roll showed an income of £178 from the shrine.[23] Subsidiary shrines were established around other relics such as Cantilupe's knife, bits of his hair-shirt, iron-link belt and shreds of his clothing, for example, in places as far apart as Leominster, Hambleden and Winchester, to say nothing of the heart at Ashridge.[24] Fragments of bone were also dispersed.[25]

Of course the main theatre was the new tomb, ever-guarded by its *custodes,* who were, however, less occupied during the fourteenth century. Whereas seventy-one miracles were registered during the single month of April in 1287, the total figure for the years 1300 through 1312 was seventy-five.[26] These tend to be more complex than the wonders acclaimed in 1287. Accidents involving infants and children are well-represented. Robert Russell accidentally drove his cart over his infant son's head, 'killing' him. After putting him to bed they measured him with string which was then used as the wick of a candle dedicated to Thomas—a common English curative technique.[27] In 1307 when the boy was examined by the canonization commissioners, they noticed that his head was rather narrow and peaked, which his father ascribed to the accident.[28] Many miracles were resuscitations of drowned children, usually pulled from rivers or ponds, though a Tewkesbury boy 'died' in a cask of beer and a London child drowned in a rain barrel by the hall door.[29] More typical was the case of the Lincolnshire parents who, unable to find their child, went frantically about *ubique lamentando et ululando;* finally it was seen in the river, to which everyone ran *ad illud horridum spectaculum.* After vows and measurement the child revived.[30] Another infant accident

21 *Reg. Swinfield,* 369-70 (Bath and Wells), Vat. Cod. Lat. 4015, fos. 260^{v}-263^{v} (Norwich, Exeter, Worcester, York), *Reg. Sutton,* Lincoln Record Soc. LX, 32 (Lincoln).

22 *Reg. Swinfield,* 358, Vat. Cod. Lat. 4015, fos. 260^{v}-261^{r} (Durham), 261^{v}-262^{r} (Winchester).

23 W. N. Yates, 'The fabric rolls of Hereford cathedral', *National Library of Wales Journal* XVIII (1973), 79.

24 Vat. Cod. Lat. 4015, fos. 88^{r-v}, 18^{r-v}, 27^{v}, 56^{v}, 35^{r}.

25 Vat. Cod. Lat. 4015, fos. 110^{r}-111^{r}—thumb-bone; J. Rosenthal, *The Purchase of Paradise* (1972), 87—finger-bone.

26 These are miracles to which a specific date can be assigned, or at least a specific year; a few are undated in the miracle-lists.

27 See Finucane, *Miracles and Pilgrims,* 95-6.

28 *AA.SS,* 621-23, 693; EC., fo. 37^{r}.

29 *AA.SS,* 646, 692; EC., fo. 36^{r-v}; *AA.SS,* 701.

30 EC., fo. 46^{r}; the manuscript contains several miracles (post-1307) not examined by the canonization commission or published in *AA.SS.*

victim was little Roger, who toddled into the dry moat or ditch around Conway castle one night while looking for his father. He revived, thanks to Thomas, even as the coroners were writing up their report.[31]

Other hazards of medieval life, involving adults, are revealed in the miracle-lists. A wine ship from Gascony, for instance, was caught in a storm in the Irish Sea. After her Bristol master advised his crew to pray to Cantilupe, the storm abated.[32] Around 1302 a man swore at the tomb that the flames threatening his house were extinguished after he bent a penny and vowed the coin to Thomas.[33] Normally, pennies were only bent over the ill or 'dead' to effect a miracle.[34] Violence, claimed by some to be pandemic in medieval society, is illustrated by a few wounding cases, like the Berkeley youth whose leg had been pierced with an arrow but was subsequently healed with Thomas' help.[35] Another kind of violence befell a Doncaster man, robbed by a forest gang who cut out his tongue. After promising pilgrimage to Thomas' shrine and experiencing a traumatic vision, the victim recovered his speech.[36]

As the foregoing shows, some miracles entailed visionary experiences, like the one recounted by a cleric of Aymer de Valence, Earl of Pembroke. His illness ended after a vow to Thomas and a vision, in which an elegantly-vested bishop three feet in height rubbed him down with a white cloth, and so cured him.[37] His physical ailment had something to do with a 'swelling' of the body which could not be remedied, either *medicis* or *surgicis*. Some of the physical problems reported in the fourteenth century were more elaborate than the simple biblical cures of 1287. A London woman suffering from stone had a penny bent over her for Thomas. Later, as she stepped into her bath, she was painlessly relieved of this burden (as big as a hen's egg).[38]

Finally, Cantilupe's powers extended to animals and birds as well as to the elements and man. A Cornish knight's falcon was trampled by his squire's horse. The knight bent a penny over it for Thomas then, cradling it in his hood or cap, he rode towards his *mansionem*. The bird recovered en route.[39] Felicia's mare dropped dead in a field; Felicia, thrusting her hand down its throat, felt no breath or pulse. They measured it to Thomas, without apparent effect. Next morning two servants sent out to skin the horse found it alive and well.[40]

31 *AA.SS*, 626-28, 630-31; Vat. Cod. Lat. 4015, fo. 189r; EC., fo. 38v-39r; the miracle was mentioned in the bull of canonization.

32 *AA.SS*, 692; EC., fo. 36r.

33 *AA.SS*, 655, 692-3; EC., fo. 36v.

34 Finucane, *Miracles and Pilgrims*, 94-5.

35 *AA.SS*, 655, 693; EC., fo. 36v.

36 *AA.SS*, 694-5; EC., fo. 38v.

37 EC., fo. 43v-44r.

38 *ibid.*, fo. 41r-v.

39 *ibid.*, fo. 43r.

40 *ibid.*, fo. 43r-44v.

Besides these unusual examples, about half of the seventy-five miracles conform to the type familiar in all medieval saints' cults: the healing of the blind, the lame, the crippled. On the other hand, the rise in reported accidents, animal cures, natural or man-made catastrophes suggests that Thomas was now being called upon in the extraordinary—as well as in the normal—pitfalls of life. People of greater social diversity, with more varied needs, than the crowds round the tomb in 1287, now turned to Cantilupe for succour. About half of the recorded pilgrims of the 1300-1312 period were men; women and infants were equally represented in the remainder. These changes in sex profiles reflect the different circumstances of the miracles as well as higher male physical mobility.[41] As for the distances, excluding two pilgrims from Hereford itself (and one from Ireland), the average of the fifty-two identifiable fourteenth-century sites (some contributing three and four pilgrims) was seventy-two miles. By the early fourteenth century, Thomas' influence extended to nearly every English county from Cornwall to Yorkshire and included the east coast of Ireland as well.[42] The miracle-reporting pilgrims who came from these diverse places told of experiences that suggest a more extensive and flexible awareness of Cantilupe as a source of spiritual power. Presumably this was true of 'ordinary' pilgrims as well.

Even so, in addition to a marked decrease in recorded pilgrims, there is other evidence that pilgrimage to the tomb was on the wane. When the canonization commissioners made an inventory of the shrine offerings in 1307, they found silver ships and golden rings, knives and anchors and precious stones and nearly 2,000 wax images of humans, animals, eyes and limbs. Yet some former shrine-keepers claimed that only a fraction of the wax offerings remained: most had been consumed with age or melted down for other cathedral uses.[43] Though some votives were presented even as the commissioners carried out their work at Hereford, it was a collection in decline.

Nevertheless, as a result of this commission which only began its work many years after enthusiastic pilgrims had ceased to crowd round the tomb to gape at miracles, Thomas was eventually canonized. Finally, at mid-century, the bones were translated back to the east end of the church, site of the first miracle announced by cathedral bells and the *Te Deum Laudamus* more than sixty years earlier. A transient increase in pilgrims and offerings no doubt followed Thomas' canonization and translation, after which the cult enjoyed an unspectacular, more dignfied, existence to the end of the Middle Ages.

41 *cf.* Finucane, *Miracles and Pilgrims,* 142-51.
42 *AA.SS,* 693; EC., fo. 37r.
43 Vat. Cod. Lat. 4015, fo. 74r-76r; *cf.* Finucane, *Miracles and Pilgrims,* 98, 180 for this inventory.

THE EFFECT OF THE PILGRIM CULT OF ST THOMAS CANTILUPE ON HEREFORD CATHEDRAL

Penelope E. Morgan

The aim of this chapter is not to give an architectural history,[1] but to show from surviving documentary evidence the effect of the pilgrim cult of St Thomas Cantilupe on the fabric of Hereford cathedral.

As christian piety began increasingly to be expressed by personal endowments of chantries, the provision of masses and obits, and by gifts to the churches, so more altars and more space became necessary, and gradually the old Norman buildings were adapted and new ones built to meet the need. The cult of saints and veneration of relics, very important features of medieval worship, became one of the chief, if not essential source of revenue for providing larger and more magnificent buildings.[2]

At Hereford attempts were made to re-promote the cult of St Ethelbert and about 1200 the chapter urged Giraldus Cambrensis, the most popular writer of his age, to compile a life of the saint to attract pilgrims and bring money which was needed for extensions at the east end including an ambulatory and Lady chapel—the latter a superb example of Early English craftsmanship which probably took over thirty-five years to build. Soon after, the Norman clerestory of the choir was replaced to give more light and the stone vault was erected. During the episcopacy of Peter de Aquablanca (1240-68) work began on the north transept: the possibility being that this arm of the Norman cathedral may never have been completed. The French style of architecture, similar to some in Westminster abbey, reflects the influence of this Savoyard bishop whose beautiful tomb is at the end of the aisle, and who left twenty marks to the work of the cathedral.[3]

At this time there were no special endowments for the fabric, although it seems to have been the practice of the chapter to allocate a canon's share of the commons for that purpose[4] and in 1246 Pope Innocent IV authorised an enforced proportionate payment from the prebendaries

1 For the architecture see G. Marshall, *Hereford cathedral: its evolution and growth,* (Worcester, [1951]); and Royal Commission on Historical Monuments England, *An Inventory of the historical monuments in Herefordshire,* (London, 1931-34), I, 90-120.

2 For a study of church building in the middle ages and its finance see C. R. Cheney, *Medieval texts and studies,* (Oxford, 1973), No. 18.

3 'The Will of Peter de Aquablanca bishop of Hereford', ed. by C. E. Woodruff, *Camden miscellany XIV,* (1926). He was also a benefactor in his lifetime.

4 W. W. Capes, ed., *Charters and records of Hereford cathedral,* (Hereford 1908), 130 n.2.

towards the building expenses.[5] This supplemented the limited income from pilgrims, indulgences, mortuary dues, legacies and gifts. There were also special appeals. In 1281 Bishop John le Breton issued an indulgence[6] to those who contributed towards the fabric of the Lady chapel and its ministers, and in 1274 the sub-dean exhorted the clergy of the deanery to give generously towards its lights, altar and ornaments.[7] Although documentary evidence of this period is scant it gives the impression that rebuilding and alterations were carried out slowly and that the chapter were struggling to raise money to meet the cost.

When Thomas Cantilupe was enthroned in 1275 the nave, south transept and treasury (now the inner vestry) were still Norman throughout and the north-east and south-east transept areas were unfinished. After his death in 1292 his bones were brought to Hereford and buried under a stone before the altar in the Lady chapel. Immediately his successor, Richard Swinfield (bishop from 1283-1316) his former chaplain and friend, in co-operation with the chapter, set about trying to secure his canonization. A new tomb was prepared in the north transept—the most recent part of the cathedral, which was easier of access and where there was more light and space. Originally intended as an altar tomb it was converted within a few years, as stories of Cantilupe's sanctity spread, into a shrine with a super-structure to hold a feretrum. The beautiful base, carved with knights and naturalistic foliage, and one small brass representing St Ethelbert, once part of a large brass memorial on the tomb, remain, but there are no records of the superstructure.[8] On Maundy Thursday, 1287, Cantilupe's bones were translated with great ceremony to this shrine, and for the next twenty years pilgrims flocked to Hereford and their offerings enabled the chapter to embark on lavish rebuilding to enhance the cathedral.

Work started almost at once after Cantilupe's death as in January 1282/3 Archbishop Pecham issued an indulgence to those who contributed to the upkeep and repair of the fabric.,[9] and other bishops did likewise between 1284 and 1291.[10] Authorities disagree as to the exact order of rebuilding. George Marshall in his scholarly and carefully reasoned history[11]

5 Hereford cathedral archive (hereafter HCA.) 2516.
6 HCA. 1396.
7 HCA. 1410.
8 For details of tomb see G. Marshall, 'The shrine of St Thomas de Cantilupe in Hereford cathedral' in *Trans. Woolhope Naturalists' Field Club,* XXVII, (1930-32), 34-50; and E. G. Benson 'The lost brass of the Cantilupe shrine' in *Trans. W.N.F.C.,* XXXIII, (1949-51), 68-76. The east end was wrongly moved away from the wall in 1857.
9 HCA. 1425.
10 HCA. 1420; HCA. 1422-1426.
11 *op cit.,* 91-92.

IV. Tomb of Saint Thomas Cantilupe in Hereford cathedral.

suggests that the inner north porch was enlarged *c.* 1250-1260, followed by the north-east transept, choir and nave aisle between *c.* 1290-1294, and the central and western towers *c.* 1295-1315. On the other hand Richard Morris,[12] who made a detailed study of the mouldings, seems to agree more with George Gilbert Scott[13] and points out a logical sequence in view of the pilgrim cult. The inner north porch (which he thinks is *c.* 1288-1290) and the nave aisle formed the main entrance to the north transept for pilgrims to the shrine and would be the first parts to be enhanced. Although Cantilupe was not canonized until 1320, it was hoped this would have taken place soon after 1306, and before 1317 plans had been made for a more sumptuous shrine in the Lady chapel as Bishop Swinfield, who died that year, left 100 marks in his will for the construction of one.[14] Hence the second stage of the building would be the north choir aisle and north-east transept making a ceremonial route for pilgrims with the tombs of former bishops lining the way. But Swinfield himself was buried in the north-east transept and other members of his family are nearby, which may indicate that this particular work was carried out during his episcopacy. Whatever the exact order, evidence points to the fact that after 1282 Hereford cathedral was the centre of feverish activity with a small army of masons, stone-cutters, carpenters and other craftsmen, and that much rebuilding was carried out in a comparatively short time. Although many masons' marks have now been obliterated or may never have been visible, only fourteen are left in the Lady chapel and crypt and two in the north transept, whereas no less than forty are still visible in the aisles, north-east transept and porch.[15]

The only fabric accounts extant for this period are those kept by John de Brecone, chaplain, for Michaelmas 1290 to Michaelmas 1291.[16] The total receipts amounted to £286.1.8½d, equivalent to at least £157,300 today.[17] Of this sum no less than £178.10.7d (=£97,900) came from the tomb of the 'Blessed Thomas' and £30.14.0d from the alms box. These two items therefore account for nearly three-quarters of the total. The number of pilgrims involved can be estimated when it is remembered that the

12 R. Morris, 'The Remodelling of the Hereford aisles' in *Journal of the British Archaeological Association, 3rd ser.*, XXXVIII, (1974), 21-39.

13 G. G. Scott, 'Hereford cathedral' in *Archaeological Journal,* XXXIV, (1897), 325-348.

14 HCA. 1068. He also gave 20 marks for glass and 50 marks for building a chapter house. The legacy was not acknowledged by the chapter until February, 1336/7.

15 Royal Commission on Historical Monuments, *op.cit.* III, 222-223.

16 HCA. 2368. See also G. Marshall, *op. cit.*, 95-101; and W. N. Yates, 'The Fabric rolls of Hereford cathedral, 1290/1 and 1386/7', in *National Library of Wales Journal,* XVIII, (1973), 79-86.

17 Assuming £1 in 1290 equals approximately £550 to-day. See H. Kraus, *Gold was the mortar,* (London, 1979), 135, 137.

average offering would probably have been less than a penny.[18] The only other large amounts were £34.17.5¾d from the sale of the canons' commons (or allowances) and £17.13.2d from the clergy of the diocese. £3.1.6d came from Lydney, £15.8.6¾d from rents and arrears; £1.8.8¼d from the bakehouse; and £4.1.5¾d from legacies, obits and mortuary dues. Sales brought in 3/- for broken silver, 3/- for lead and 3d for wool. This emphasises how much the chapter relied on income from pilgrims for their building operations.

The expenses throw much light on the activities of that year. Master Hugh the mason (probably a part-time overseer) had a fee of £5.0.0d per annum, and some idea of the number of men employed is shown by the fact that the wages of hired masons amounted to £117.3.5¼d, and of stone-cutters and boys to £75.7.10d. The charges of smiths for their work came to £11.3.3¾d and ironwork for eight windows cost £4.0.0d. George Marshall[19] suggests that these were the four in the transept, two in the choir aisle and two in the north nave aisle between the north transept and the porch; but Richard Morris[20] thinks they were all in the aisles. Plasterers' wages and work accounted for 10/10d, lime cost £10.3.9½d and miscellaneous items such as bowls, ropes, wattle, etc. totalled 17/10d. The wages of carpenters and the cost of timber came to £5.19.1d, glass cost 12/1½d and the glaziers' wages for repairing were 8/6d. One of the most costly items was lead showing that the roofs were being covered in this material, probably replacing thatch. John de Brecone paid £14.12.6½d for lead, and in addition twelve loads were bought by the treasurer for £21.0.0d,[21] not included in the accounts. There is also a receipt dated 11th November, 1291 from Richard Tyrel of Little Marcle for £4.0.0d in part payment of £10.10.0d for lead he had sold to the stewards of the chapter.[22] Carriage costs were low—only £21.5.7¼d—as wood and stones were brought from Ayrcrop (at Allensmore), Aconbury and Lude (Lyde) all near Hereford. A quarry at Aycrop with right of way cost 3/6d. John de Brecone, who was probably clerk of the works, had a salary of £3.0.0d and his clerk 10/-d. Eight pence was paid for parchment bringing the grand total expenditure to £270.19.0¾d. The wages of workmen are

18 R. C. Finucane, *Miracles and pilgrims,* (London, 1977), 180. This refers to figures suggesting that about 1,200 Hereford-bound pilgrims passed through Worcester alone each year.

19 *op.cit.,* 96.

20 R. Morris, *Decorated architecture in Herefordshire,* (unpublished doctoral thesis, 1972), 62.

21 One cart-load was approximately 19 cwt. sufficient to cover about 160 sq. ft., therefore the total sum for lead would cover approximately 4,160 sq. ft. See L. F. Salzman, *Building in England down to 1540,* (Oxford, 1952), 263.

22 HCA. 2530.

recorded for each quarter[23] showing how much less work was done during the winter. From December to March the masons were paid £10.18.0d; whereas between July and December the total was £56.18.10d.[24]

In July, 1307, Hugh the barber, the sixth witness called on behalf of the chapter before the commission of inquiry into the life and miracles of St Thomas held in London, reported that many legacies had been received, and out of the oblations at the tomb a beautiful bell-tower had been built and the church refurbished.[25] When the commission moved to Hereford later in the year it recorded that the offerings at the tomb had been so bountiful that they had provided for the necessary outlay on two new 'naves' and on part of the great tower (*fuerunt cathedralis ecclesia de duabus navibus ampliata, et fabricatum in parte maximum campanile*).[26] Does the word *navis* refer to 'a bay' or 'an aisle'? Then came disaster. The additional weight of the heightened tower with its beautiful ball-flower ornament was too great and the foundations began to give way. To add to the difficulties, money was becoming scarce as fewer pilgrims came to Hereford, and in 1319 the chapter appealed to Pope John XXII[27] to allow them to appropriate the revenues of the church of Shinfield with its chapelry of Swallowfield in Berkshire to the fabric account of the cathedral which then required great expenditure to save it from ruin. They stated that the old foundations had been considered sound by skilled architects and that they had expended large sums of money to a total of 20,000 marks (£13,333.13.4d) and more on many superstructures of sumptuous workmanship, but that now, owing to weakness of the foundations it was threatened with ruin and the only remedy was to rebuild from the foundations. The expense of this, and also the cost of the canonization of St Thomas had weighed heavily on them. The state of the cathedral must have been a little exaggerated as there is no evidence that it was re-built from the foundations. As a result, the Pope issued a bull on the 26th January, 1319/20[28] allowing the chapter to appropriate the rents, amounting to £20 per annum, to the fabric fund to help with the expenses of

23 In 1280 London master masons, carpenters, tilers and plasterers were paid the following rates daily:

Michaelmas to Martinmas	4d in all or	1½d and food.
Martinmas to Candlemas	3d ,, ,, ,,	1d ,, ,,
Candlemas to Easter	4d ,, ,, ,,	1½d ,, ,,
Easter to Michaelmas	5d ,, ,, ,,	2d ,, ,,

See Salzman, *op.cit.*, 69.

24 It is worth mentioning that Mr. A. Pailing, the present stonemason working on the cathedral, estimates it would take him a year to quarry, carve and erect one of the four-light windows in the nave aisles.

25 Vat. Cod. Lat. 4015, fo. 28v.

26 *ibid.*, fo. 313.

27 HCA. 1320.

28 HCA. 1858. The Chapter had held the advowson since 1269, HCA. 1397, HCA. 1145.

rebuilding 'so long as the work shall last'. The income from Shinfield continues to be allocated to the fabric fund to-day! ! ! The same year the pope issued an indulgence[29] to all penitents contributing to the work.

Then, at last, in October, 1320, came the bull of canonization[30] which it was hoped would inaugurate a new wave of popularity to help fill the coffers. On the 18th November, 1320, Walter Reynolds, archbishop of Canterbury, wrote to all the clergy of the diocese exhorting them to contribute towards building a shrine to St Thomas and to maintain the fabric.[31] An appeal was also made to the whole country by Edward II who issued Letters Patent on the 20th November, to all his bailiffs concerning the collection of alms for the shrine and church, and instructing them to raise the greatest possible levies.[32] The archdeaconry of Norfolk contributed no less than £45.4.2d.[33] Bishops issued indulgencies[34] and John de Aquablanca, the dean, who died in 1320 left 20/- towards a new tomb after canonization.[35]

Immediately work on the new shrine was expedited. On the 6th December, 1320, John de Werlyngworthe, goldsmith of London, gave a receipt for £10 for making sundry ornaments for the shrine.[36] (It was probably he who became a goldsmith of note in Exeter in 1327.[37]) The following March, Adam, a dealer in marble, received £10 in part payment of £40 owing for marble supplied for the shrine.[38] Adam of Corfe settled in London and died there in 1331, but as Adam the marbler he undertook to pave four bays of the new Lady chapel of St Paul's in 1313 and also supplied marble columns for St Stephen's chapel.[39] In 1321 William Sprot of London had £80 for electrum[40] and Michael the image maker of London gave a receipt on the 19th June for full payment of his work in fashioning the shrine according to an agreement, and also for his expenses in coming to Hereford, staying there and returning to London.[41] It is clear that some of the best craftsmen available were employed on the new shrine in the Lady chapel. Leland refers to St Thomas being 'rychely

29 PRO, *Calendar of Papal Registers, Papal Letters II, 1305-1342,* 196.
30 HCA. 1445.
31 HCA. 1444.
32 HCA. 1435; PRO, *Calendar of Patent Rolls, 1317-1321,* 526.
33 HCA. 1446.
34 HCA. 1428-1431.
35 HCA. 2883.
36 HCA. 1440.
37 C. J. Jackson, *English goldsmiths and their marks,* (London, 1905), 130.
38 HCA. 1437.
39 J. Harvey, *Medieval craftsmen,* (London, 1975), 130.
40 Capes, *op.cit.,* 195. Electrum was probably a kind of brass known as latten, such as used for monumental brasses.
41 HCA. 1436.

shrined'[42] and it must have been a magnificent erection, which, however, was destined to remain un-used until 1349, and was completely destroyed at the Reformation.

But even after canonization St Thomas never regained popularity, and following the dramatic death of Edward II in 1327 no doubt many pilgrims were diverted to Gloucester. By 1336 the numbers of pilgrims had decreased to such an extent that Pope Benedict XII issued a mandate to reduce the tax of twenty marks previously made on the wax offered at the shrine; the decrease in devotion having reduced the yearly amount to barely six pounds of wax.[43] Fewer pilgrims meant less money. In 1324 the chapter sold (or mortgaged) for £20 to Thomas Chandos, archdeacon and canon, one of the six books left by Alan de Creppinge to the library 'on condition that they should not be removed'.[44] Things must have been bad! Some help may have come from Lady Joanna de Bohun's endowment to the Lady chapel as any residue was to be devoted to the fabric[45] and then in July, 1329, Adam de Orleton, then bishop of Worcester, agreed to pay an additional £20 rent for his lease of Shinfield, which he had held for several yers, having heard of the ruinous state of the cathedral. The additional rent was to be used for the fabric and for no other purpose![46]

Thus the rebuilding of the cathedral, started in such lavish style when money was pouring in from pilgrims, had to be curtailed and the arrival of the Black Death in 1348/9 probably halted all progress for a few years, for it was not until the 25th October, 1349, that the saint's relics were moved to the new shrine. This probably gave rise to a brief revival of the cult, but by 1355 Bishop Trilleck was offering to try and procure indulgencies from all the bishops assembled in parliament towards the fabric. He also appointed an agent to collect alms and ordered non-residents in the diocese to pay a portion of any lease made of their churches. Fines levied at his visitation were also to be allocated to the same cause.[47] This all shows how desperate was the need for money.

The final decline of the cult is also clearly shown by comparing the accounts for 1290/91 with those for 1383/84[48] the next surviving set. The total receipts were £75.7.8½d which included the £40 from Shinfield. The shrine only produced £2.13.4d and the alms box £3.0.0d. The total expenditure was £40.10.7½d for small items and repairs, including a tiler

42 *Itinerary of Wales, c. 1536-1539,* ed. by L. T. Smith, (London, 1906), 48.
43 PRO, *Calendar of Papal Registers, Papal Letters, II,* 531.
44 HCA. 2885.
45 HCA. 3202; HCA. 2165; HCA. 1817.
46 HCA. 1375.
47 HCA. 2453.
48 HCA. R.621.

for six weeks @ 3/6d per week; two carpenters for nine weeks and one day @ 2/- per week; two masons with assistants @ 3/6d per week; a plumber and one assistant for six weeks work on the nave of the Lady chapel @ 10/- per week. In 1386/87[49] receipts from the shrine had dropped to 26/8d and there was only 19/4½d in the alms box; the total income being £78.15.7d. The expenditure was £55.8.4d on small items of repair only. There was no income from the shrine by 1446/7.[50]

Some work continued after 1349, but at a much slower rate and on necessary re-building and completion rather than enhancement. On 9 April, 1359 the chapter entered into a contract with John of Evesham, a mason of Worcester, to work on the cathedral and instruct others for the rest of his life for 3/- weekly and a white loaf daily. If ill he was to receive the same sum for two weeks and then 1/- weekly until fit. He was also granted a house in Castle Street.[51] In 1364 Thomas de Cantebrugge agreed to build a chapter house and the chapels of St John and St Michael [in the south east transept] within seven years.[52] When it is remembered that Bishop Swinfield left money for building a chapter house in 1317[53] it is clear that after about 1320 the chapter must have been struggling for finance or the work would have been completed long before. An agreehent with Thomas Deuyas, mason of Hereford, for building the 'upright werke' of one wall of the cloister near the chapter house[54] probably drawn up about this time was not implemented and work on the new cloister was delayed until 1412[55] and it may not have been completed until about 1490.[56]

In conclusion it is no exaggeration to say that the cult of St Thomas Cantilupe had an enormous effect on Hereford Cathedral. Without the resulting financial aid there would never have been sufficient money for so much re-building and enhancement, for ever since that time the chapter has had great difficulty in finding funds to keep the fabric in repair.

49 HCA. 2371.
50 HCA. 2370.
51 HCA. 2372.
52 HCA. 2374. The re-modelling of the south-east transept was delayed partly by the Black Death.
53 HCA. 1068.
54 HCA. 2375.
55 HCA. 2369.
56 G. Marshall, *op. cit.*, 130ff.

A SAINT IN THE CALENDAR: THE EFFECT OF THE CANONIZATION OF ST THOMAS CANTILUPE ON THE LITURGY

by Philip Barrett

In April 1320, Pope John XXII issued a bull of canonization for Thomas Cantilupe and appointed 2 October as his feast-day.[1] This was kept locally as a principal double. Shortly before the first opportunity to keep the feast, Adam de Orleton, bishop of Hereford from 1317-1327, wrote to the archbishop of Canterbury, Walter Reynolds, asking for the feast to be observed 'in your city, diocese and province so that the first coming feast may be kept with all devotion and solemnity'.[2] Later that same month, he called upon the faithful to celebrate the feast and promised indulgences to penitents who visited the shrine.[3] The date of the saint's death, however, was not 2 October but 25 August, and this day, known as the Deposition of St Thomas, was observed as a semi-double. This was obligatory only in the cathedral.[4] A third feast-day was added in 1349 when John de Trillek, bishop of Hereford from 1344-1361, translated the saint's relics from the north transept to a new shrine in the Lady Chapel on 25 October.[5] This day was also kept as a principal double.[6] Thus, by the middle of the fourteenth century, Thomas Cantilupe was commemorated on three separate days in the Hereford calendar. The purpose of this essay is to give a brief examination of the texts which were written and chosen for these three days.

We will examine first the propers for the Mass. The introit for the Deposition is *Statuit ei,* but both the other two feasts have a specially written introit, *Gaudeamus omnes.* The one for the Translation is clearly based on that of the main feast, which is, in turn, based on that of St Thomas Becket. The psalm, however, is different: *Domine Deus noster* on 2 October and *Cantate Domino canticum novum* on 25 October. The Kyrie *Conditor* is prescribed for both the October feasts. A different collect is used for all three feasts, each of which is characterised by a particular felicity and confidence in its choice of words. The collect for 25 October is loosely based on that of 25 August. The Epistle for 25 August and 2 October is Ecclesiasticus, chapter 44, verses 20-23, but on 25

1 E. M. Jancey, *St Thomas of Hereford* (Hereford 1978), 17.
2 *Registrum Ade de Orleton* . . . ed. A. T. Bannister, Canterbury and York Society (hereafter C & Y Soc.), (1908), 139-140. Translation in E. N. Dew, *Extracts from the cathedral registers,* (Hereford, 1932), 45-6.
3 *ibid.,* 142-143.
4 *The Hereford Breviary,* ed. W. H. Frere and L. E. G. Brown, Henry Bradshaw Society (London, 1904) I, 426.
5 *Registrum Johannis de Trillek* . . . ed. J. H. Parry (C & Y Soc.), (1912), 147-8.
6 *The Hereford Breviary, op. cit.,* I, 426.

October some verses from Isaiah were preferred (Isaiah, chapter 68, verses 10, 11, 12 & 14). The gradual on 25 August and 2 October is the standard *Ecce sacerdos magnus,* with an identical verse after the alleluya: *Tu stirps praeclara vita.* The feast of the Translation, however, has a different text: *Exaltent eum in ecclesia plebis.*

The sequences for 2 October and 25 October are very interesting, and may be based on some of the wording used in the bull of canonization.[7] The sequence for 2 October, *Magnae lucem caritatis,* begins in the familiar 8.8.7.D. metre, to which it returns after some lines of 8.7. The sequence for 25 October, *Novi plausus incrementum,* is rather longer and employs an 8.8.7 metre for each of its eighteen verses.

The same gospel, Luke, chapter 11, verses 33-36, is used for all three feasts, which also share a common offertory, *Veritas mea.* The secret for 25 August and 2 October is identical, *Gloriosi pontificis tui Thomae,* but 25 October uses instead *Hostias et preces.* A similar divergence is found for the communion text, which on 25 August and 2 October is *Beatus servus,* while 25 October has *Magna est gloria,* while for the post-communion prayer the first two feasts use *Sumpta Domine,* while the Feast of the Translation uses *Munera Domine.*

The octaves of both the October feasts were observed, but shared common texts. The epistle was *Ecce sacerdos* and the gradual was *Inveni David,* but with *Tu stirps praeclara* as the alleluya verse, as on the feast. A different (and much shorter) sequence, *Summi regis in honore,* was provided. I am grateful to Dr Christopher Page for pointing out that this sequence is clearly based on the one used during the octave of St Ethelbert the King (20 May), who was, with Our Lady, a patron of the cathedral. There are some minor differences in some of the other texts. The texts used at the votive mass of St Thomas are derived from those used on 25 August and during the octave of 2 October.[8]

The texts used at the offices on the three feast-days are much more difficult to summarise, and the task is further complicated by the fact that one of the manuscripts, a small 15th century breviary in Worcester cathedral library, has some marked differences from the other sources. Most of the material is individually composed, but some texts are identical with those used in the mass, while others are repeated at various points during the offices on the three feasts.

7 25 August uses the sequence for 2 October.

8 For the mass texts, *cf. Missale ad usum percelebris ecclesiae Herefordensis,* ed. W. G. Henderson (1874, new ed. 1969), 314-5 (Deposition), 333-6 (Feast & Octave), 347-50 (Translation), 403-4 (Votive mass).

First, we shall consider the texts which are also used at mass. We have seen that *Ecce sacerdos* was used as the gradual on 2 October, and it is also employed as the chapter at both first and second Vespers for the feast of the Deposition and for the main feast. It is also used as the chapter at Lauds on 2 October and at Vespers during the octave. The collects used on all three days are the same as those at mass, while the sequence *Summi regis,* provided for use during the octave of 2 October, reappears as an alternative to the hymn *Gaude mater et ecclesia* at second Vespers on 2 October. The Worcester breviary used the gradual text *Tu stirps* as an antiphon to the Magnificat at first Vespers of this feast. *Gaude mater ecclesia* is the usual hymn at Vespers, but *Iste confessor* is used at Matins on 2 October and *Jesu redemptor* at Lauds on that day. The same antiphon to the Magnificat, *O pater pietatis,* is used at first Vespers for 25 August and 2 October, but this is replaced by another, *Sicut fragrant* for second Vespers of these two feasts. A rubric for 25 October adds that everything at the offices on that day should be as on 2 October, with the exception of the readings and the collect.

Some of the readings are directly inspired by the bull of canonization. For example, the third reading at Matins on 2 October uses the words found in the bull: *'Abstinens etiam a vino sepius, sciens quod in ipso lubricum latet carnis, sciens etiam quod Deus promittur in objectum et premium mundis corde; a juventate sua castitatis pulchritudinem adamavit'.* (Often going without wine, conscious that in it lies dangers of the flesh, knowing also the reward God promises to the pure in heart, from his youth he embraced the beauty of chastity). The next two readings are from the passages which follow immediately in the bull, and the second reading uses the sentence which immediately precedes the one quoted above. Again, the antiphon *O pater pietatis* continues with the words *O gemma presulum,* a phrase which is also to be found in the bull.[9] The remaining readings give a succinct account of various episodes in the saint's life, his death in Italy and the journey of his bones back to England, and the circumstances surrounding their translation in 1349.

The compiler of these services is unknown. Bishops Orleton and Trillek are unlikely to have undertaken the task personally, though they must have encouraged one of their household or someone on the cathedral staff to undertake the work. Something of the amount of work involved can be glimpsed from the successful attempt by Edmund Lacy, bishop of Hereford 1417-20, and later bishop of Exeter, to introduce the feast of St Raphael on 5 October.

9 The texts of the offices are in *The Hereford Breviary, op. cit.*, II, 309-11 (Deposition), 345-54, 361 (Feast), 380-3, 385-6 (Translation). The text of the papal bull is in W. W. Capes, ed. *Charters and records of Hereford cathedral* (Hereford, 1908). A partial translation is given by E. N. Dew, *op. cit.*, 50-52.

Authorising the feast for use in the diocese of Hereford, Thomas Spofford (bishop of Hereford 1422-48) related how Lacy 'has provided and published his own history of the said blessed Raphael, with nine lections, antiphons, responds, collects and chapters, with complete Mass and prayers adapted thereto, collected from the sacred codes of approved reading, to the praise of God and in memory of the said heavenly spirit Raphael, after the manner of a simple feast of nine lections, to be sung annually for ever in his cathedral of Exeter and anywhere else in his diocese, as devotion shall prompt, together with plain chant and notes and tones and small notes added. . . We order and decree the commemoration or feast of St Raphael to be included in the other feasts of nine lections of our cathedral, with nine proper lections, hymns, responses, antiphons, versicles, chapters, collects and invitatory, with mass for the proper. . . .'[10]

Lacy's Exeter register refers to the authorisation of the observance of the feast at Ottery St Mary, and says that the office having been compiled by the bishop, it was examined and approved by John Snetysham, chancellor of Exeter cathedral, acting as apostolic delegate, together with Thomas Gascoyne, chancellor of Oxford university and five other masters in theology, and by the minister and definitors-general of the order of Friars Minor in England, and other theologians of the order, to whom the bishop had submitted it.[11]

One may, however, hazard a guess—yet to be substantiated by evidence—about the authorship of the propers for 25 August and 2 October. The chancellor of Hereford cathedral in 1320 was Robert of Gloucester, doctor of civil law at Oxford university. Born around 1252 he remembered Cantilupe's Oxford days[12] and was appointed by him as a canon of Hereford by December 1279, when Cantilupe granted him a house near the cathedral.[13] He was a member of the cathedral foundation until his death over forty years later in 1322. He was a member of Cantilupe's household and was sent by Bishop Swinfield as his proctor to the Roman Curia in 1283, where he stayed for at least two years.[14] For a while he was chancellor to Archbishop Winchelsea. He was an important witness at the commission of inquiry into the canonization of Cantilupe in 1307 and is supposed to be the author of a metrical chronicle of English history.[15] He

10 *Registrum Thome Spofford, Episcopi Herefordensis* . . . ed. A. T. Bannister, C & Y Soc., (1919), 267-79; *cf.* E. N. Dew, *op. cit.*, 113-115.

11 *The Register of Edmund Lacy, bishop of Exeter,* 1420-1455, ed. G. R. Dunstan, C & Y Soc. (Torquay, 1967) III, 340-4, and related documents on following pages.

12 *The Register of Thomas de Cantilupe* . . . transcr. R. G. Griffiths, introd. by W. W. Capes, Cantilupe Soc., (1906), xiv.

13 *ibid.*, 244.

14 *Registrum Ricardi de Swinfield* . . . ed. W W. Capes, C & Y Soc., (1909), 66, 96, 98, 99, 101.

15 A. B. Emden, *Biographical register of the university of Oxford* (Oxford, 1958), II, 773-4.

was clearly a senior figure in the Close at Hereford, one who had venerated Cantilupe all his life and who lived long enough to receive the news of his canonization. He would be with his literary gifts, the obvious person for Bishop Orleton to turn to for help in compiling the liturgy of the saint, and one may tentatively ascribe it to him. There is, however, no verbal correspondence between his evidence and the unattributed readings and propers, which may have come from a report to the Pope by the commissioners of the process of canonization.

There is no such likely candidate for the authorship of the propers for 25 October. Indeed, it should be remembered that special liturgies were often composed in advance of the actual canonization of a saint, and even for some who failed to achieve canonization. For example, an office was composed for the feast of John Dalderby, Bishop of Lincoln, who died in 1320, although repeated efforts during the next few years failed to achieve his canonization. Another example is that of Simon de Montfort, in whose honour some Franciscans composed an office.[16]

The liturgies composed for the three feasts of St Thomas of Hereford give us a good insight into the way in which such services were put together in the late middle ages. Patterns from other feasts are used, but not slavishly, and the obvious honour and esteem in which St Thomas was held shines through the words in which his sanctity was celebrated.[17]

16 D. H. Farmer, *The Oxford dictionary of saints* (Oxford, 1978), 422-3, 426.

17 This essay has been based on the printed editions of the missal and breviary referred to in footnotes 4 and 8. Since these texts were published, a number of other Hereford mss. have come to light. Three of these are in the British Library: the so-called Dewick missal (Add. MS. 39675), an incomplete Gradual (Harl. 3965) and an Ordinal (Harl. 2983). An early 15th century Breviary at the Bodleian Library (Ms. Laud Misc. 299/752)) has some material for the feasts of St Thomas. Another volume (MS. Rawl. c. 301) includes a mass of this saint, and MS. Lat. liturg. b.7, nos. 13 and 15 has a fragment of an office in his honour. A further fragment is in the Gloucestershire Record Office. This is described in appendix III of the article by Professor Trowell and Mr. A. Wathey in the present volume and illustrated in plates V and VI.

JOHN BENET'S 'LUX FULGET EX ANGLIA - O PATER PIETATIS - SALVE THOMA'.

The reconstruction of a fragmentary fifteenth-century motet in honour of St Thomas Cantilupe

by

Brian Trowell and Andrew Wathey*

The motet here reconstructed and published for the first time has enjoyed a greater share of good luck than most other such incomplete remnants of late medieval English music. Of its original three voices, the whole of the tenor part and almost a quarter of the contratenor are missing: and although the only known copy offers us a fairly accurate text for the surviving music, its scribe had no more than an elementary knowledge of Latin, and made no fewer than seventeen mistakes in transcribing the words. This suggests that the verses were quite unknown to him, and that he may perhaps have been copying them from an English exemplar in an unfamiliar handwriting.

With over two-fifths of the original words and music missing, one could not normally hope to attempt a plausible reconstruction. A chain of fortunate circumstances has nevertheless enabled us to present a version of the music in which only 66 semibreves out of 1248 have had to be freely invented, just over 5% of the whole; of the verbal text, 347 syllables may be restored with complete confidence, to which a hypothesis amounting to a virtual certainty enables us to add a further 29, just over 7% of the whole. The following pages will explain the steps which have led to this happy conclusion, and then go on to offer a hypothesis suggesting who may have commissioned the motet, and for what occasion.

*The opening part of this article formed the basis of an unpublished paper which Brian Trowell read at the Annual Conference of Research Students in Music in Oxford in December 1980. The essential final step in reconstructing the motet (i.e. the identification of the tenor *cantus firmus*) could not then be taken, for none of the known versions of the liturgy for St Thomas Cantilupe transmitted the plainsong melodies along with the texts. Shortly before delivering the paper, the speaker learned from Andrew Wathey that the latter had discovered two sources containing the music of four of the antiphons whose texts are employed in the motet. Wathey had also reconstructed the missing tenor, and was now able to show that it presented a version of *Salve Thoma.* His discoveries, so generously made available, proved to be of such importance in their own right that Trowell felt it essential to invite him to collaborate in the preparation of this article. Most of the first draft was the work of Trowell; Wathey then suggested further additions and improvements, and provided the account of the newly-discovered chants with facsimiles and transcriptions which forms Appendix III.

Benet's composition, one of three such occasional motets that survive from his pen,[1] is the penultimate item in a manuscript containing vespers music and motets that was probably compiled in the 1440s for the chapel of Leonello d'Este, Duke of Ferrara; the motets may have been performed as memorials or votive pieces at the end of Vespers.[2] The volume is now kept, together with a few similar but later musical mss, in the Biblioteca Estense in Modena, where it has the callmark *a*.X.1.11 (formerly lat. 471); in musicological literature it is known under the siglum *ModB*.[3] The motet occupies the last opening in the source. The top voice or discantus stands on fo. 135ᵛ, headed with the composer's name, 'Benet'. The opening phrase of the discantus, and the composer's name in the same spelling, are also entered in the contemporary index on p. viii. What is preserved of the middle voice or contratenor is copied at the top of fo. 136ʳ, and underneath that would have been the bottom voice or tenor; the lower half of the leaf, however, has been torn away.[4]

We cannot argue from the presence of this motet in a Ferrarese manuscript that St Thomas Cantilupe was particularly venerated in Italy, even though some of his mortal remains were interred in the monastery of Santo Severo, near Orvieto. *Lux fulget* is simply one of a sequence of over fifty English compositions, many of them similar occasional motets, that were collected for a music-loving connoisseur at a time when the 'new art'[5] of the English school, led by John Dunstable, Leonel Power and John Benet, was much sought after in Burgundy, South Germany, Austria and North Italy. A good many of the works brought together in *ModB*, including the motets of Guillaume Dufay and Dunstable, employ an unusually complex and mathematical method of construction now known as 'isorhythm': it was undoubtedly a taste for learned and elaborately-contrived music, rather than any special concern for the saints and occasions celebrated in the accompanying texts, that guided the selection

1 The others are for St Alban and St Mary Magdalene; there is also a *Sanctus Jacet granum* (and perhaps a *Gloria* and a second *Sanctus* based on the same chant) for St Thomas of Canterbury. See B. Trowell, article 'Benet, John', in *The New Grove Dictionary of Music and Musicians*, (22 vol.), ed. S. Sadie (Macmillan, London, 1980), II, 481 f. All three motets survive as *unica*.

2 See C. Hamm, and A. Besser Scott, 'A study and inventory of the manuscript Modena, Biblioteca Estense, *a* X.1.11 (ModB)', *Musica Disciplina* 26 (1972), 101-43, esp. 114 f.

3 In the *Répertoire international des sources musicales* it now rejoices in the longer siglum I-MOe *a* X 1.11.

4 It is highly unlikely that a fourth voice is also missing; though Dunstable composed some four-voiced isorhythmic motets, Benet's other motets, like almost all his music, are composed for three voices; his only four-voiced work is a canonic *Kyrie Deus creator omnium*.

5 It was called an 'ars nova' by Johannes Tinctoris, the leading musical theorist of the 1470s, in the dedication of his *Proportionale musices* (*c.* 1476): see C. E. H. de Coussemaker, ed., *Scriptorum de musica medii aevi nova series* (4 vols.), 1864-76, IV, 153-5.

of such pieces. The impressive series of English compositions at the end of the source were probably copied *en bloc* from some such book as the now lost 'livre de motez a la maniere de france' that once belonged to Dunstable's patron, John, Duke of Bedford.[6] Dunstable is easily the leading composer represented in the 'English' fascicles of *ModB*, which is the sole source for seven of his eleven isorhythmic motets; and there is also a work by John Pyamour or Piamor, who had served, it seems, as Master of the Children of the Chapel Royal and who ended his career as clerk to Bedford, presumably in the chapel that the latter maintained as Regent of France.[7] Ann Besser Scott has suggested that the English music may have been collected more directly from English musicians visiting the Council of Ferrara (1438-9) in the retinues of the English magnates;[8] but although the bishops and noblemen visiting the Council of Constance (1414-9) had certainly taken their choirmen and instrumentalists with them, it was decided to abandon this practice at the next great church council, that of Basle (1431-49), and to set up a special conciliar chapel instead.[9] This procedure was likely to have been followed, in the absence of evidence to the contrary, at Ferrara also.[10]

It is not surprising that English church historians concerned with St Thomas Cantilupe and Hereford cathedral should have remained for so long in ignorance of Benet's motet. The source had been known to the English scholar William Barclay Squire, who in 1892 made a diplomatic copy of the Dunstable works it contained and a thematic catalogue of those by other English composers, and contributed a letter on the subject to *The Times* of 21 February, 1893;[11] but it was not until 1916 that the first short catalogue of the contents of *ModB* was published, and in an

6 'Item ung livre de motez a la maniere de france couvert de cuir blanc' (P.R.O. E 154/1/33, fo. 10v): information privately communicated by Mrs Jenny Stratford, from a document which she hopes shortly to publish.

7 See J. Harvey, *Gothic England*, 2nd ed. (revised), (Batsford, London, 1948), 87.

8 'English music in Modena, Biblioteca Estense *a*.X.1.11 and other Italian manuscripts', *Musica Disciplina* 26 (1972), 145-60, 153 f.

9 For Constance, see M. Schüler, 'Die Musik in Konstanz während des Konzils 1414-1418', *Acta Musicologica* 38 (1966), 150-68; for Basle, M. Tegen, 'Baselkonciliet och kyrkomusiken omkr. 1440', *Svensk tidskrift for musikforskning* 39 (1957), 126-31.

10 Lewis Lockwood has drawn attention to a singer and instrumentalist variously called 'Johannes de Anglia' and 'Johannes ab arpa de Anglia' employed at the court of Ferrara in 1449 and 1450. ('Dufay at Ferrara', *Dufay quincentenary conference* ed. by A. W. Atlas (Brooklyn, NY, 1976), 1-25, 7). The harp may tempt us to speculate that he was a Welshman from the diocese of Hereford, but it is very unlikely (since he was evidently a secular instrumentalist) that he was Johannes Benet or any kind of learned musician capable of composing or understanding a motet as complex as *Lux fulget*.

11 His diplomatic copy and catalogue are now in the British Library as Add. MS 36490; and see A. Hughes-Hughes, ed., *Catalogue of the Manuscript Music in the British Museum* (3 vols, London, 1906-9) I, 356 f.

Italian journal.[12] In 1955 Brian Trowell published a list of Benet's works, pointing out the connection with St Thomas;[13] his unpublished doctoral dissertation of 1960 discussed the English music and attempted a rather unsatisfactory reconstruction of *Lux fulget,* without identifying the liturgical texts.[14] A proper catalogue of *ModB,* by the American scholars Charles Hamm and Ann Besser Scott, at last appeared in 1972[15]; they had evidently made their own reconstruction of *Lux fulget,* identifying this antiphon from *Analecta Hymnica*[16] and suggesting that the tenor *cantus firmus* resembled the Alleluia *Ego sum pastor bonus.* Dr Scott's dissertation, which we have not yet been able to consult, may contain this reconstruction and perhaps other relevant matter.[17]

A brief examination of the surviving music reveals that *Lux fulget,* like many other such occasional motets, is isorhythmic in construction: the restoration of the missing tenor voice, as we shall show, therefore presents few difficulties. We have set out the music in Appendix I in such a way that the repetitions of the same rhythm ('iso-rhythm') to notes of different pitch is obvious to the eye. The motet is composed in three sections, each in a different metre, beginning respectively at bars 1, 65, and 97. Half-way through each of these sections, the rhythmic values of the notes in the first half begin to be repeated: the rhythm of bars 33-64 exactly copies that of bars 1-32; bars 81-96 copy bars 65-80, and bars 113-128 copy bars 97-112 (we have numbered every fifth bar for ease of reference).

Motets of this kind, composed in the 'classic' manner of Sturgeon, Dunstable, Forest and Benet, always contain three statements of the same tune in the tenor; by a notational trick of proportional time-signatures, the tenor notes and rests lose part of their value on each repeat, diminishing in the proportion of either 9: 6: 3 or, as here, 6: 4: 3.[18] The former proportion is an arithmetic progression; the latter employs the harmonic

12 *Bollettino dell'associazione dei musicologi italiani,* serie viii, *Catalogo delle opere musicali. . . Città di Modena, R. Biblioteca Estense,* ed. P. Lodi, (Parma, n.d. [1916]), 15-17; reprinted Forli Editore, Bologna, 1923.

13 'Some English contemporaries of Dunstable', *Proceedings of the Royal Musical Association* 81 (1954-55), 77-92, 91 f.

14 *Music under the later Plantagenets,* unpublished Ph.D. dissertation, University of Cambridge, 1960.

15 See note 2; for *Lux fulget,* see pp. 142 f. of the article.

16 But not, it seems, the other antiphons: see *Analecta Hymnica Medii Aevi,* edd. G. M. Dreves, C. Blume, and H. M. Bannister, (55 vols. Leipzig, 1886-1922), XIII, 248-51.

17 A. Scott, *Coherence and calculated chaos: the English composers of Modena, Biblioteca Estense MS a X.1.11 (lat. 471),* unpublished Ph.D. dissertation, University of Chicago, 1969.

18 See the discussion of isorhythm and other proportional schemes in B. Trowell, 'Proportion in the music of Dunstable', *Proceedings of the Royal Musical Association* 105 (1978-79), 100-41, especially 101-4.

mean, for the proportion between the outer terms (6: 3 = 2: 1) is the same as the proportion between their respective differences with the inner term (6-4 = 2; 4-3 = 1). Thus, in bars 9-12, the first note of the tenor is worth 12 of the crotchets in the upper parts; in bars 69-70, on its first repeat, the same note has been made duple and imperfect and is now worth only 8 crotchets; on its second repeat in bars 101-2, its value has been halved from that of the first statement to only 6 crotchets.

In each section, then, the upper parts present a fresh pair of rhythmically analogous variations over the same tenor, which shrinks in length from section to section. We may represent this form schematically thus:

discantus } contratenor }	AA′ BB′ CC′
tenor	DD′ > DD′ > DD′

By aligning the upper parts for each section above each other as in Ex. 1 we can discover, using our knowledge of fifteenth-century harmony, what the possible pitches are for the missing tenor notes: the same tenor must provide a satisfactory basis for the harmony of all three sections of the motet, fitting against AA′, BB′ and CC′. Most pieces of this kind open with a more florid duet for the upper voices while the tenor rests: here we can tell that the tenor begins in bar 9, the first bar of the top line of Ex. 1:

The second and fourth notes of the tenor, it will be seen, present us with some ambiguity: in each case, the tenor note could be either D or F. Isorhythmic tenors, however, usually begin with a long note worth six, nine, twelve or even eighteen crotchets (semibreves in the original notation, for we have quartered the note-values in our edition). It will be useful, for purposes of comparison, to give the passages in equivalent rhythm to Ex. 1 (i.e. bars 41-52, 85-90 and 117-22); see Ex. 2:

Here, only the single pitch F is possible for all the first four tenor notes. If we are looking for a long note to begin the tenor with, it is likely that these Fs must all be tied together to produce it, and that the equivalent note at the beginning of Ex. 1 will equally be a single long D. Following this procedure we are able to establish beyond doubt the pitches and durations of all the tenor notes (and rests) except one, the sixth tenor note of Ex. 2, which might be E or G; if it is a G though, the change of rhythm that this necessitates will give us two repeated Fs at the equivalent point in Ex. 1.

Our analytical reconstruction is made a little harder by the presence of five minor errors in the copying of the contratenor part, but the logic of the process makes it possible to recognise and correct them. The missing portions of the contratenor present a more difficult problem, but our task is made much easier by two things: first, we now possess the missing tenor for the last section, and this greatly restricts the choice of notes open to the contratenor in the three-part passages; second, the isorhythmic repeat within each section enables us to tell exactly what the rhythm of the contratenor must have been for bars 93-6 (cf. bars 77-80) and for bars 119-24 (c.f. bars 103-8); as a bonus, a few note-tails are visible in bars 97-8, which in turn help us to restore bars 113-4.

The stylistic coherence and strictly isorhythmic method of the music, then, allow us to reconstruct the musical text with a high degree of certainty. What of the verbal text? Analysis of the metres and rhyme-schemes had suggested that the texts of the discantus and contra were probably not single poems specially written by one man, but a compilation of six different texts of the kind familiar from late medieval rhymed offices; and so indeed they turn out to be. All six are prominently placed as antiphons to *Magnificat* at first or second Vespers for the synodal Feast of St Thomas (Oct. 2) and its octave, preserved in the Hereford breviaries;[19] the same liturgy is repeated for his Translation (Oct. 26), and two of the antiphons also occur in the service for his Deposition (Aug. 25). The discantus employs four antiphons in the sequence *Lux fulget ex Anglia, Sicut fragrant orto florum, Puer mersus morti datus* and *Tu stirps preclara,* outlining the Saint's birth, the flower-like fragrance of his life and his miraculous saving of a drowned youth, and offering a prayer for his intercession. The rather less agile contratenor has two antiphons, *O pater pietatis* and *Salve Thoma,* the latter shorn of its last four words. Since these four missing words cannot have been intended to serve for the whole of the missing music, which covers 109 semibreves, there must have been another antiphon following *Salve Thoma.*

What can the missing antiphon have been? Assuming that in perfect time the composer's rate of word-setting was constant, there ought to be half as many syllables in the 32 bars of the final section as there are in the 64 bars of the opening section. In the discantus part, this proportion is almost exactly observed: 53 syllables to 107. The opening section of the contratenor has 65 syllables, which would lead us to expect 32 or 33 in the final section. It is impossible to fit 'gratie', the final word of *Salve Thoma,* into the middle section; it must therefore have spilled over into the final section (musical and textual divisions often fail to coincide in such motets as this). That means that we are looking for a text of 29 or 30 syllables. There is only one other antiphon to *Magnificat* in the rhymed office for St Thomas, *Syon psalle iugiter,* and it has 28 syllables. It would fittingly complete the sequence beginning with *O pater pietatis* and *Salve Thoma,* which both seek intercession through St Thomas's piety and pastoral love; *Syon psalle* shows him sweetly singing amid the angelic choirs, and this would also chime in beautifully with the final verse of the discantus: *'duc nos ad premia cara'.*

19 *The Hereford Breviary,* ed. W. H. Frere and L. E. G. Brown (3 vols.), Henry Bradshaw Society, vols. XXVI, XL and XLVI (London, 1904, 1911, 1915); the antiphons have lost their final Alleluias; for page references see Appendix II.

Like *Sicut fragrant* and *O pater pietatis, Syon psalle* also does duty as a memorial or psalm antiphon. The latter two do not seem to have been included in the small ms breviary now in the Chapter Library at Worcester (MS Q 86); *Tu stirps preclara,* on the other hand, is omitted from the printed breviary of 1505. Since the index of antiphons provided by Wordsworth and Brown is not entirely reliable, Appendix II sets out the various uses of all these items in *The Hereford Breviary.* Its text allows us to sort out all the passages garbled in *ModB;* in one case, however, the motet offers a better reading: 'angelicus' is to be preferred, for both metre and sense, to the breviary's 'anglicus'.[20] Most of the scribal errors in *ModB* seem to have arisen from a misreading of contractions or an unfamiliarity with English proper names. The motet's text for *O pater* is slightly nearer to the version used as a Magnificat antiphon on the principal feast-day ('claritatis', 'purgans') than to the version given for the Deposition ('charitatis', 'purgatos'). Finally, though Wordsworth and Brown prefer the reading *Syon psallite,* we should note that the reading is *Syon psalle* on the one occasion in the breviary when it is used as a *Magnificat* antiphon: the perhaps less logical plural verb for a collective subject occurs in two earlier placings.

Before leaving the verbal text, it is worth noticing that the scribe of *ModB* used a capital letter on each of the three occasions when the start of a new isorhythmic section or repeat in the discantus happened to coincide with the beginning of a line of verse: this suggests that he understood both the isorhythmic structure of the music and the verse structure of the text. It is also worth recording that John of Tynemouth, writing in the second quarter of the fourteenth century, added the words of the antiphon *Lux fulget* after his account of St Thomas Cantilupe in his *Sanctilogium Angliae.*[21] If this were the best-known of the set, that would explain its prominent placing as the first antiphon of the top part in the motet.

It was at this point in the investigation that Andrew Wathey's discovery of the music for the antiphons supervened; it enabled him to identify the reconstructed tenor as the opening phrase of the antiphon *Salve Thoma,* whose words appear in the contratenor. The identification allows us to sort out the problem raised in connection with Ex.2 above:

20 All save one of the English sources consulted have 'anglicus' for the second verse of *Lux fulget,* including Bodleian Lib., MS e Musaeo 2 (see App. III); but the latter has an extra ligature for the missing '-gel-'. John of Tynemouth (see note 21) has 'angelicus' but gives no music. The first lection of the first nocturn of matins for St Thomas' Day repeats St Gregory's pun: 'Thomas natione anglicus, angelicus vero' (*The Hereford Breviary,* II, 347).

21 See C. Horstmann, ed., *Nova Legenda Anglie* . . . 2 vols. (Oxford, Clarendon Press, 1901), II, 373, citing British Library, MS. Cotton Tib. E. i, part 2, fo. 74; John died *c.* 1348, so that this is the earliest known source for *Lux fulget.*

the sixth note must indeed be a G, tied to the previous G, and the two Fs in Ex. 1 must also be a single note. One variation between the chant and the tenor must be recorded: between the two Gs in bars 51-57 (and their recurrences in bars 90-93 and 122-5), the version of the chant which Wathey discovered has an F: see Ex. 3.

While there would be room, harmonically speaking, for an F lasting three beats in bar 53, that is not the case in bars 91 and 123; nor would the rigidity of the isorhythmic scheme permit anything except a rest in the bars in question. Either Benet based his tenor on a variant version of the chant, or else he deliberately excluded the note F at this point because an extra note would not have allowed him to cadence in the correct mode on to a D at the end of each section: strict isorhythm would have forced him to finish his pattern one note earlier, on an E. Dunstable, faced with a similar problem in his isorhythmic motet *Gaude virgo salutata,* solved it by adding the final note at the very end of the work as an extra *longa,* after the completion of the isorhythmic scheme.[22] We may also note here that the opening of the discantus, which is recalled at the beginning of the second section, seems loosely to ornament the *Salve Thoma* chant; and that in bar 75 the discantus appears to signal the arrival of the text *Puer mersus* by quoting the first three notes of its plainsong (for which see Appendix III).

22 See M. Bukofzer, ed., *John Dunstable: Complete Works = Musica Britannica* IV, 2nd ed., revised by I. Bent, M. Bent, and B. Trowell (London, Stainer & Bell, 1970), 74-77.

Can Benet's stylistic orientation and scanty biography help us to suggest a date and occasion for *Lux fulget?* His works number about twenty (there is some doubt raised by conflicting attributions to Power and Dunstable), and they have come down to us in some fifty copies.[23] Only four are to be found in the rather fragmentary English manuscripts of the time. (Benet seems to have been too young for a work of his to be included in the Old Hall ms). The remainder survive in manuscripts apparently or certainly copied in Cambrai, Basle, Vienna, the Imperial Chapel, Trento, the Veneto and Ferrara, most of them between about 1425 and 1465. The sources rarely give his Christian name; his surname is variously spelt Benet, Bennet, Benett, and even Bonet and Bonnet, though the commonest form is Benet (which musicologists have preferred to adopt in order to distinguish him from the Elizabethan composer, John Bennet). His nationality is sometimes specified as English. He was plainly a disciple and imitator of the great John Dunstable, so much so that Brian Trowell once believed that they might be the same man. Benet's music is of such high quality that it is not surprising that continental scribes sometimes attributed his works to Leonel Power (d. 1445) or John Dunstable (d. 1453).

Of Benet's life we know very little. A John Benet of London, clerk, was appointed master of the six choristers of St Anthony's Hospital in the City of London in 1443, a post which may have become vacant by 1449: this man must have been a competent musician. Also in 1449, a John Benet was entered as an existing member, together with Agnes his wife, in the register of the London Gild of St Nicholas (which includes the names of several composers amongst those of the parish clerks); no date of death is given. The will of a John Benet, chaplain, proved in Norwich in 1457, makes no mention of music and otherwise allows no identification.[24] From these scanty facts, from Benet's musical technique, and from the likely dating of the manuscripts in which his music is preserved, allowing for some time-lag in the case of the continental mss, one may deduce that Benet flourished from *c.* 1415-50.[25]

23 For sources of information in this and the next paragraph, consult the works cited in notes 1 and 13.

24 District Probate Registry, Norwich, 31 and 32 Brosyard.

25 A search through the relevant registers of the bishops of Hereford reveals only one local John Benet. Since, however, he was a Benedictine monk of Great Malvern he probably took his surname from his order. Nicholas, Bishop of Dunkeld, ordained him successively acolyte and subdeacon in Ledbury church on March 14, 1404 and June 13, 1405, and the suffragan ordained him priest in the conventual church of Leominster on September 18, 1406, after which he vanishes. (See *Registrum Roberti Mascall, Episcopi Herefordensis* (1404-1416), transcribed by J. H. Parry, with introductory note by C. Johnson, Canterbury and York Society (hereafter C & Y Soc.) XX (London, 1917), 126 and 133). It is inconceivable, though, that this religious priest could have abandoned his vows and order and re-emerged in mid-century as a married clerk in only minor orders.

We can hazard an informed guess about the likely occasion for the motet, and speculate as to who commissioned it. The most probable liturgical occasion would have been a jubilee or centenary of an important date in St Thomas' history. He died in 1282, on 25 August; his bones were brought back from Italy to his beloved Hereford and translated to his tomb in the north transept in 1287; he was canonized in 1320. These dates offer us the following jubilees or centenaries falling within the likely period of composition of the motet: 1420 as the centenary of his canonization; 1432 as the sesquicentenary of his death; 1437 as that of this translation. There appears to be no surviving record of any special celebration in any of these years.

If the motet is indeed to be connected with Hereford cathedral, then the most likely date would seem to be 1420; not merely because the centenary of St Thomas' canonization would probably have taken precedence over the other occasions, but also because in the period leading up to it the bishop of Hereford was Edmund Lacy, the only bishop between 1404 and 1448 whose career and record of patronage show a particular leaning towards music, musicians and an interest in the liturgy.[26] He had been a canon and prebendary of St George's Chapel, Windsor, from 1401 to 1417 and Dean of the royal household chapel from 1414 to 1417. These two institutions contained some of the leading composers of the time, whose works he would thus frequently have heard; as an ecclesiastic close to the king, he would also probably have been familiar with the household chapels of other magnates, which contained composers such as Power (with Thomas, Duke of Clarence) and Dunstable (perhaps already with John, Duke of Bedford). In June, 1417, two months after his consecration as bishop, we find Lacy presenting Richard Blythe, a clerk of the Chapel Royal, to a Hereford prebend; and on April 28, 1419 he presents John Dunstapylle, clerk, to another.[27] If this was indeed the great composer, which seems likely enough, one may perhaps imagine the latter serving as an intermediary, if a motet were to be commissioned, and bringing Benet's talents to Lacy's attention.

26 See *Dictionary of National Biography,* Supplement, III, 74, and A. T. Bannister's introduction to *Registrum Edmundi Lacy, Episcopi Herefordensis* (1417-1420), transcr. by J. H. Parry, C & Y Soc., XXII (London, 1918); also A. B. Emden, *A biographical register of the University of Oxford to A.D. 1500,* 3 vols., (Oxford, Clarendon Press, 1957-9), II, 1081 ff.

27 *Reg. Lacy . . ., op. cit.,* 113, 115. The name is *not* spelt Dunstavylle: a photograph of the entry from the bishop's register clearly shows a faint descender to the 'p'. Blythe may have been the composer mentioned in a motet by Johannes Alanus; he is traceable in the royal household chapel from 1413, and was probably an older man nearing the end of his career, since he is reported dead in 1420. See B. Trowell, 'A fourteenth-century ceremonial motet and its composer', *Acta Musicologica* 29 (1951), 65-75, 70 f.

Lacy's will has unfortunately not been preserved. We can show that he possessed an organ: in July 1440, when he had been bishop of Exeter for twenty years, he gave to the then bishop of Hereford, Thomas Spofford, a pair of organs left at Whitbourne, to be assigned by him to any church or chapel he pleased: [28] presumably they had remained at Whitbourne since the time when Lacy had been bishop of Hereford. His own household chapel, when he was bishop of Exeter, was probably capable of supporting the performance of polyphonic music. The will of a Jacob Michell, dated 1438 and proved in 1439, bequeathed to one John Bosovseke 'quaternum meum cum canticis de Musyke qui quidem quaternus est in capella reverendissimi patris et domini domini mei Exonien*sis* episcopi', with the proviso that Lacy had to give his permission for its removal from his chapel: 'cum eiusdem domini supportacione benigna'.[29]

We do not know when Lacy began to plan his new liturgy for St Raphael the Archangel, though it may conceivably have been in his mind while he was bishop of Hereford. If so, he had to wait some twenty years before the new ceremony was finally approved, and it did not reach Hereford until 1445.[30] One wonders whether it is a coincidence that the day he chose for it was October 5, three days after the Feast of St Thomas and of course within its octave. As bishop of Hereford, Lacy cannot have learned before the New Year of 1420 that he was destined for Exeter; we may surely take it that a man who was in later life to show such an interest in developing the liturgy would not have failed to plan well ahead for a particularly splendid celebration of a day so important to his cathedral as the centenary of St Thomas Cantilupe's canonisation.[31] And if John Benet, as a rising young composer, had been invited to write a polyphonic motet for performance at the end of First Vespers on October 2, would we be wrong to suspect the guiding hand of Lacy in the liturgically inspired selection of all seven antiphons to *Magnificat* as the texts which Benet was to dignify with his sonorous and elaborate music?

28 *Registrum Thome Spofford, Episcopi Herefordensis* (1422-1448), ed. A. T. Bannister, C & Y Soc., XXIII (London, 1919), 234.

29 *The Register of Edmund Lacy, Bishop of Exeter, 1420-1455,* 5 vols., ed. G. R. Dunstan, C & Y Soc. (Torquay, 1963-72), IV, 34.

30 *Reg. Spofford, op. cit.,* XI and 267 f. For its acceptance in Exeter in 1443, see *The Reg. of Edmund Lacy, op. cit.,* V, x, which also shows that after his death Lacy himself came to be regarded unofficially as a local saint.

31 For a study of the jubilee celebrations for another English St Thomas, see R. Foreville, *Le jubilé de S. Thomas Becket du XIIIe au XVe siècle, 1220-1470: Etude et documents* (Paris, 1959).

NOTES TO APPENDIX I

MUSIC

Note-values have been quartered; square slurs above the notes show ligatures; half-brackets show coloration. Parts not named in ms. Original clefs C2 C4 [C5]. Discantus: bar 36, note 3, *c* in ms; 128 is a conventional final *longa.* Contratenor: 17,4 *a* (perhaps this should stand); 18,1 *b;* 49,2 *d;* 87,4 *a;* 88,2 *g;* 93,5 *custos* indicates *b* as first note of next line; 93,5-103,2 torn away, but rhythm of 93,5-96,3 reconstructed from 77,5-80,3; surviving note-stems suggest values and contour of 97,1-98,2 and therefore analogous rhythm of 113,1-114-2; 108,2-128 missing, but rhythm of 119,3-124,1 copied from 103,3-108-1 and harmony of tenor and discantus insists on the low *c* in 122 and 125.

Tenor: editorially supplied; the version of the chant used by Benet apparently lacked an *f* between the second and third *g*s of 'bone'; original notation of the tenor was probably as follows:

Ex. 4

[Time-signatures would have been 2C, 2C, O (one for each statement)]

TEXT

The underlay of text beneath the notes in the ms is generally not very accurate, and has been slightly adjusted in many places. Punctuation and capitalisation are editorial, with full stops separating the antiphons; u/v and i/j have been standardised.

Discantus: 7-8 'angelicus' must be right, for the metre; 24-5 'gratio'; 36 'ad'; 43-50 'fragrantis otto floris cade*n*t ora*n*ter lilio'; 54 'moris'; 55-6 'excelsa'; 58-9 'gaude*n*t'; 68-71 'curas contrittoru*m*'; 72-4 'post ac patria'; 78-9 'tandi'; 83-5 'ex om*n*ia'; 87 'statui'; 92-6 'so*m*pnis exitatus'; 107-9 'herserdia*m*'; 115 'ac sciencia'; 121 'ara' erased?

Contratenor: 75 'at*que*'; 81-8 'fero gratis'; 93-128 missing; Magnificat antiphon *Syon psalle* editorially supplied.

APPENDIX I

Isorhythmic motet 'Lux fulget ex Anglia - O pater pietatis - Salve Thoma': John Benet

35
40
et post hoc ex - i -lium ac feli - cem transi - tum iun-ge nos be-a -
te cur - ren - - - - - - - - - - ti - - - -
I,2
45
-tis. Sic-ut fra - grant or - to flo - - rum, can - dent, cu-rant
-um, nos pur - - gans [a] pec - - ca - - tis gau - - - - de- re
pa - - - - - - - - stor
50
55
li-li- a, Tho - -mas per ex - empla mo-rum fragrat in ec-cle-si -
cum be - a - - tis fac in per - pe - - - - tu-
bo - - - - - - - - - - - - - - - -
60
-a, can - -det cho - ro con- - - fes-so - rum;
-um. Sal-ve Tho - - - - - - ma, pa - - - stor
- - - - - - - - - - ne.

Flos-vi-te mun - di-ti-a, culpas cu-rat con - - tri -torum,po- li pre-stat
bo - ne Chri.- - sti gre - gis et pa - tro - - - -
II,1 Sal - - - - - - - - -
premi - a. Pu - er mer - sus morti da - tustan - dem Tho - me
- - - ne, ac doc - - - - - tor ec - cle - si - e,
- - ve Tho - - - - - - ma,
men-su - ra-tus est apud Ox- - o - ni-am, qui statim re- su-sci-
o - - pem que - so fer e - -gro - - - tis,
II,2 pa - - - - - stor
- ta - - tus, ut a som - - nis ex - ci - - ta - - tus.
at - - que men - - ti - bus [de - vo - tis con-fer lu - men
bo - - - - - - - - - - - - - - ne.

De - i per po - ten - - - ti - am, cum re - vix - it,
gra - - - - - - - - ti - e. Sy - - - - on psal-le
III,1
Sal - - - - - - -
cla-mans dix-it: e-a- musad Her for- di - am. Tu [stirps] pre-cla- - - ra, sac-
iu - gi - - ter con - cen - ti - bus so- - - - - - no - - ris,
- ve Tho - - - - - ma,
- - ra vi - ta, sci-en-ti- a cla - ra, pon-ti - - fi-ca - lis
Tho - - - - - - - - - mas can - - - tat dul-
III,2
pa - - - - stor
a - ra, duc nos ad pre-mi - a ca - - - - ra.
- ci - - ter cum an - ge-lo- rum cho - - - - - ris.]
bo - - - - - - - - - - - - - ne.]

APPENDIX II

The order of antiphons in the motet is:

DISCANTUS	CONTRATENOR	TENOR
Lux fulget ex Anglia	*O pater pietatis*	[*Salve Thoma pastor bone*]
Sicut fragrant orto florum	*Salve Thoma pastor bone*	
Puer mersus morti datus	[*Syon psalle*]	
Tu stirps preclara		

The following table shows how these appear to be deployed in the Feasts of St Thomas, following *The Hereford Breviary;* page references are to Vol. II. The order for the translation on 25 October is the same as that for the Feast Day and the service is not repeated under that date. All are antiphons to *Magnificat* unless followed by an asterisk.

	PRINTED BREVIARY (1505)		WORCESTER CATHEDRAL MS Q.86 (Saec. xiv)	
DEPOSITION: 25 AUGUST				
Vespers	*Syon psallite**	309		
	*O pater pietatis**	310		
Second Vespers	*Sicut fragrant*	311		
ST THOMAS' DAY: 2 OCTOBER				
Vespers	*Syon psallite**	346		
	O pater pietatis	346	*Lux fulget*	345
			Tu stirps	345
Second Vespers	*Sicit fragrant*	351	*Sicut fragrant*	351
			Salve Thome [sic]	353
			Puer mersus	353
			Lux fulget	353
			Tu stirps	353
OCTAVE				
October 3-6, 8				
Vespers	*Syon psalle* [*sic*]	353		
	Salve Thoma	353		
	Puer mersus	353		
	Lux fulget	353		
St Osyth: 7 October				
Vespers memorial	*O pater pietatis**	362		
Sunday within Octave				
Vespers	*O pater pietatis*	364		
St Dionysius: 9 October				
Vespers memorial	*O pater pietatis**	365		
Second Vespers memorial	*Sicut fragrant**	369	*Sicut fragrant**	369

APPENDIX III

This appendix presents the available plainsongs of the antiphons whose texts are used in *Lux fulget / O pater pietatis / [Salve Thoma]*. Ligatures are transcribed as slurs; plicas are indicated as a smaller note after the main pitch. Punctuation and capitalisation are mainly editorial.

SOURCES

Gloucestershire Record Office, GDR Fragment 14

Described in N. R. Ker, *Medieval Manuscripts in British Libraries,* Oxford, 1969-, II.971. This bifolium was used as a cover for one of the volumes of visitations in the long series of Gloucester Diocesan Act Books.

Folios 1-1v (Plates V and VI) preserve most of Second Vespers for the Feast of St Thomas, and follow the fourteenth-century breviary Worcester Cathedral MS Q.86, (fo. 300) in placing the Matins Responds for the Octave directly after the final antiphon to *Magnificat*. The contents of fos. 1-1v are as follows:

fo. 1	Hymn	[*Summi regis*] (end only)
	Versicle	*Amavit eum*
	Antiphon	*Sicut fragrant*
	Psalm	*Magnificat*
	Antiphon	*Puer mersus*
fo. 1v	Psalm	*Magnificat*
	Antiphon	*Salve Thoma*
	Psalm	*Magnificat*
	Respond	*Hic est Abel*
	Versicle	*In presenti*
	Respond	*Thomas primus* (beginning only)

Oxford, Bodleian Library, MS e Musaeo 2

Described in F. Madan and Others, *A Summary Catalogue of Western Manuscripts in the Bodleian Library at Oxford,* Oxford, 1895-1953, II.655-6. See also O. Pächt & J. J. G. Alexander, *Illuminated Manuscripts in the Bodleian Library Oxford,* Oxford, 1966-1973, III.60, where the manuscript's decoration is dated *c.* 1370-80.

Lux fulget appears (with Versicle *Ora pro nobis* and Reading *Deus qui ecclesiam tuam*) in the Commemoration of St Thomas of Hereford on the Feast of St Remigius (October 1). Lessons of St Thomas with St Leodgarius follow.[32]

NOTES TO TRANSCRIPTIONS

Lux fulget

line 2: MS *anglicus,* set to the last two ligatures and final *g*; *vir,* at preceding line-end, allotted extra *c-d* ligature. See note 20, page 166.

line 6: MS *da.*

line 9: MS *ad.* Cotton Tiberius E. i reads *ac.*

Puer mersus

line 9: MS *herefordiam.*

32 For Thomas with Leodgarius see also Oxford, Bodleian Library, MS Laud misc. 299, fo. 467.

A MOTET BY JOHN BENET

LUX FULGET Music: MS e Musaeo 2, p.919

A MOTET BY JOHN BENET

SICUT FRAGRANT Music: GDR Fragment 14, fol. 1

A MOTET BY JOHN BENET

PUER MERSUS Music: GDR Fragment 14, fol. 1

A MOTET BY JOHN BENET

SALVE THOMA Music: GDR Fragment 14; fol. 1^{v}

V. Gloucestershire Record Office, GDR Fragment 14, fo. 1
Second Vespers for the Feast of St Thomas.

VI. Gloucestershire Record Office, GDR Fragment 14, fo. 1v
Second Vespers for the Feast of St Thomas.

THE RELICS OF ST THOMAS CANTILUPE

by Dom Illtud Barrett

Before his death near Montefiascone in Italy on August 25th, 1282, St Thomas had expressed a wish to be buried in his own cathedral church of Hereford. His body was, therefore, boiled so that bones and flesh could be separated. This distasteful substitute for embalming was forbidden by Pope Boniface VIII in 1300 under pain of excommunication, but we know that over a century later the body of King Henry V was similarly treated after his death at Vincennes in 1422. The flesh and viscera of the saint were buried in the Abbey Church of San Severo near Orvieto, while heart and bones were brought back to England. The heart was taken to the chapel of the canons of Ashridge, and before the end of 1282 the bones were buried in the Lady Chapel of Hereford cathedral beneath a large flat stone. The bones had suffered considerably in appearance because of the boiling to which they had been subjected. Dom Ethelbert Horne of Downside wrote in 1947, 'On account of the more oily parts of the body getting boiled into the substance of the bones, these became of a dark colour, and after their preservation for many years, they tended to lose what we know as ordinary bone-colour and to become a yellowish or reddish brown'[1] This helped the identification of the relics many centuries after the saint's death.

Even before the bones of St Thomas had been laid in their first tomb, small relics had been removed from the body, for we hear of such relics being in the possession of his family as well as pieces of clothing and other personal impedimenta. It is likely that other parts of the body may have been detached for this purpose when it was moved to its new tomb in the north transept of the cathedral in 1287, and to its shrine in 1349, for our medieval forebears had a consuming passion for relics which we perhaps find remarkable or even macabre. In any case, there in the great shrine at the east end of the cathedral lay the bones of St Thomas until the shrine was totally destroyed in the 16th century by order of King Henry VIII.

Devout persons in Hereford were determined that the bones of St Thomas should not be defiled or desecrated, and they were removed from the shrine before its destruction. Their subsequent history is well documented, and fully set out in an article by Father John Morris, S.J. in 'The Month' of January 1882. The first custodian whose name we know is the Reverend William Ely. Born in Herefordshire, Ely had been ordained priest in Queen Mary's reign, and appointed President of St John's College,

1 E. Horne, in *The Clergy Review,* XXVIII, (1947), 91-104.

Oxford, in 1559. During the reign of Elizabeth I, he returned to his native county, and must have exercised his priesthood for some time: he died in Hereford gaol in 1609. We know the names of the priests and custodians of the relics who succeeded William Ely. The relics were held in honour, and were privately venerated by the large numbers of Roman Catholics who lived in and around Hereford. The relics were even carried through the streets in a private procession by night to ask the saint's intercession in averting the plague which threatened the city. The procession had the desired effect, and the plague ceased, but in what year did the procession take place? Richard Strange, who published his life of St Thomas in 1674, says that it was 'even in our time, not many years ago',[2] so Father Waterworth, S.J., in charge of the Catholic mission at Hereford in 1846, places the procession in 1665, though the 1879 edition of Strange's *Life,* suggests that it took place in 1610. It has been estimated that perhaps a fifth of Hereford's population in the 17th century retained their attachment to the old religion, and their veneration for St Thomas Cantilupe was very strong.

During the Civil War, the relics were dispersed in 1642 to prevent their seizure by Parliamentary troops, but were recovered by a Mrs Ravenhill, a Roman Catholic lady of Hereford. Certainly, in 1668, Father Richard Barton, rector of the Jesuit College of St Omer, spoke of 'the box in which the venerable head of many of the bones of the saint, rescued long since from the fury of the heretics, are religiously preserved by the Catholic priest at Hereford, in England, and exposed to the public veneration of the faithful, as much as can possibly be done in that country amongst heretics.' Before this date, however, the relics of Cantilupe were being dispersed. Father Cuffaud was the first Jesuit known to have been in charge of the Catholic mission in Hereford, and it was he who gave an arm bone of the saint to Father John Poyntz *alias* Stephens, who gave it to his sister, Mary Poyntz, on November 12th, 1651. Miss Poyntz was then living in Paris, and was instructed by her brother to give the relic to the English Provincial of the Society of Jesus should anything happen to him. This was the relic that was placed in the Sodality Chapel of the College at St Omers on September 1st, 1668, and on October 1st of the same year, the local bishop allowed it to be publicly venerated. The relic accompanied the Fathers when the College was transferred to Bruges, and after the suppression of the College was in the possession of the bishop of Bruges. All knowledge of the relic is now lost, as the property of the bishop was sold on December 17th, 1795. It is possible that somewhere in Belgium the relic may yet exist in its silver, glass and ebony reliquary.

2 *The Life and Gests of S. Thomas Cantilupe, Bishop of Hereford*... Collected by R.S.S.I. (Ghent, 1674. Reprinted Burns and Oates, London, 1879). The reprint was edited by Canon Vincent Dolman, O.S.B., parish priest of the church of St Francis Xavier, Hereford.

The other relic given away by Father Cuffaud has had a happier history. It is a *tibia* or right shin bone given in 1664 to Mr Evans living in North Wales. Father Evans, also known as Father Humphrey Brown, was at the time the Jesuit Superior of his brethren in North Wales, and resided at Holywell. The priest's house and chapel at Holywell was known as the Old Star Inn during the penal times, and was something of a Catholic pilgrimage centre. The relic of St Thomas remained there for one hundred and seventy-one years, until in 1835 it was transferred to Stonyhurst. There it may be seen in a handsome reliquary made, Father John Morris tells us, by Hardman of Birmingham: 'a glass cylinder enables the reliquary to be seen, and the two ends are ornamented in silver with the singular armorial bearings of the Cantilupes.'[3]

There remains one other notable relic of St Thomas Cantilupe, and this is his skull, preserved in the abbey church of St Gregory the Great at Downside. The fascinating history of this relic is in the archives of Downside, in an account written by Dom Gilbert Dolan. One of the monasteries founded by the English Benedictines on the Continent during the age of persecution was the abbey of Lamspring in the diocese of Hildesheim in Germany. About the year 1670, Brother Peter Street, a laybrother of this community, was visiting his sister, and found that the head of the saint was in her house near Hereford. The Streets were a well known Herefordshire family, and Brother Peter on finding the head there and 'not thinking it kept and exposed with dew public veneration, brought the same to Lamspring.'

Dom Benet Gibbon, a distinguished monk of the Lamspring House, and one of the members of the royal monastery at the palace of St James in London, established by King James II, has left an account of the arrival of the relic, and its subsequent history, which is now in the Downside Archives. In it, Dom Benet states that the bishop of Hildesheim had given permission for the public veneration of the saint's relic to be made annually on his feastday, October 2nd. He also states that the Catholic clergy of Hereford wrote to Abbot Gascoigne of Lamspring, demanding the return of the head. Dom Benet Gibbon was told to reply to the letter, and informed the clergy of Hereford, that the relic would only be returned if a responsible person was sent to whom it could be entrusted. 'No answer being given, it there remains.' Dom Benet's account was written in 1720, and this is the last reference to or knowledge of the head of St Thomas at Lamspring that we have until 1881. The monastery had been suppressed by the Prussian Government in 1803, and the abbey church had become a parish church with a resident priest, though the books and furniture of the church had been respected.

3 J. Morris, 'English relics, I: St Thomas of Hereford', *The Month,* XLIV (Jan.-Apr., 1882), 125-6. For an illustration of this relic, see R. C. Finucane, *Miracles and Pilgrims,* (London, 1977), plate 15.

Many inquiries had been made during the nineteenth century about the fate of the relic, but the answer from the parish priest was always the same—that the head of the saint was not in the former abbey church Consequently, in September 1881, Dom Gilbert Dolan, a monk of Downside, went to Lamspring to search for the relic himself. Dom Gilbert tells us that a complete search of the church, all its altars, the chests and cupboards of the sacristy was carried out by himself, the parish priest, and the lay sacristan. It was fruitless. Finally, when Dom Gilbert was about to give up in desperation, the parish priest suggested that they have one more try: there was one remaining place where the relic might be. All three went to a small space behind the High altar and reredos where there was a very large cupboard, which seemed to be empty. The parish priest stood on a chair and searched the higher shelves, but they too were empty. A table was produced, and the chair placed on that so that the parish priest could search the topmost shelves of all. 'Standing on the chair thus elevated (for no ladder was at hand), the parish priest to his astonishment and that of the sacristan and myself, brought into the light two very old and broken boxes, containing various relics, and attestations of relics, and conspicuous at the top of one of the boxes was an ancient skull, the lower jaw of which was missing. The skull was covered, as were the other relics, with dust and cobwebs, but bore unmistakeable marks of a portion of the forehead having been cut off with some sharp instrument.' Dom Benet Gibbon stated in 1720 that a piece of the skull had been cut out so that Lamspring would retain a relic of the Saint even if the head had to be returned to Hereford, so there was no doubt that this indeed was the relic venerated as the head of St Thomas Cantilupe. Like the relic at Stonyhurst, the skull too had the unmistakeable colouring caused by the boiling after the saint's death.

Part of this relic, now in the Lady chapel of the abbey church at Downside, was given to the monks of Belmont Abbey, Hereford, on the occasion of the centenary of the monastery in 1959. It may well be the very piece cut from the front of the skull at Lamspring, and is kept above one of the altars in a handsome reliquary designed by Dom Theodore Bailey. Each year on October 2nd, the custom observed at Lamspring is followed at Belmont, and the relic is placed on a decorated table flanked by two lighted candles to be venerated during Mass and Vespers.

Fr John Morris tells us in his article of 1882, how Dean Merewether thought that the relics were still in the saint's tomb in the north transept of Hereford cathedral in 1846, and actually opened it, though the Jesuit Father Waterworth, in charge of the Catholic mission, and a friend of the dean's, knew that he would not find them. Indeed this tomb had been opened as recently as 1813, when a ring, a seal, and the head of a crozier were found, and removed. Unfortunately, all these articles were stolen from the cathedral in 1838, and were never recovered.

In 1947, Abbot Ethelbert Horne, the Downside archivist, wrote a description of the skull, which may be repeated here. 'It is certainly of fine form, having a massive and high forehead and is of considerable width above the eyes. The lower jaw is missing and there are no teeth left in the upper. A large piece of the right side of the forehead has been deliberately sawn out and this must have been done by a surgeon and by one who knew exactly what was wanted. It was a difficult and delicate piece of work, and it has evidently been done with great care, the correct instruments for such an operation being used. When Abbot Gascoigne replied to the Hereford clergy that they could certainly have the relic back again if they would send a responsible person to fetch it, but that he should keep a portion of it at Lamspring, he probably expected that someone might come suddenly and that he must therefore be prepared beforehand to remove the portion he wanted to keep. If this surmise is correct, it will account for the large piece that has been sawn out of the forehead. The general colour of the skull is the same as that of the Stonyhurst relic and suggests that it underwent the same treatment after the Saint's death. It has been well described as a yellowish-brown, 'like very old parchment'. Small pieces of bone have been cut or broken off from every part of the skull, evidently for relics.'[4]

We have seen that in 1668, Father Richard Barton spoke of all St Thomas Cantilupe's bones still being in Hereford, and in Catholic hands. All, except the Downside, Stonyhurst and Belmont relics are now lost. 'The apathy of the eighteenth century', wrote Father John Morris, 'has undone much that the care and zeal of the seventeenth century would have secured to us.'[5]

I acknowledge with deep gratitude the valuable help of Dom Philip Jebb, archivist of Downside abbey, and of Father F. J. Turner, S.J., Librarian of Stonyhurst college. Both have given me photostats of MS material in their archives, and have drawn my attention to articles and books, particularly the article by Fr John Morris, S.J. in 'The Month' for January 1882, and the article by Dom Ethelbert Horne, F.S.A. in the 'Clergy Review' of August 1947.

4 E. Horne, *op. cit.*

5 J. Morris, *op. cit.*

THE RADIANCE OF SANCTITY

by Norman S. Rathbone

Above the shrine of St Thomas of Hereford, in the north transept of his cathedral, now hangs an ornament fashioned in shining and coloured metals which the craftsman who devised and made it has called a nimbus. It is not itself a source of light illuminating the tomb of the Saint as a precious object to be admired by visiting eyes. It reflects a hidden light which issues from the tomb itself. In a remarkable and imaginative way it suggests the radiance of sanctity, that spiritual brightness and supernatural light which shines upon the world in the lives of holy men and women. The radiance of holiness like the odour of sanctity is the symbol of the divine presence, a grace and power manifest in the saint. Moses, descending from Sinai, must veil his face to conceal its mysterious and perilous brightness. Stephen's judges saw his face shining as an angel's; and the corpse of Hereford's own martyr and saint, Ethelbert, the king was accompanied by strange lights. In another poetic figure it is sometimes related of the bodies of the saints that they have exhaled delicious fragrances, the odour of sanctity, a sensible sign of the supernatural sweetness of their souls.

Such language is an attempt to express the meaning of holiness. It is a word, an idea, of profound implication and religious significance; and at the same time it eludes a precise definition. It cannot be described simply in moral or personal, let alone physical terms. Yet it is impossible to speak of God, or of divine things, or of the divine presence in the human soul, without making use of the word and concept of the holy.

In its most primitive sense it is that religious word, which gathers into itself man's basic experience of the supernatural, the 'other', as something which attracts yet terrifies, the *mysterium tremendum et fascinans,* the numinous.

Caves and mountains, stones and streams, trees and beasts, may carry within themselves a divine power and presence. A dark cavern is the aboriginal cathedral. Apollo speaks in the awe-inspiring vale of Delphi. Horeb is the mount of God, and the place of transfiguration. Such are the commonplaces of human faith; perhaps here is the ultimate source of religion, the primal theology of which all else is the development and explication. There is no need to point out that such religion easily develops into superstition and magic, that the notion of holiness can become materialised and petrified, the divine fire can turn to ashes. This is specially dangerous when the holy presence and grace shining through a human heart and mind become formalised into a function or an office or a power. The thaumaturge, the sorcerer, the priest, may be the vehicle of supernatural forces and powers. But such men are truly holy only in so far as they are as persons, partakers of the divine nature, holy as God is holy.

It was thus that righteousness, to use the Old Testament term, came to be seen by the prophets of Israel and no less by the wise men of the Gentiles to be the essential quality of the saint. Moral holiness, purity of heart, uprightness of character, distinguish the truly saintly man. Sacred men are not the same as holy men. The former may have still some part to play in religion, but holiness of life is the essential. So sanctity achieves a truly personal character. The 'holy one of Israel' is the name of the righteous judge of all the world.

But once more the idea of the holy lay open to corruption or at least diminution. As the primitive sense of the numinous declined easily into superstition, so the moral understanding of holiness was sometimes debased into a barren legalism. The perilous ascent of the holy mountain where God is, was turned into a dreary slavery. Law, obedience, conscience, right and duty, can and do exist without holiness, without the living presence of the Spirit.

It is at this point that the Gospel enters the world. In Jesus, the 'Holy One of God', as the demons recognise, the veritable truth and depth of holiness is displayed. Awe, the numinous, is still there. People are astonished, afraid of him. Righteousness is there, for he is the holy and the just one. But holiness in him consists in the unity of the Son with the Father, the perfect response of love to the love of God. The holiness of the saints consists in nothing else than a participation in the holiness of Christ through the Spirit, and in this alone. No predisposition of temperament, no achievement of virtue, no insight or mystical elevations, by themselves are the ingredients of holiness. The saint in the time-consecrated phrase, is the friend of God. He possesses the power and impetus to give himself utterly to God in responsive love. Belonging to God, he turns to his Father in heaven with generous self-donation.

So it is that the first saints to be honoured in the church were the martyrs. By their death they gave all it is possible to give. Ignatius on his way to Rome to be ground by the teeth of the lions, Polycarp refusing all concessions to his venerable age, and offering himself as a Eucharistic loaf in the fire; and the countless others who suffered and died, are marked with the holiness of the Christ in his passion. After them, in other ways, the virgins and ascetics, when persecution abated, and martyrdom became a rarer manner of self oblation, follow the same path of love. And together with them, bishops whose entire vocation is charity; and priests and layfolk, men and women, the simple and learned, an unnumbered host, make up the great company of the friends of God.

It is clear then that holiness is not a virtue as one of the virtues, nor an achievement like learning, nor a discipline, nor even a special grace like contemplation. It is rather a radiance which shines in the life of those who love and are loved by God. Eric Gill's aphorism 'The artist is not a special kind of man, but every man is a special kind of artist', may be adapted for our purpose. The saint is not a special kind of man, but every Christian is called to be a special kind of saint. To be a saint does not demand a particular kind of personality or profession. But in every personality, every profession not false or debased, or twisted or inhuman, sanctity can shine.

So the saints display such diversity in life yet such unity in aim and direction. Sanctity is like their common humanity. It is indeed human nature raised to its perfection by the grace of charity. For just as human love draws out the best in a man's personality, concentrating and intensifying its powers; so too in an infinitely more potent fashion, divine love inspires him to heroic achievement. Of course there is the possibility of extravagances, of strangeness and awkwardness. The lives of the saints show many examples but these are mere surface aberrations, and not the essentials of sanctity.

So far we have said nothing of the question of canonization; the enrolling of a christian in the calendar of saints, the according him a place in the public cultus of the church. In fact all this is of peripheral concern to the question of holines. Popular veneration, the miracles at shrines, pilgrimages, invocation of the blessed, the ecclesiastical processes which canonization has involved in the Western church since the middle ages, or the less formalised proceedings of the Eastern church are the tributes of the fellow citizens of the saints, the accolade which the Church militant bestows. Birthday honours are for the few, but loyalty and devotion are for all.

Such an accolade honoured our holy bishop in his own times and after his decease. To-day we look rather for the evidence of his holiness less in miracles than in his consecration to his pastoral office; his care for the young and the poor; his concern for a trained clergy to shepherd his flocks; his defence of the rights of the church against secular opposition which, in his age, was thought of as the defence of the rights and dues of God. In giving himself wholly to his pastoral care, in the love of Christian people, he fulfilled in a special way the vocation to holiness.

It may well be that by this course of practical, devoted, loving service St Thomas will most encourage those who still honour him today.

His personality is less vivid to us that that of other bishops who were his near contemporaries, and of other saints of his times. We do not know him as we know Hugh of Lincoln, or the rugged scholarly Grosseteste, or Francis, or Elizabeth of Hungary. He left no intimate writings, we have no portraits; but he is certainly among the number of those who shine as lights in the world and whose holiness is still an example and inspiration to the pilgrim church.

APPENDIX

A SERVANT SPEAKS OF HIS MASTER: HUGH LE BARBER'S EVIDENCE IN 1307

by Meryl Jancey

The evidence produced at the inquiry for the canonization of St Thomas Cantilupe in 1307, survives in a manuscript, Vat.Cod.Lat. 4015, in the library of the Vatican. It takes the form of replies made by witnesses to a number of set questions designed to establish that Cantilupe's life demonstrated certain clearly defined qualities essential to a well-understood ideal of sanctity and that alleged miracles could be authenticated. This material has been made available in the entry for Cantilupe, published in 1765, in the great continuing work of the Bollandist fathers, the *Acta Sanctorum*. This is like a great quarry from which stones can be pulled to build up our knowledge of Cantilupe but it has some limitations. The form of the evidence demanded re-arrangement in which, although what was important for proven sanctity has been carefully retained, the context of some of the information is not clear, and the total narrative of any one witness's testimony broken.

The original record is not easy to use, largely because of its wearisome repetition, and its evidence needs to be approached with some caution. The witnesses were somewhat inhibited by having to fit their testimony to a strict pattern. Then, they had to bring to memory events of many years ago. Cantilupe had been dead for 25 years when the inquiry was held. This could cause difficulties about details of names, times, and places. Again, the men who could be called to speak for him in 1307 were all younger than Cantilupe. Many of them had served, in varying degrees, under his authority. The relationship of young men to an older one, or of servants to a master, does not always lead to full understanding by the one of the other. Cantilupe is unlikely to have opened his whole mind to these much younger men. Much of what they say seems to be recording an awed observation rather than an understanding sympathy. Their testimony stands, however, as a remarkably consistent study of a man whose reserve and austere rectitude did not blind those who knew him to the gentler aspects of his character which were often revealed in an exquisite courtesy and forbearance. In spite of the common form which they all followed, the testimony of each was the record of a personal experience coloured by the response of each to the saint and by the degree of intimacy each could claim.

The evidence of Hugh le Barber is one of the longest pieces of testimony given at the inquiry. A brief abstract of the main points of his information is taken from the record of the hearing. Great care was taken to distinguish between firsthand and hearsay evidence and to get specific examples of general statements. Not every instance of this is given here, nor is every question indicated in cases where Hugh had nothing to say. The concern is not with the form of the evidence, but with one man's contribution to the total body of information for Cantilupe's character and manner of life.

Men of many ranks of life spoke for Cantilupe. Hugh had been a relatively humble servant, speaking from his observation of the general tenor of life in Cantilupe's household. He had known Cantilupe for a very long time. This fact is of great importance for one especial point. He was able to explain that the loving charity, saintly devotion and austere practices shown in the last stage of Cantilupe's life, had been exercised in its former phases. There had been no sudden conversion when he became bishop of Hereford in 1275.

Hugh le Barber came forward on behalf of the dean and chapter of Hereford to speak as the sixth witness before the commissioners then sitting in London in July 1307. His evidence was to take several days. He was a man of seventy and upwards, and described as of Ely. Like all the witnesses, he first established his credentials and the grounds of his knowledge. He had met the lord Thomas some fifty five years ago at the university of Paris, where he served as his barber. He was afterwards with him for several unbroken spells, part of which was spent at the university of Oxford, where he looked after his room and made his bed.

The articles of inquiry fell into three groups. The first concerned Cantilupe's life and virtues, which were discussed under six main heads. The first of these covered his parentage, birth, and early life. Hugh could here only repeat what was generally known, but added that he believed the lord Thomas was baptized in the parish church of his father's manor of Hambleden, where a chapel had been built, in which was [later] placed a painted figure of the lord Thomas. A pilgrim cult centered there on a little knife which Hugh had seen and knew for one the lord Thomas had used at table. He had heard it said that miracles were worked through it. As the lord Thomas was about forty years old when he first knew him, he had no personal knowledge of his earlier life, but believed it had been virtuous. He had heard so from Master Peter de Botevilt, and Dom William Daubeney who had been with him. They said that his dislike of bawdy songs and smutty jokes was such that it was said of him that he ought to have been a woman, not a man.

There then follows, in answer to further questions under the first head and to questions under the second as to Cantilupe's life before he became bishop, a fairly general account of his master's routine. A chaplain, member of the household, said Mass every day. The lord Thomas was sociable and hospitable to all ranks of men at the universities. He fed five poor people in his house, and sometimes as many as thirteen. From the fragments of his table he kept two poor scholars and used his influence to get livings for them. Two such, on his return from Paris, he beneficed himself. As chancellor of the university of Oxford, he was severe with unruly students, confiscating their arms and refusing the right to carry such except to those who were of good repute. Hugh saw twenty bows and long and short swords which had been confiscated, and was himself given a long sword which had belonged to Roger de Horn, a particularly riotous student. He could not speak of the lord Thomas' life when he was chancellor of the king because he was himself at that time with Peter de Montefort, kinsman of the lord Thomas, but he had heard that he bore himself in that state justly, well, and wisely. Hugh accompanied him on visits to his benefices, seeing for himself that feasts were made, many alms given, food sent to the sick, ruinous buildings made good, and rights of the livings restored. He was able to specify building works carried out at Hampton near Warwick, and at Doderhull, where also dues of salt were recovered for the rectory. He added that the lord Thomas never entered upon litigation unless he knew he had the right.

The third question concerned Cantilupe's excellence of life. He was very faithful and truthful, said Hugh. This meant more than mere veracity, and included abstinence from all extravagance in speech. Whenever the lord Thomas wished to give emphasis, the only oath he was heard to use was 'By Saint Dewy', [David], a saint, it is explained, in Wales. He never changed his words, there was no duplicity in his words or deeds. He not only never lied, but did not speak slanderously to take away anyone's reputation. As an instance of this Hugh described, as though he had been present, how the lord Thomas reproved his brother-in-law Robert Tregoz for speaking shamefully of a young woman sitting at table with them.

Hugh gave a fairly detailed account of Cantilupe's practices in fasting, particularly on vigils of the feasts of the Blessed Virgin. He was always abstemious in eating and drinking. He was never drunk, and hated drunkards and luxury lovers. He stayed up late at night over his studies and rose up before his household to say matins. Hugh often heard him say matins and the other hours, and Mass, on Sundays and feast days, *cum nota.*

Hugh was then asked if he lay in Cantilupe's chamber. He explained that he did so, with Robert the chaplain, only when the secretary, Roger de Kirketon', was absent. Otherwise, Hugh lay outside. The lord Thomas' bed was not shut off from whomsoever was in the room. He lay in the bed, which was not furnished with a mattress, but had a quilt folded on top of bedding, on which sheets were laid. These were the circumstances as he knew them when the lord Thomas was at the universities, not after he became bishop or while he was chancellor of the king because he was not with him then. He knew of these things because he made the bed and was often about the room after the lord Thomas was in bed. Every day he cleaned the sheets from lice. There were so many that he could not keep the bedding nor Cantilupe's clothing free of them. They kept coming, in spite of changes of bedding and clothing. He took Cantilupe's boots off and ministered to him, and discovered lice *ad abhominationem.* He was so puzzled about this, that he asked Roger the secretary about it. He replied that some men had lice naturally. One day at Oxford, when the lord Thomas had gone out to the schools, Hugh discovered between the sheets a hair belt, made of grey-coloured hair, knotty and spiky, two hands' breadth wide and long enough to encircle a man's waist. The whole thing was alive, *tota repleta,* with lice. He could clean it only with a sharp point. He then laid it beneath the foot of the bed. When the lord Thomas came back from the schools to say his hours with his chaplain and companions, he called his secretary to him, and shut the door of his room. Then Roger, who had an affection for Hugh, came out, and asked him to swear to keep secret what he would be asked. Hugh said that he would do so if he knew what it was. Roger asked if he had found anything in or near the bed. Hugh described the finding of the belt, and vowed he would speak of it to no-one. This vow he kept while the lord Thomas was alive. In reply to further questioning, he said he did not know of any other hairshirt in the lifetime of the lord Thomas, but after his death Dom William de Montefort, dean of London, who was one of the executors of his will, gave into Hugh's care a certain knotty hairshirt which the lord Thomas had given him. It was about fourteen years before the lord Thomas became bishop that Hugh found the belt, at some time, he thought, between midsummer and michaelmas.

Asked about other austerities, Hugh replied that the lord Thomas was no hypocrite. He did not shew himself off as of more excellent life than others. He conformed in outward apparel and in the furniture of his bed to what was suitable. He wore a mantle in the house, at dinner, and had furred clothing and bed coverings.

When he was at the universities of Paris and Oxford, the lord Thomas frequently went to the houses of the orders of friars preachers and minor. Brother Robert de Kylwardeby, of the order of friars preachers, later archbishop of Canterbury and then a cardinal, was a particular friend, visited him in manors belonging to him, and preached and heard confessions in his household.

The fourth set of questions concerned Cantilupe's life as bishop, inquiring into the way he governed himself, the church and people committed to him, his diligence in visitation and correction, in preaching and celebrating the Mass, his care for the spiritualities and temporalities of his episcopal office.

It was commonly known, said Hugh, that as bishop the lord Thomas lived a disciplined life (*rexerat bene se*). He knew from Robert Deynte, now dead, then his chamberlain, that the lord Thomas wore a hairshirt at that period of his life and lived austerely. He himself did not at that time make his bed or look after his room. For two and half years after the lord Thomas became bishop, he had the care of the castle of Lydbury. He then gave specific examples of Cantilupe's government of the church committed to him and his recovery of its rights. Gilbert, earl of Gloucester had long claimed hunting rights over Malvern chase, to the prejudice of the rights of the church of Hereford. The lord Thomas entered into litigation against the earl. Hugh was present when the Earl uttered *multa verba imperiosa et superba,* threatened the lord Thomas, called him clergiaster, and said he would castigate him as he would all such. The lord Thomas replied that his threats would not hinder him from seeking his rights and those of his church.

Matters seem to have been halted by a royal suspension of a final sentence of the court. From Hugh's account it would seem as if the court and the parties then went to some part of the disputed ground. There, the lord Thomas went to where his clergy were, put on his full canonical dress, with mitre and cross, saw that the priests were vested, and went forth with them carrying lighted candles, to where the judges were placed, with the earl. Then, after extinguishing the candles, the lord Thomas pronounced a general sentence of excommunication on the earl and all those who disturbed his right and that of the church of Hereford in the chase. The earl mounted his palfrey and took himself off with his people and those who had gathered there. Judgment was given for the lord Thomas and the church of Hereford. The lord Thomas then caused many huntsmen and hunting dogs to come there on that day and for three days following, and there was no more trouble. The lord Thomas had with him many barons and noblemen of his kin. Hugh named some of them, but could not remember the date.

Hugh gave as another example of the recovery by Cantilupe of the rights of the church by instancing his successful litigation against Peter Corbet, Baron of Caus. Corbet usurped the church's rights by taking away beasts from the lands and pastures belonging to Bishop's Castle and

Lydbury and holding them to ransom. Another example was the restoration to the see of Hereford of three Welsh vills, the names of which were so foreign-sounding Hugh could not remember them. He had heard Robert de Wodeford, then constable of the castle at Lydbury, say that they were worth in rents a third part of the Hereford bishopric. In the time of predecessors of the lord Thomas, the Welsh had occupied these vills and made war in the neighbourhood. The witness was there when a thousand armed men were plundering in the area. The lord Thomas came, and in a castle of the see which from ancient times controlled the Welsh near those vills, solemnly excommunicated them. Many lighted candles were thrown into the ditch. When the Welsh who were coming to invade the bishop's land, saw the multitude of candles in the ditch, they were stupefied with terror. Within a few days, the greater part of the vills signified to Hugh and to others who were on the side of the lord Thomas in the castle of Lydbury, that they wished to make peace. They came to give help against the Welsh who were desirous of taking the three vills, and their families and cattle were taken for protection into the castle. The lord Thomas recovered the rights of the see, and held the three vills in peace.

He could say nothing about the lord Thomas' controversy with Frater John Pecham, archbishop of Canterbury, because he went to Rome.

He replied to further questions under this head of Cantilupe's life as bishop, that he saw and heard that the lord Thomas visited his diocese, preached, celebrated mass, confirmed children, corrected the clergy, and performed all the offices of a bishop, but could give no specific examples. When asked, he said that the lord Thomas was elected with agreement as bishop of Hereford, and that he had heard from John de Clare, of the order of friars minor, formerly of the household of the lord Thomas, that his predecessor in the see, Dom John le Breton, predicted publicly that the lord Thomas should succeed him.

The fifth set of questions in the first group of inquiries into Cantilupe's life and character was arranged to provide evidence of his practice of the particular named virtues of discretion, prudence, humility, holiness, gentleness, patience, kindness, sobriety, sedulousness in meditation, justice, fear of God, pitifulness, peaceableness. Last of all, inquiry was made into his sufferings from persecution and adversities.

As to discretion and prudence, Hugh could speak only in general terms. He knew of his humility from personal experience. The lord Thomas spoke humbly to the poor and called them his brothers. He frequently chided Hugh and others of his household when they did not call them brothers. One day, when the lord Thomas was at a meal and had before him half-a-dozen poor people, he sent Robert le Whytacre of his household to the gate, to see if there were any brothers there and to bring two of their number up. Robert went to the gate and found no men in religious orders there, which was what he thought was meant by brothers, so returned and told the lord Thomas there were none. To this the lord Thomas replied by saying, 'what, none like these', pointing out the poor men eating before him. Robert answered that there were twenty such, and was then asked to bring up five of them. This happened at Hampton in the diocese of Worcester, in the presence of Hugh and many others, about sixteen years before the lord Thomas became bishop.

He was humble in dress and bearing, but nevertheless made use of good clothing for himself and his household, and had beautiful palfreys. He was not ashamed to conform to what was suitable.

He was meek and gentle as a lamb, debonair, patient and kind. Hugh knew this from his manner of living and because he never knew him angered. When he reproved Hugh or any of his household and any made a rough reply he taught them charitably so that they should mend their ways. Asked if he showed patience with the earl of Gloucester, Hugh replied that the strongest words he spoke were 'Lord earl, Lord earl, say what you please about me, I will not let the rights of my church go by on account of your menaces'. When the witness was threatened by Roger de Horn, the unruly student previously mentioned, about his wearing the sword which had been Roger's and refused to be daunted, the lord Thomas, who was present said, smiling, to Roger, 'it does not seem that he fears your threats'.

Hugh repeated, as he had said before, that the lord Thomas lived soberly. He diluted his wine so that it was half water. He was very fond of pie made of Severn lampreys. Occasionally he had it brought before him, smelt it, and asked if it were well done, and had it put for others to eat. This was known to Hugh, not of his own observation but by what he had heard from a knight whose name he could not remember, who said it took place at Kemeseye near Worcester. He had himself seen and heard that the lord Thomas liked partridge and other little birds, but he either abstained totally from them, or ate only a mouthful. He had heard and seen this at many places—at Oxford, Snyterfeld, Hampton, Schirebourne—but could not remember specific times because it happened so often. The lord Thomas did not drink strong beer. Asked if this abstemiousness was affected in order to gain praise, Hugh answered that the lord Thomas was no hypocrite. He made it seem as though he was taking good ale and food, and gave it away or had it put for alms. In the same way with anything especially nice to eat, of which there was not a plentiful supply, he would give it to his companions and those eating with him, and if any remained, have it put for alms. He never took more than a mouthful himself. When soup was served, he put bread in it, and gave the bread away in alms.

Hugh knew that he was chaste from the way he talked. He never observed anything in him of lewdness. He had no women, however old, engaged in his household, and did not freely meet with women, even of his own kin, except occasionally when they had a meal with him.

To the question whether Cantilupe was sedulous in prayer Hugh said yes, and that he knew this because he would not permit anyone to speak, unless they were very great, when he was engaged in saying his hours nor would he turn his head to reply at such times. As to his devotion, Hugh said he saw him weeping greatly at Mass, so much so that a priest wiped his eyes and dried his tears with a cloth when he was celebrating. Hugh saw this happen four or five times in the church of London when the lord Thomas, as canon, was in residence and celebrating at the high altar. He said also that he had great compassion for the sick. When any of his household were ill he visited them personally and often, had great care taken of them, and medicines prepared for them. Hugh knew this from his own experience when he was ill for a year and four months at Hampton, Kemesey' and Aston. He could not carry in his memory the names of all such sick men whom the lord Thomas visited. When the lord Thomas went to places where he had benefices he had inquiry made about any sick and sent to them the better and more delicate food from his house. This happened at Hampton, Snyterfeld, Schirebourne, Kemesey'. When the lord Thomas was at Oxford he did the same for poor scholars, whose names Hugh did not remember. All this was many years before he became bishop.

For the whole time that the witness was with him at the universities of Paris and Oxford, on Maundy Thursday, he washed, dried and then kissed, the feet of thirteen poor people, fed them, and gave them one or two silver pennies. He gave away his clothes, for the love of God, to poor priests. Asked if these were given to priests serving in his own benefices, Hugh said sometimes to them and sometimes to others. He himself, by orders of the lord Thomas, gave a mantle made of *bluet,* lined with furs, to a vicar who was not in the service of the lord Thomas, but he could not remember the name, as this happened 46 years ago. When the lord Thomas was at the university of Paris, and Hugh was with him, fifty five years ago, he gave to William Plantefolie, who spent his time frequenting taverns and playing at dice, a mantle, surcoat, furlined hood and also a tunic *de bono blueto de Ipre* on condition that he abstained for a year from gaming and from frequenting taverns.

When he was at the universities he often sent Hugh and Roger de Kirketon with bedding and shoes for the poor whom he called his brothers.

When the lord Thomas could not go himself to his benefices, he made arrangements for corn or beans and pease to be supplied to the poor. Hugh knew of this from the bailiffs of those places by whom the food-stuffs were supplied, and also, himself, had been responsible for the threshing of the corn and beans to be given to the poor. He mentioned places at which this food was given out—Doderhull, Hampton, Aston, Wyntringham, Dyghton, and gave the names of bailiffs that he could remember—William Wyther, Alan de Kymberle, Robert de Wodeford, William de Kymberley. Asked about the quantity given on these occasions, Hugh replied that this varied according to the number of the poor and the degree of their poverty, but normally the quantity was a measure of corn or beans and pease corresponding to what a horse would eat in one night. When the lord Thomas made allowances of food at Oxford, he sent a sackful of fragments to poor prisoners. When he was journeying in places where bridges needed repair, he gave alms for this purpose. He knew of this at one especial time at Twyford, when such alms were given by one of the companions of the lord Thomas, William de Albanus. Hugh saw and heard that in many places when lepers and other wretched creatures came running for alms, he gave to them.

To the questions whether Cantilupe forgave those who had offended him, Hugh answered yes. He, and another of the household, wanting to go out one night and unable to pass through the gate which was shut, climbed over the wall . . . This happened at Hampton, where the lord Thomas was staying. The next day, the lord Thomas wished to dismiss them, but when they sought pardon, forgave them, but with the warning that if it happened again, they would be dismissed. Hugh received his pardon on another occasion. They went to London, where the lord Thomas was giving dinner to the lord Edward and other great ones of the realm. Hugh had charge of a silvergilt drinking cup, but allowed it to be stolen by a respectable-looking serving man. The lord Thomas forgave him, after having rebuked him for his carelessness.

The lord Thomas was very sedulous in contemplation, studied much and pored over his books. It displeased him to be much interrupted at his studies. Hugh often saw him in chapel kneeling and prostrate, and believes that at those times he was pleading with God. Asked if this was by day or by night, he replied that it was by day, before Mass, or afterwards, while he was at the universities.

When asked if Cantilupe was just and God-fearing, Hugh said that he knew that he was from talking with him. He never entered upon litigation unless his case was good. When he was sure of this, he pursued the cause vigorously to the end. He was greatly displeased to hear of any injustice. His fear of God was noticeable in his hatred of liars, luxury lovers, and unjust and evil men.

He was licensed in Theology. Robert de Kilwardeby, his confessor, commended him for his virtue, and this Hugh heard for himself in the church of St Mary in Oxford.

He was pitiful, as has been described, and peaceable. He would have no troublemakers in his household. He was a peacemaker. He healed a discord between two priests, one called Peter, the other Robert, at Hampton. Hugh was present when they ate together with the lord Thomas on the day peace was made between them. At Snyterfeld he reconciled John de Ludham, a servant, with the friends and relations of Matilda de Valoynes, daughter of Dom John de Cantilupe, brother of the lord Thomas. There had been a betrothal without the knowledge of Matilda's relations. This was before the lord Thomas became bishop.

As to his sufferings, Hugh could only speak of some twenty times that he was ill, and took medicine and was cured. He was sixty when he died.

The second group of questions, concerning Cantilupe's reputation, the common voice about him, the provenance of his fame, was not dealt with in Hugh's evidence. He had more specific knowledge to impart under the third head, the questions concerning the miracles.

He knew nothing, he said, of miracles during the life of the lord Thomas, but after his death he did. When he and his wife were living in London, they dined one night with Master James de Hulles and John de Baldok', executors of the will of Master William de Montefort, formerly dean of London, and kinsman of the lord Thomas. As they were returning home, Hugh suddenly felt a sharp pain, and his right eye was as though filled with ashes. Up to that time he could see well enough to thread a needle. He was much afflicted all that night with pain in his eye. The next morning when he went to the church of St Paul's and reached the gate leading to the place where the bread and beer for the canons was put, he had a similar pain and similar loss of sight in the other eye. This lasted for eight days. He sought medical help from a surgeon, Master Robert, who put a plaster over his eyes, but after this, he was much worse, and his face so changed that it was as if he had leprosy. Eventually this improved, but he remained blind. When he went to church he had to be led by the hand by one or other of his sons, Roger or William. He prayed to the Blessed Mary and to St Thomas that they would ask God that he might recover his sight sufficiently to see the elevation of the Host, to go about, and to play at chess and dice. His wife Juliana then had him measured to St Thomas, and wax eyes were sent by William de Baldok to Hambleden, the birthplace of the lord Thomas. Two days afterwards his sight was sufficiently restored for him to see the hens walking about near him in his house. He was measured again, and the measurement was sent to Hereford, to the tomb of the said Thomas, by Joan, wife of William le Hasteler of Kyngeslane, a place five English leagues outside Hereford. After eight days from the first measuring he could go about without being led and could see the Host raised by the priest at the altar, however far from the altar he might be.

Afterwards, within the year, he went to the church of Hereford, because of the pilgrimage there, carried oblations to the tomb, and visited Dom Philip Walense', rector of the church of Stretton with whom he was acquainted and with whom he used to play at chess and dice when he came to London. When he went to stay at his house, he played chess and dice and could see the marks on the dice.

Hugh was asked if he could explain what had brought this affliction upon him, if he had been a wicked man. He replied that when he was young he had been dissolute. The lord Thomas, when he was with him, urged him to mend his ways. When he became blind, he was devout, and thanked God for the punishment.

His recovery could not have been by natural means.

He was asked if he knew of other miracles worked through the lord Thomas. He believed, knew, heard and saw that this was so, and that many persons claimed miracles had been done for them by the merits of the lord Thomas. Pilgrims flocked to Hereford. There is not a saint in England, he said, towards whom men have such devotion as to the said saint Thomas de Cantilupe, and more pilgrims flock to him than to any other saint in England. He went on to say that in the church of Hereford in which he rests are many 'ymagines' of silver and wax, and sticks and crutches, more than could be carried in a six horse cart. He had seen them in the church of Hereford, and they attested the miracles which God worked through the said saint Thomas. He said also that from the oblations which the faithful brought to the tomb there had been made at the church of Hereford a beautiful great bell-tower and the church was restored, and many in England made legacies in their wills on account of this devotion.

This brought Hugh's evidence to an end. The concern of the commissioners at the end of each piece of testimony was to make sure of the honesty and incorruptibility of the witness. Hugh's testimony was allowed, for any distrust on account of his poverty was disregarded by the commissioners in the light of his devotion, general appearance and age. He had spoken in French.

SELECT INDEX OF NAMES